D0948668

SKORZENY: HITLER'S COMMANDO

SKORZENY: HITLER'S COMMANDO

Glenn B. Infield

St. Martin's Press
New York

For Bill

CONTENTS

vii

CONTENTS

ACKNOWLEDGMENTS

During the years of research required for this book, I was helped by so many persons and organizations that to try to list them all is impossible. In addition to those listed in the bibliography who aided me by providing personal information about Otto Skorzeny and his activities both during and after the Third Reich, I want to thank Judi Billingsley who hunted through the archives in Washington, D.C., for important facts never previously uncovered; George Owens of the Central Intelligence Agency; Robert Wolfe, Donald Spencer, and Mark Steinitz of the National Archives; Daniel P. Simon of the Berlin Document Center; Louise E. Foster of the Defense Intelligence Agency; Blair P. Hall of the Department of State; Thomas H. Bresson of the Federal Bureau of Investigation; and Thomas F. Conley of the U.S. Army Intelligence and Security Command.

When dealing with intelligence activities and the world of clandestine operations, violence, and terrorism, many individuals who are willing to give information are not willing to be identified for fear of retaliation. To these persons I am very grateful.

Nor could I not emphasize the cooperation given me by Otto Skorzeny himself prior to his death in 1975. Obviously, he would not speak about many of his postwar activities, but his information concerning many of the mysteries of the Third Reich were fascinating and not available from other sources.

There would not have been a book if it had not been for the encouragement, patience, and help given me by my wife, Peggy. To her and all the others—thanks.

INTRODUCTION

While I was doing research for my previous books, the name Otto Skorzeny kept appearing on documents I studied in Germany, Spain, France, Italy, and England, as well as in the United States. I knew the name because of the publicity Skorzeny had received when he rescued Benito Mussolini from an Italian mountaintop prison in 1943. But, many of the documents that referred to him had nothing to do with this mission. My curiosity aroused, I did some further research on the man and came to a startling conclusion. Otto Skorzeny not only played an important role in Hitler's Third Reich but also in the postwar world; in fact, he was the Hitler-link to the present-day-terrorism rampant around the globe.

During the Third Reich, Skorzeny learned an important truth that he never forgot: an act of terrorism, committed by a minimum number of persons, is very often more effective than a large-scale, complex military operation. Terrorism, during the Third Reich and today, has been defined in various ways, and yet there is no universally accepted definition. The National Foreign Assessment Center of the Central Intelligence Agency defines international terrorism as "the threat or use of violence for political purposes when such action is intended to influence the attitude and behavior of a target group wider than its immediate victims and its ramifications transcend national bound-aries."[1]

Skorzeny, as an SS-*Standartenführer* (colonel) with Section VI of the

1

Reichssicherheitshauptamt (Reich Central Security Office), certainly used "violence for political purposes" and "transcended national boundaries." One of his most important assignments was to direct secret agents in foreign and neutral countries. Terrorist attacks, kidnappings, and assassination were standard operating procedure for him and the agents in his command. He and his men were called "Hitler's Commandos" by the Western Allies in an effort to compare Skorzeny's agents to the irregular forces that were used by England and the United States. Groups such as Orde Wingate's Raiders, David Stirling's Long Range Desert Groups, Popski's Private Army (Lieutenant-Colonel Peniakoff), and William Donovan's OSS achieved fame and limited success for the Western Allies, long before Skorzeny's name was known outside the Third Reich, but these units were military in nature and their targets were almost exclusively military. Skorzeny, on the other hand, had as many political targets during World War II as military. Hitler and Skorzeny understood that at times the military power of a country could be overcome if one man was dealt with. The German generals were unconvinced at first. They believed that the only way an opposing military power could be defeated was on the battlefield. Skorzeny's forays in Italy, Hungary, France, Denmark, and other countries changed their minds.

Skorzeny's wartime exploits interested me greatly, but so did his activities after World War II. His name was linked with a whole series of mercenary, undercover, and terrorist activities ranging from Biafra to Egypt to South America. According to reports, he had been associated with Juan and Evita Perón in Argentina, Gamal Abdel Nasser in Egypt, and Francisco Franco in Spain. Rumor had it that Skorzeny worked for the CIA, that he trained American soldiers in Spain for duty in Korea. According to the confessed train robbers of the Glasgow-to-London night mail-train, Skorzeny had financed the operation, which resulted in a take worth $7 million on the night of August 6, 1963. And I knew it was true that when a French resistance fighter berated Skorzeny about his wartime activity for Hitler many years after the end of the Third Reich, Skorzeny declared: "I am proud to have served my country and my Führer."[2] Obviously he was no apologist for Hitler! I felt compelled to meet and talk with this man.

As I walked down the dark hall on the fourth floor of the office building located at Montera 25-2 in Madrid, hunting Skorzeny's office several weeks later, however, I was apprehensive. Even when I recalled that Skorzeny himself had called my room at the Palace Hotel that morning and, in his booming voice, had invited me to come over to his office, I was still concerned about meeting him face to face. Two days earlier, I had visited Albert Speer in Heidelberg, Germany, and his comments about Skorzeny added to my anxiety. Speer, of course, was Hitler's Minister of Munitions and Armaments and very close to the Führer. After spending twenty years in Spandau Prison, he had written his memoirs. While visiting with Speer, I had mentioned that I would be flying to Madrid to see Skorzeny, thinking he would be delighted, since he and Skorzeny were undoubtedly the two most famous Nazis still alive. Instead of being happy, however, he frowned and looked at me for a few moments in an icy silence.

"Skorzeny doesn't like me," Speer said.[3]

I was shocked. "Why doesn't he like you?"

"He thinks I have turned against Hitler."

I didn't know what to say, so I remained silent.

Speer continued. "I think that is why he doesn't like me. When you see him, will you please ask him? Tell Skorzeny I admire him."

As I walked down the dark hall in Madrid, I wondered how Skorzeny would take Speer's query. After all, this was the man alleged to have hung Hitler's would-be assassins of July 20, 1944 on meat hooks with wire, and allowed them to slowly strangle. And, when asked in 1944 what should be done about the prostitutes in Berlin, he answered: "Bury them!"

There was no nameplate on the door. My knock was answered by a young woman who spoke only Spanish. I handed my card through the narrow opening of the chain-locked door and, a moment later, I heard Skorzeny's powerful voice tell her to invite me inside. Standing beside a wooden desk was a huge man easily identifiable as Skorzeny by the duelling scar on his left cheek. It was this scar that had resulted in the nickname of "Scarface" used by those who disliked and feared him. Four inches over the six-foot mark in height, heavier than his wartime photographs indicated he was during the Third Reich, Skorzeny was an impressive sight as he greeted me. His appearance verified everything I had read about him. His gray-black hair nearly matched his pants. He had a green turtleneck sweater under his brown sports coat, a sweater that he wore, I discovered later, to hide the scar on the back of his neck where he was operated on for cancer in 1970. I noticed that he moved slowly and had difficulty sitting down. The cancer operation had completely paralyzed him from the waist downward, and the doctors had predicted he would never walk again. Skorzeny ignored their prediction. With the help of a former SS officer who became a physical therapy expert after the Third Reich, he was taking small steps within a month after the operation. By the time I visited him, only the slowness of his movements gave any indication of his former paralysis.

Skorzeny was a very easy man to talk with, a very interesting conversationalist. When he discovered that I was a former combat pilot and had flown many missions over Germany during World War II, he immediately told me about his hazardous glider flight to rescue Mussolini, and the dangerous takeoff from an Italian mountain peak in the small Storch aircraft carrying the pilot, Mussolini, and himself. I soon discovered that he told it as it had happened, not the way he thought I would like to hear it. Not once did he say Hitler had duped him, as other Nazi survivors had told me. He told me instead about reviewing a French television show prior to its broadcast at the request of the producers. The documentary dealt with the German campaign in North Africa, and in one segment of the show a former German army officer was narrating. When this officer stated that Hitler did not send the German army the war material they needed to fight the campaign, that the Führer left his soldiers in the lurch, Skorzeny protested vehemently to the producers. The producers were so impressed—and you have to remember this was a documentary being presented by a nation that had been at war with Germany—that they invited Skorzeny to appear on the program. He explained to the viewers that Hitler *did* send the required materials, but Allied planes and ships prevented delivery.

It became very obvious to me that Skorzeny had definite views about his role in World War II, views that had not changed during the decades after the fighting stopped. He ignored the fact that the world now considered his Führer the monster of the twentieth century, that anyone who had a good word for Adolf Hitler in the 1970s was immediately classified as a man of similar ilk. There was no doubt in my mind as the afternoon wore on that Skorzeny thought Hitler had been absolutely correct in most of his actions during the Third Reich, the Jewish holocaust excepted. Nor was there any doubt in my mind that Skorzeny considered his terrorist activities in behalf of Hitler ethical. Putting these two facts into a present-day perspective it was understandable that Skorzeny was credited with organizing the postwar brotherhood of Nazi survivors, *Die Spinne*, that aided the Hitler loyalists escape the Western Allies' net and protected them during the years after the Third Reich. In light of his belief that his Third Reich terrorism was justified, his alleged worldwide terrorist activities after 1945 should not come as a surprise.

It was nearly the dinner hour when I stood up and extended my hand to Skorzeny. As we walked toward the door, I decided it was time to ask him about his relationship with Albert Speer, as Speer had requested. I explained briefly that I had been in Germany and had visited Speer. Despite the fact that Skorzeny's smile faded at the mention of Speer, I asked my question.

"Speer says you do not like him and he would like to know why."

Skorzeny glared at me. "I believe that if I am loyal to a man when he is winning I should also be loyal to him when he loses."[4] Suddenly the smile returned, producing a dimple in one cheek and accenting the duelling scar on the other. "But I am a peaceful man who doesn't like trouble," he continued. "Tell Speer I like him. I like everyone."

Skorzeny had impressed me very favorably during our long conversation, but I wasn't entirely convinced that he was a peaceful man who didn't like trouble. I decided to find out what the documented records and people intimately acquainted with him had to say.

This book reveals what I discovered. This is the true story of Otto Skorzeny.

THE FÜHRER AND SKORZENY

I

"I am proud to have served my country and my Führer."

1 THE MOST DANGEROUS MAN

On a warm summer's day in 1944, Otto Skorzeny stood at the edge of a Luftwaffe airbase at Lärz and watched technicians and ground crewmen attach a V-1 to the underside of a Heinkel III bomber. The V-1 *Vergeltungswaffe* (reprisal weapon), developed by German scientists at the secret rocket base at Peenemünde, was a pilotless jet-propelled missile that Hitler was depending upon to destroy London and other British cities. It had a speed of 400 miles per hour and carried a ton of explosives that detonated on contact. The V-1 that Skorzeny, chief of Hitler's special forces, was looking at was different, however. It had been adapted for a Hitler commando attack known as "Operation Suicide." Instead of being pilotless, this particular missile had a seat large enough for a man. The plan developed by Skorzeny was for a volunteer pilot to crash the V-1 and its load of explosives into a target, destroying both target and pilot.

Skorzeny looked at the major standing a few feet away from him on his left. Heinrich Himmler, Reichsführer of the SS *(Schutzstaffel)*, and Skorzeny's superior, was taking no chances. He had sent the major to Lärz to observe the test and to send a complete report to him. Hitler had not approved "Operation Suicide" yet. In fact, the Führer was not even aware of the conversion of the V-1s for Skorzeny's test. If everything worked out well, Himmler would take credit for the plan when it was presented to Hitler as one opportunity remaining to change the course of the war. If the plan was a fiasco and Hitler discovered it,

Himmler would put all the blame on Skorzeny. Skorzeny's stare made the major nervous and he walked back toward the headquarters.

With a loud roar the Heinkel III bomber moved down the runway with the modified V-1 swinging slightly under its wing, gained speed, and lifted into the air a hundred feet before the end of the strip. Skorzeny watched as the plane climbed higher and higher, waiting for the release of the V-1. Suddenly the missile with the man in it dropped free of the bomber and began to descend in a series of tight turns. At first it appeared the pilot had the V-1 under complete control, but gradually the angle of descent increased until it was diving straight toward the ground. Skorzeny watched impassively as it disappeared from sight behind a hill. A few seconds later there was a column of black smoke spiraling skyward. An ambulance, its siren blowing, raced toward the crash scene followed by several vehicles filled with Luftwaffe personnel. Skorzeny turned away from the smoke and motioned for his aide to join him.

"We'll need another pilot," he said quietly. "Have him sign the release."[1]

Without another word he turned and walked to his Mercedes, got in and drove away.

A Luftwaffe fighter pilot standing nearby, Gustav Morder, shook his head in disbelief. "Doesn't he give a damn that a man was just killed?"[2]

No one answered.

The following day Skorzeny was back at Lärz watching another test flight of the piloted V-1. The pilot in the missile brought it down safely in a fast, rough landing that brought a smile to Skorzeny's face. By the end of the week, after several more successful flights, Himmler joined him at Lärz accompanied by Joseph Goebbels, Hitler's Minister of Propaganda. Both wanted in on the glory they felt would result from Skorzeny's plan for "Operation Suicide" when it was presented to the Führer. Goebbels even wanted a copy of the release signed by the volunteer pilots which stated:

> I hereby voluntarily apply to be enrolled in the suicide group as pilot of a human glider-bomb. I fully understand that employment in this capacity will entail my own death.[3]

Goebbels intended to glorify the suicide pilots and Otto Skorzeny, the man who had planned the operation. In this instance, however, the

Western Allies invaded Europe before the manned V-1s could become operational and the plan was abandoned. Yet, it was because of such unorthodox operations during World War II that Skorzeny became Hitler's favorite commando and the most publicized adventurer of Nazi Germany. To Americans he was known as "the most dangerous man in Europe."

Skorzeny's mundane life prior to Hitler's Third Reich certainly gave no indication that he would become the greatest adventurer of Nazi Germany. He was born on the twelfth of June, 1908, in Vienna, the son of Anton who died in April 1942, before his son became known worldwide, and Flora Sieber, who survived the Third Reich with her son. He had one brother, Alfred, who remained in Vienna throughout the war years and also outlasted the Nazi regime. Vienna, in 1908, was the mecca of music and art, the city to which an eighteen-year-old art student by the name of Adolf Hitler had moved from his home at Linz. Skorzeny's father had a successful engineering business during these pre-World War I days, and the family lived very well. Young Skorzeny had little interest in art or music, and it soon became apparent to his father and mother that it would be best for the boy to follow in the footsteps of his father and become an engineer.

World War I brought an abrupt change in the fortunes of both Vienna and Skorzeny. The sparkling, cosmopolitan city that was the capital of the Hapsburg dynasty and a center for banking and finance, as well as fashion and culture, became the first war capital of World War I in 1914. When Austria declared war on Serbia, it became a city of impending doom. The gaiety and bright lights quickly faded and Skorzeny's father soon lost his business. When World War I ended in defeat for Austria and unemployment and inflation were rampant, Skorzeny had his first experience with the spartan life that would become a ritual for him during World War II. When he once complained to his father that he had never tasted real butter, Anton told his fifteen-year-old son: "There is no harm in doing without things. It might even be good for you not to get used to a soft life." [4]

It was a prophetic statement.

When, after the war, he was asked by Colonel Howard A. Brundage, U.S. Army, at Nuremberg, Germany, on September 11, 1945, what schools he had attended, Skorzeny stated: "Elementary, secondary, and technical high school." [5] He was, of course, understating his education and some of his actions during these formative years of his life. The record indicates that Otto Skorzeny graduated from the *Technischen Hochschule in Wien* (University of Vienna) on December 11, 1931, as an engineer. His engineering skill was invaluable to him later during the planning of his commando and terrorist missions, but of even more importance was the duelling experience he received while attending the university. The first extracurricular activity joined by Skorzeny after his admission to the University of Vienna was the *Schlagende Verbindungen* (duelling society). The duel originated in Germany as a form of judicial combat used to administer justice or settle a dispute. The university students, however, didn't have to suffer a slight to have an excuse to fight a duel. It was more like a sport to them and none of the students took it up more enthusiastically than Skorzeny. He fought his first duel during his initial year at the university and before he graduated he had fifteen such "sabre combats" to his credit and a distinctive scar on his left cheek that gave him the title of "Scarface" to the Americans during World War II.

"I was often grateful later for the self-discipline we learned in our student club," he said. "I never felt under more pressure than I did at eighteen when I had to fight my first duel under the eyes of my fellow students. My knowledge of pain, learned with the sabre, taught me not to be afraid. and just as in duelling when you must concentrate on your enemy's cheek, so, too, in war. You cannot waste time on feinting and sidestepping. You must decide on your target and go in."[6]

Skorzeny became known as the student who was willing to fight a duel anytime with anyone. He also became a target for those who wanted to gain prestige on campus. His reputation grew as his victories piled up, until he was finally cautioned by both his father and university authorities that he should spend more time with his books and less with his sword. What really convinced him that they might be right, however, was a duel he fought with a friend over the love of a campus beauty. They both were bloodied, but a week later she married a fellow neither had heard of.

His books had little interest for him. He didn't like to read, he didn't like to study. He managed to get passing marks in the subjects he was forced to take in order to get his engineering degree—math, physics, drafting—and his thesis, titled "The Calculation and Construction of a Diesel Engine" was accepted by university officials as a requirement for his diploma but was not considered outstanding.

After graduating, Skorzeny worked for several engineering firms in Vienna and then opened his own. He was moderately successful with his business, married Emmi Linhart (whom he had met at a swimming pool) and moved into an apartment on Aichholzgasse Strasse in Vienna. But he was restless, not content with his routine life, so when the new party of Adolf Hitler, the *Nationalsozialistische Deutsche Arbeiterpartei* (NSDAP or Nazi), began recruiting members in Austria Skorzeny signed up. One of the main attractions of the Nazi party for Skorzeny was the road races held periodically. He promptly entered his own racer and won three gold medals. Otherwise, according to him, he carried his party card but was not active in the organization. His parents were staunch opponents of the Nazi party, especially after the murder of the Austrian chancellor Engelbert Dollfuss by SS gunmen on July 25, 1934. When, in July 1936, Germany and Austria signed a treaty giving the Austrian Nazis legal status, the strain between parents and son was less, but rumors of a Nazi coup fired the controversy from time to time. Skorzeny, spending most of his time with racing cars, engineering business, and new wife, ignored the rumor at first. When Hauptmann Joseph Leopold, a prominent Austrian Nazi, casually informed the private secretary of Sir Oswald Mosley, the British fascist leader, early in January 1938 the Nazis were going to take over the government in the spring and the conversation became public, Skorzeny just laughed.

"I knew that without help from Germany we Nazis in Austria couldn't possibly overthrow the government of Chancellor Kurt Schuschnigg."[7]

Nor did he pay much attention when Hermann Göring, Hitler's number two man in the Nazi party, boasted that after the spring of 1938 the Third Reich would no longer have to pay for the raw materials obtained from Austria. To a man of action such as Skorzeny, words were harmless. Only the sword or the gun made an impression. Skorzeny vowed after the war that he was unaware of the secret plans Hitler had for Austria. On February 12, 1938, the Führer summoned Schuschnigg to the Berghof, his mountain retreat in the Bavarian Alps near the town of Berchtesgaden, and compelled the chancellor of Austria to sign an agreement clearing the way for *Anschluss* (union). After returning to Vienna, Schuschnigg tried to delay the inevitable Nazi takeover of his country by Hitler by scheduling a plebiscite on the question of Austrian independence. Angered by the chancellor's action, Hitler, on March

11, demanded Schuschnigg's resignation in favor of Artur Seyss-Inquart, the leading Austrian Nazi, and sent German troops to the Austrian-German border. Seyss-Inquart promptly was installed as chancellor since Schuschnigg had no alternative, but Hitler was not satisfied. At the urging of Göring, Seyss-Inquart sent a telegram to Berlin requesting German troops to invade Austria to restore order. On March 12, the German army crossed the border and Skorzeny suddenly found himself a member of the ruling political party of Austria.

The very day that Seyss-Inquart was named chancellor of Austria by President Wilhelm Miklas, after Hitler forced the resignation of Schuschnigg, Skorzeny was involved in an incident at the presidential palace that conflicts with his denial of ever having taken an active part in the Nazi party prior to the war. Seyss-Inquart, the new chancellor, was speaking to a large and enthusiastic crowd in the city square near the Vienna Gymnastic Club, an organization that supported the Nazis in Austria. Skorzeny was at the club listening when suddenly he was summoned by the director of the organization, Anton Dubas, who told him President Miklas had just passed near the crowd on his way to the presidential palace and there was going to be trouble. Several carloads of armed Nazis, later identified as SS members, were following the presidential entourage and were going to try to take over the palace by force.

"Try and smooth things over, Skorzeny. You're a sensible fellow," Dubas said.[8]

Skorzeny jumped into his car, one of the ones he used for road racing, and tried to catch up with the presidential convoy and the trailing Nazis. They had too big a head start, however, and had reached the palace by the time he arrived. President Miklas, well guarded by Austrian soldiers, was walking into the building. The Nazis were leaping from their cars and running after him. Skorzeny shoved his way past the gun-carrying Nazis, hurried into the palace, and caught up with President Miklas on the staircase. The startled Austrian soldiers surrounded him immediately only to discover a moment later that they, too, were surrounded—by armed Nazis. A shooting spree seemed inevitable.

"Quiet!" Skorzeny shouted.[9]

Both the Austrians and the Nazis were confused by the loud order from the huge, scarfaced man standing on the staircase wearing civilian clothing. They quieted down although the guns were kept cocked.

Finally President Miklas asked Skorzeny to identify himself. Skorzeny told him he was a representative of Seyss-Inquart who had come to the palace to prevent bloodshed, and the new chancellor would verify his identity. Skorzeny put through a telephone call to Seyss-Inquart, explained the situation to him, and the new chancellor assured President Miklas that Skorzeny represented him and was trying to maintain order. The president was satisfied but there was still a problem to be solved. Who was going to control the palace? The Nazis and the Austrians looked at Skorzeny for orders. Wisely he directed the Austrians to maintain security inside the building and the Nazis to mount guard outside. The crisis was over.

According to Skorzeny he was involved in the incident merely because he *happened* to be at the Vienna Gymnastic Club that day and because director Dubas thought he was a "sensible fellow." However, in May 1945, when *SS-Obergruppenführer* (Lieutenant General) Gottlob Berger, who specialized in security problems while serving in the *Reichssicherheitshauptamt* (Reich Central Security Office), was captured at Berchtesgaden and queried about Skorzeny, he indicated it was no accident Skorzeny was on the scene that day.

"Skorzeny belonged to the SS and the Gestapo," Berger told his American interrogator. "In 1935 or 1936 he was one of the first in the Austrian Nazi party. He was very active during the *Anschluss*."[10]

Berger's testimony refutes Skorzeny's claim that he had played little or no part in the Austrian Nazi party until 1939.

In addition, when Skorzeny was questioned at Nuremberg after the war about his friendship with Ernst Kaltenbrunner, the leader of the Austrian SS at the time of the *Anschluss*, he admitted he had known Kaltenbrunner since 1929.

"I met a Miss Elder at a party in Linz. It was a large party and Kaltenbrunner was present. Later he and Miss Elder married and through his wife I remained acquainted with him."[11]

Asked about his friendship with Kaltenbrunner after 1929, he couldn't recall the details of their meetings. When the interrogator asked Skorzeny if he had any contact with Kaltenbrunner in 1938, the year of the *Anschluss*, Skorzeny nodded.

"I saw him in 1938 when he came to Vienna. I was invited to his house several times. My wife accompanied me."

From this evidence it appears that Skorzeny was very active in the Nazi party in Austria in 1938, a member of the SS and Gestapo at the same time, and wasn't interested in the party only because of the road races the Nazis sponsored.

In 1939, when the war started, Skorzeny volunteered for the Luftwaffe, since he had done some private flying. At thirty-one years of age, however, he was considered too old for flight training so he spent the next five months training in a communications depot in Vienna. He didn't like the training, didn't want to be a communications expert, and made it his business to tell every officer he met just how he felt. Finally, in March 1939, a few weeks after his daughter Waltraut was born, Skorzeny was transferred to the *Waffen SS* (Armed SS). At that time the *Waffen SS* was looking for personnel with a technical background and since there were no openings for technical officers in the Luftwaffe, Skorzeny volunteered for the transfer in hopes of becoming an officer. He was a noncommissioned officer at the time of the transfer but was immediately classified in the *Waffen SS* as a *Fähnrich* (officer-cadet) who, if he proved himself in the ranks, would be commissioned.

Skorzeny, with his civilian-adventurer attitude, had a difficult time proving himself to his military superiors. He was posted with the *Division Reich* as a technical expert with an artillery regiment, and it was his responsibility to keep the division's tanks and other vehicles operational. He did so but his unorthodox methods continually got him into trouble and went on his record. When he needed treads for his tanks and none were available through normal supply channels, he organized a "scavenger group" and led them to another division's warehouse at night to steal the necessary treads. On another occasion his trucks were halted because of lack of tires. This time he was in a hurry so he obtained the tires at a depot at gunpoint. The tanks and trucks kept moving, but Skorzeny's personnel record was soon filled with reprimands and warnings. His chances of ever becoming an officer diminished each day.

If he wasn't getting into trouble in the field, he was causing an uproar while off duty. He had been on his good behavior for several weeks after the reprimand he had received for obtaining the tires at gunpoint. His commanding officer had told him his only chance to get his promotion to officer rank was to behave himself. Unfortunately, Skorzeny and several of his friends decided to spend a few off-hours in a small café in Holland and after a few drinks Skorzeny's promise to his commanding officer was forgotten. When he and Hans Jaeger, a fellow sergeant in the *Division Reich*, saw a portrait of Prince Bernhard of the Netherlands hanging in the café, they demanded it be taken down. Skorzeny and his companion were aware that years earlier the prince had served in the SS but later had denounced Hitler and fled to London with exiled Dutch officials. When the café owner refused to take the portrait from the wall, Skorzeny promptly shot it down with his pistol.

"That was a mistake," Jaeger said. "The next day Skorzeny was called before the general, given a hellish dressing down because he had aggravated the newly conquered Dutch citizens, and was confined to his barracks for six weeks. His promotion to officer was tabled indefinitely." [12]

The SS contribution to the victory on the western front in 1940 was not as great in numbers as the contribution of the German army—three and a half divisions compared to a hundred and forty—but in quality it was outstanding. The SS was determined to show the regular army troops that they were equal or better on the battlefield. Skorzeny and his fellow SS members under the command of *Gruppenführer* (Major General) Hans Jüttner recklessly raced through Holland, matching every victory of the German army and in many instances outshining the regulars. But behavior such as Skorzeny's couldn't be ignored.

Skorzeny's confinement to barracks because of the café escapade came to an abrupt end, however, when during the night of March 26–27 the Yugoslav government of Prince-Regent Paul was overthrown by a group of army and air force officers who thought the prince was much too friendly with Hitler. In Berlin Hitler was furious. He summoned his generals, including Jüttner, and announced: "I will make a clean sweep of the Balkans." [13]

His Directive No. 25, issued the day after the Yugoslav revolt, read:

> The military putsch in Yugoslavia has changed the political situation in the Balkans. Yugoslavia, in spite of her protestations of loyalty, must be regarded for the time being as an enemy and therefore crushed as quickly as possible. [14]

Skorzeny's regiment rushed from the western front to Temesva in southwestern Rumania and invaded Yugoslavia on April 1, 1941, only eleven days after the palace revolt. Skorzeny soon discovered that the campaign in the east was entirely different than the romp through

Holland had been. Casualties were high and for the first time Skorzeny, who was supposed to be the technical expert assigned to keep the regiment's vehicles in repair, found himself fighting face to face with the enemy. Three days after the invasion of Yugoslavia, he was repairing a truck when he saw a group of enemy soldiers walking toward the vehicle. He quickly motioned for the men with him to hide in the nearby shrubbery while he slipped behind a large tree. Waiting until the Yugoslavs were standing around the disabled truck, Skorzeny aimed his rifle at them and told them they were prisoners. His companions, mostly mechanics, joined him, their guns trained on the enemy. The Yugoslavs, taken by surprise, offered no resistance, so Skorzeny and his men marched them back to regiment headquarters. His prisoners totaled fifty-four soldiers and three officers! Skorzeny's past transgressions in Holland were forgotten and he was made an officer on the spot.

The campaign in Yugoslavia was over within a month and the members of Skorzeny's regiment, as well as the remainder of *Division Reich,* anticipated a lull in the activity. They had no forewarning that Hitler was determined to attack Russia. German citizens first learned of the Führer's plans at seven o'clock on the morning of June 22, 1941, when Hitler's public announcement was broadcast over all German radio stations:

> Weighed down by heavy cares, condemned to months of silence, I can at last speak freely—German people! At this moment a march is taking place that, for its extent, compares with the greatest the world has ever seen. I have decided again today to place the fate and future of the Reich and our people in the hands of our soldiers. May God aid us especially in this fight![15]

Camped on the shore of the river Bug, Skorzeny and his SS companions learned about the planned Russian invasion a few hours earlier and in a more abrupt manner. Jüttner briefed them just before midnight.

"We will cross the river at five A.M. Our destination is Moscow!"[16]

Skorzeny was shocked. He thought the Soviet-German nonaggression pact, signed in Moscow in August 1939, was still in effect. The consensus of the men of his regiment had been, up to that minute, that they had permission to move through Russia to reach the Middle East so they could attack the British Eighth Army from the opposite direction from Rommel's Afrika Korps. Now their only consolation was the fact that Russia, too, would be surprised.

That comforting thought faded the next dawn when they crossed the Bug River. The Soviet troops were waiting and, while *Division Reich* was able to push them back, casualties were high. There were two infantry regiments, one engineering battalion, one tank brigade, a reconnaissance battalion, and Skorzeny's artillery regiment in *Division Reich*. All suffered heavy losses. In addition to the miserable weather, the mud, and the enemy, Skorzeny also had to battle gall bladder trouble. During the early winter of 1941 he was not feeling well and took refuge in a Russian house that had been evacuated by the owners. While he was resting, trying to regain his strength and recover from a spell of dizziness, Russian artillery shells fell in the vicinity. The first barrage missed the house, but a second barrage exploded much closer and Skorzeny was hit in the back of the head by shrapnel. Knocked unconscious, he lay there several hours until he was discovered by other SS men and taken to a nearby aid station. His treatment consisted of a bandage, a few aspirin, and a glass of schnapps.

Skorzeny rejoined his regiment a few hours after being treated at the aid station, but his health went from bad to worse. Gall bladder attacks and continual headaches plagued him and, in January 1942, he was put on a hospital train headed for Germany. He promised his friends he would be back in a few weeks. He was completely unaware that fate and Adolf Hitler would change those plans.

2 HITLER'S COMMANDOS

During the first two and a half years of the war, Adolf Hitler depended upon the German armed forces for his intelligence needs and any clandestine warfare assignments required. The *Abwehr* section of the German High Command, the organization responsible for secret missions, was under the command of Wilhelm Canaris. A small, volatile man who held the rank of admiral, Canaris was fifty-five years old in 1942 when Skorzeny was invalided home from the Russian front. He was a brilliant leader of courage and skill, who had carried out many secret missions for the German navy during World War I, but Hitler was not satisfied with the work of the *Abwehr*. Yet, the Führer was very careful about any move to oust Canaris because the admiral was an influential member of the *Oberkommando der Wehrmacht*—OKW— (The High Command of the Armed Forces), and even in 1942 Hitler didn't want to antagonize the military commanders any more than was absolutely necessary. He still respected the OKW sovereignty, but he was convinced a move had to be made.

Meanwhile, Skorzeny had reached Berlin from Russia and, while Hitler was trying to devise a way to circumvent the *Abwehr* and Admiral Canaris without alienating the OKW, was admitted to a hospital. After several weeks of treatment for his wounds, exhaustion, and his gall bladder, he was discharged. Instead of being returned to the *Division Reich* in Russia as he had expected, however, he was assigned to the newly formed Fifth Panzer Regiment in France. He remained with this unit until February 1, 1943, when once again he was returned to a hospital. The doctors examined him carefully and decided he was no longer fit for front-line duty. It was a depressing period for the action-loving Austrian, further saddened by his father's death during his initial hospital stay. The inheritance of his father's successful scaffolding and trestle business was little consolation. Discharged from the hospital in March, Skorzeny was sent to a repair depot on the outskirts of Berlin to sit out the rest of the conflict.

Several hundred miles south of Berlin, in the mountains of Bavaria, a decision was being made that would abruptly change the course of Skorzeny's life. On March 30, Hitler asked Himmler to meet with him at the Berghof, the Führer's mountain retreat on the Obersalzberg near Berchtesgaden. Six days earlier an agent belonging to Canaris's *Abwehr* section had been arrested in Munich after it was discovered he was involved in a currency racket. During the search of the agent's quarters, treasonable evidence linking the *Abwehr* and the Vatican was uncovered. When Hitler was informed, he concluded it was time for him to make his move. He decided that Himmler's SS would assume much of the responsibility previously delegated to the *Abwehr*. As usual, Hitler camouflaged his action by having a parallel organization established in the SS rather than disbanding the *Abwehr*.

When the SS was reorganized in 1939 the *Geheime Staatspolizei* (Gestapo)—Secret State Police—and *Kriminalpolizei* (Criminal Police) became a part of the new *Reichssicherheithauptamt* (Reich Central Security Office), commonly known as RSHA. The Criminal Police section was known as Amt V and was under the command of Artur Nebe, while the Gestapo became Amt IV under the command of Heinrich Müller. A third section of the RSHA was Amt VI controlled by Walter Schellenberg, an intimate associate of Himmler. Amt VI dealt with foreign intelligence but had been seriously hampered in its efforts by the military arm of intelligence, the *Abwehr*. Now Hitler made it clear to Himmler that he wanted Amt VI to play the dominant role in intelligence and clandestine warfare. A special unit was to be established to handle the sabotage and subversion assignments that the military was too "squeamish" to handle, a unit to be designated Amt VI-S.[1]

Skorzeny was cooling his heels in the repair depot on the outskirts of Berlin early April 1943, when he was handed a directive which ordered him to appear at RSHA headquarters at nine o'clock the next morning.

When the puzzled Skorzeny arrived at the headquarters he was ushered into the office of a major who, after swearing him to secrecy, explained the reason for summoning him.

"He told me the *Abwehr* had a special unit called the Brandenburg Battalion which was entrusted with certain special missions," Skorzeny said. "Hitler was not satisfied with the operations of this battalion and wanted the RSHA to form a second unit to undertake such missions. He asked me if I would be interested in commanding the new unit."[2]

Skorzeny was approached for the position because of his former close association with Kaltenbrunner, chief of the RSHA. Kaltenbrunner had succeeded Reinhardt Heydrich in May 1942, when Heydrich was assassinated by Czech resistance fighters. The former Austrian SS leader had never forgotten Skorzeny and the way he had intervened during the *Anschluss* to prevent a pitched battle between the Nazis and the Austrian soldiers guarding the president at the palace. When Hitler ordered the new commando unit formed, he immediately suggested Skorzeny.

On April 20 Skorzeny was promoted to captain and assigned to Amt VI-S. Schellenberg, who was in charge of the entire Amt VI section, gave him a personal briefing. The appearance and background of the two men were completely different. Skorzeny was a huge, bluff, and rough-looking man with a scar that ran from his left ear to his chin. His uniform never seemed to fit properly. He spoke loudly, interrupted others, and had a quick temper. Action was much more important to him than planning and he had a tendency to start an operation without proper preparation, in the belief that he could bull his way through to success. Schellenberg, on the other hand, was a bright young intellectual who had studied both medicine and law at the University of Bonn. Thin and of medium height, he was always correctly dressed and polite to perfection. His voice was soft but persuasive and he had a disarming smile. Yet, he had courage equal to any man in the RSHA and had proved it several times. In November 1939 he had abducted two English intelligence officers, Captain S. Payne Best and Major R. H. Stevens, from a Dutch border village named Venlo; had tried to kidnap the Duke and Duchess of Windsor in Portugal; and was involved in listing prominent persons in England on the Hitler "black list" (to be dealt with later).

Schellenberg was sitting behind his special desk that actually was an office fortress, one that Skorzeny would duplicate later for his own headquarters. Two automatic guns were built into it which Schellenberg could fire at will by pushing a button. Another button activated a siren to summon guards to surround the office and guard all exits.

"He told me he wanted me to take charge of the schools being established to instruct agents of the new unit and to convert an SS battalion called Oranienberg into a sabotage and subversive organization renamed *Jagdverbände* 502 (Hunting Group). All orders were verbal. Nothing was written on paper."[3]

Skorzeny discovered the very first day that his assignment to head Hitler's commandos was fraught with many dangers besides those presented by the enemy. The chain of command, for instance, was never clearly outlined to him. Theoretically, since his new unit, the AMT VI-S, was a section of the RSHA, Kaltenbrunner was his overall commander. He soon discovered it wasn't that simple. Schellenberg, supposedly under Kaltenbrunner's command, was such an intimate associate of Himmler, who controlled the entire SS, that Kaltenbrunner was often completely ignored when missions were assigned Skorzeny. In addition, the German armed forces had to be appeased so the OKW also had a finger in the pie. This meant that Skorzeny often had to deal with Canaris, the head of the *Abwehr*, who despised the SS organizations and was secretly plotting against Hitler. Consequently, one of Skorzeny's most difficult tasks was trying to get his orders properly defined so he could obtain the necessary equipment and manpower from the various officers whom he had to consult before he could perform a mission.

"For matters dealing with the schools established at The Hague, Heinrichsburg near Belgrade, and at Neustrelitz, I had to consult with Schellenberg," Skorzeny explained. "Anything pertaining to the Jagd units, however, I had to meet with the OKW. Then, of course, Himmler had the last word about everything. It was very confusing."[4]

The interrogation of Skorzeny at Nuremberg in 1945 clearly indicated the difference in the chain of command between the Nazi commandos and the United States commando unit, William Donovan's Office of Strategic Services (OSS). Donovan made all the decisions for the OSS—financial and operational—although the Joint Chiefs of Staff of the military forces had overall responsibility for the unit. In the Third Reich, however, it was much more complex, as Colonel Brundage, the interrogator, discovered.

Q. Was Himmler your chief?

A. Over Schellenberg, it naturally went up to Himmler.

Q. Directly to Himmler from Schellenberg?

A. No, Schellenberg, Kaltenbrunner, Himmler.

Q. Did Kaltenbrunner have anything to do with your schools?

A. He did not concern himself with them. He did not visit any of them.

Q. What did he have to do with your Jagd battalions?

A. He had nothing to do with them.

Q. Well, he was directly over Schellenberg.

A. But Schellenberg didn't have much to do with the Jagd battalions. For instance, I received financial support from him but in a military way he had nothing to do with the matter.

Q. Did you have the authority to initiate your own action without consulting Schellenberg?

A. Of course, if I received an order from the OKW then Schellenberg was not asked. Otherwise, I had to ask him.

Skorzeny also took direct orders from Hitler and had personal access to the Führer, which gave him a way to circumvent Schellenberg, Kaltenbrunner, and the OKW if he so desired or thought advisable to accomplish his mission. When, as often happened, Hitler gave him a blanket directive ordering all other officers to cooperate with Skorzeny so that the commandos could complete an assigned mission, Skorzeny didn't hesitate to take advantage of the directive. This resulted in Skorzeny's becoming the most hated man in the SS by both the military and officers of other sections of the SS. Skorzeny, in turn, hated military officers with a passion and declared at every opportunity that "there is no such thing as a military officer's code of honor; it is only a cloak for cowardice in the face of the enemy."[5] Such remarks were countered by the charges that for Skorzeny, protected by his influence with Hitler, no law existed and he did as he pleased. Because of this leeway in his chain of command, Skorzeny developed a loner approach to his special missions and became a mystery man even among his Nazi associates.

The first man Skorzeny recruited to help him organize the commando unit was Karl Radl, a college friend. Radl had the finesse to deal with the other SS and military units which Skorzeny lacked and very quickly recruited some of the best men available. Together—Radl by sophisticated maneuvering and Skorzeny by bellowing and threatening—they obtained experts from the SS Parachute Battalion, the Wehrmacht's secret Brandenburg Battalion, the Waffen SS, and any other unit that caught their attention. Skorzeny was fortunate enough to find an area for his headquarters at Friedenthal near Oranienberg, northeast of Berlin. Originally he had an office in the Berkaer Strasse in Berlin but Friedenthal, with its meadows surrounding a small castle that dated back to the days of Frederick the Great, was much more suitable for training his commandos. He had barracks, a hangar, mess halls, training schools, and an athletic hall erected. Drill grounds were laid out. Skorzeny and Radl established their offices on the ground floor of the castle and their sleeping quarters on the third floor.

In addition to the experts Skorzeny recruited from other military and SS units, he also brought SS personnel convicted of various offenses to Friedenthal. Many of the men came from the prison camp at Chlum, Czechoslovakia. A large number of the convicts proved unsatisfactory for commando operations and were sent back to their prisons. Others were integrated into the Jagd units.

Training was difficult, both physically and mentally. Each man was expected to have a basic knowledge of rifles, grenades, and artillery pieces; had to be able to operate motorcycles, motorboats, automobiles, and locomotives; be able to parachute from an aircraft; and be an expert swimmer. Many were taught foreign languages. All were taught sabotage techniques and how to use secret weapons. Skorzeny obtained supplies of German-developed secret weapons from both the SS workshop and laboratory located in Douglas Strasse, Berlin-Schmargendorf, and the military installation based at an abandoned factory at Quenz. Among the equipment provided him were hexagonal incendiary bombs made of Nipolit about one foot long and an inch in diameter; clockwork delay fuses with an eight- to twenty-eight-day maximum delay; another delay fuse containing a selenium cell and a battery that would function either when light hit the cell or when light ceased to fall on the cell; a delay fuse set off by a high-frequency radio signal; a railway pressure igniter for attachment to a rail which was activated by the first train passing by and had a maximum time delay of fourteen days; and other equipment designed for specific purposes.

Himmler also gave orders that Skorzeny was to have the use of *Kampf Geschwader (KG)* 200 (Combat Squadron). This elite squadron flew deep penetration missions and special flights which required suicide bombs, remote-controlled bombs, gliders, piloted V-1s, and *Flugz̧uge* (pick-a-back) aircraft—a combination of a piloted plane attached to the top of pilotless lower plane which was launched in the air and guided to the target by the pilot in the top plane. However, each mission involving KG 200 had to be approved by Himmler or Schellenberg after being proposed by Skorzeny.

With a headquarters established, experts recruited to man his commando organization, and a supply of Germany's most secret weapons, Skorzeny should have felt ready for action, but he didn't. He was aware that both the British and the Americans had a head start on him as far as commando operations were concerned. At first he depended upon his friend Kaltenbrunner to explain to him just what type of missions he should prepare for and how the Americans and British had handled similar missions. He requested a meeting with Kaltenbrunner, but the RSHA commander with whom he had associated so closely in Austria prior to the war was now curt and unfeeling. He merely reiterated that as far as the schools were concerned Skorzeny was to deal with Schellenberg. Operations?

"You are an SS leader," Kaltenbrunner told him. "You are supposed to know how to organize and lead such a battalion. Use the British commando and Brandenburg Battalion techniques as an example."[6]

The entire discussion lasted less than five minutes. Kaltenbrunner didn't ask him about his wife, didn't invite him to any social affairs as he had in previous years. Skorzeny needed help more than ever as he left RSHA headquarters.

During the next two weeks Skorzeny studied every captured British commando document he could locate, analyzing the procedures used by them. He also traveled from Friedenthal to Holland to attend an espionage course being taught by an *Abwehr* officer. It was during this visit that Skorzeny was amazed to discover the large number of Allied planes that flew over occupied Europe every night, dropping agents and supplies or picking up agents. He learned that more than half the supplies dropped to enemy agents was actually recovered by Germans waiting on the ground. In addition, many of the enemy agents were captured while trying to get the supplies, and some of these agents were willing to shift allegiance to Germany, if the pay was right. From these "double agents" Skorzeny learned a great deal about the techniques and equipment used by the British commandos, much of which he adapted for use by his own organization. The fact that the

British had some weapons not available in Germany bothered him for a time but he also solved that problem.

Learning that several British radios, dropped for use by the enemy agents, had been captured by the German intelligence agents and that the Germans with the help of "double agents" were in contact with Great Britain, Skorzeny saw an opportunity to get the secret weapons he wanted. He ordered the "double agents" to ask their contacts in England to drop such weapons for use by the Dutch underground. The *Abwehr* agent in charge of the espionage course scoffed at the idea and refused to cooperate. Skorzeny, however, contacted Schellenberg and was given approval to try the idea. Within the next week the British had dropped a silent revolver and a silencer for a Sten gun, two items Skorzeny wanted very badly. To test the revolver, he fired at a rabbit running a few feet ahead of the skeptical *Abwehr* officer. The officer never heard the shot and was completely confused when the rabbit fell dead at his feet. Skorzeny had the last laugh.

In June when Skorzeny returned to Germany, he attended a meeting in the office of Canaris, commander of the *Abwehr*. Schellenberg told him that the purpose of the meeting was to discuss how the *Abwehr* and the new commandos could coordinate their future special operations and share their intelligence files.

"We were ushered into a dimly lighted office and invited to sit down in deep armchairs," Skorzeny said. "Canaris, a bald man of medium height, had colorless eyes and an expressionless glance that traveled ceaselessly from one to another of us, then periodically fixed on some imaginary spot on the wall."[7]

Skorzeny had approached the meeting with the anticipation that the experienced intelligence man, and especially Canaris of the *Abwehr*, would be willing to assist the new SS commando unit. Instead he found only resistance.

"Canaris was like a jellyfish: stick your finger into the gelatinous mass and the moment you withdrew it, the mass resumed its former shape as though nothing had happened. For three deadly hours we attempted to get answers but Canaris never ceased to find—or invent—new reasons to postpone any decision. I left with new proof of his ill will."[8]

Canaris didn't want Skorzeny to succeed because any such success by the new SS commandos would be a bad reflection on his old-line army unit, the *Abwehr*. Kaltenbrunner was having too many problems trying to control the RSHA and keep in the good graces of Himmler and

Hitler to risk his reputation and career on an adventurer such as Skorzeny. Schellenberg, ambitious and clever, planned to maneuver himself into a position where he could take credit for Skorzeny's success, if any, but avoid responsibility for his failure if the commando operations were a fiasco. The Führer didn't like failures.

On July 26 Skorzeny had lunch at the Hotel Eden in Berlin with a friend from Vienna. After lunch he called his office to check on his mail. His secretary didn't take time to answer his query about the mail.

"You are to report to the Führer's headquarters," she said excitedly. "At seventeen hours a plane will be waiting for you at the Tempelhof airport."[9]

The time for action had arrived.

3 THE RESCUE OF BENITO MUSSOLINI

Skorzeny boarded the Ju-52 Hitler had sent to fly him from the Tempelhof airfield in Berlin to *Wolfsschanze* (Wolf's Lair) at exactly five o'clock on the afternoon of July 26. He had no further explanation for the sudden and surprising order to report to Hitler, but as the plane droned eastward through the heavy cloud cover he suspected it had something to do with the turn of events in Italy. The day before there had been unconfirmed reports received in Berlin from Italy that a change in government had taken place. The reports at first were very short and confusing. At 7:00 A.M. on the morning of July 26, however, the German radio announced that the Duce, Benito Mussolini, had resigned; King Victor Emmanuel had taken affairs of state into his own hands, and Marshal Pietro Badoglio was now head of government. Skorzeny was shocked. Mussolini and Fascist Italy had been Hitler's Axis partner since 1936, and the Führer and the Duce had become symbols of world power and invincibility. The resignation of Mussolini would have serious repercussions in Germany.

Skorzeny's plane touched down at the airport in Rastenburg, East Prussia, at three minutes before eight o'clock. A car was waiting and he was quickly driven through the various security checkpoints to the innermost area of the Wolf's Lair, to Hitler's quarters. In a small building used by the Führer as a teahouse, Skorzeny was introduced to five Wehrmacht officers who also had been ordered to report to Hitler. In a few minutes all six were greeted by the Führer, who asked them to give a short resume of their careers. Skorzeny was the only Austrian among the six officers and the only one who was familiar with Italy through private trips he had taken before the war.

When Skorzeny completed the short review of his career, Hitler looked at him in silence for a few seconds. His eyes traveled over the big Austrian's body and lingered on the vivid scar on Skorzeny's left cheek. Suddenly the Führer asked: "What is your attitude toward Italy and the Italian people?"[1]

Skorzeny was blunt. "I am an Austrian and our attitude toward Italy is prejudiced by the happenings in the previous World War and by South Tyrol."[2]

A faint smile appeared on Hitler's face and he dismissed the other five officers.

Hitler took Skorzeny into a private room and verified what Skorzeny had thought was the purpose of the meeting—the events in Italy. Hitler was worried about the fate of Mussolini, whom no one had seen since his resignation. He was also worried that the new Italian government would desert Germany and join the Western powers.

"The House of Savoy will betray us this time," Hitler said, referring to King Victor Emmanuel, who had taken affairs of state into his own hands. "Although all official German authorities in Rome assure me that a desertion of Italy from the Axis is unthinkable, I feel these authorities have been deceived by the Italians and do not see the situation correctly. A monarchy which shows itself to be so unthankful to the savior of Italy, to the man who gave it an empire, who even betrays him, will also not keep faith with the country with whom it is allied for the second time. But I will keep faith with my friend Mussolini and will never permit him to be handed over to the Allies."[3]

Skorzeny listened, well aware that Hitler was troubled about the disappearance of the Duce and the possibility that Italy would change sides in the war, but he was unable to see what part he personally played in the situation. The Führer continued talking about Mussolini.

"The Duce is, in my view, the last Roman. He is the last visible symbol of the proud old Rome that once ruled the world. His life, his rise, and his deeds are only comparable with those of an old Roman ruler. The Duce is more to me than a confederate, more than the representative and founder of Italian fascism. He has come close to me as a human being as few men before. He is my great friend. And I never leave my friends in the lurch.

"You, Skorzeny, will free my friend Mussolini and prevent the terrible fate which our enemies have conceived for him. You and your men are relieved from duty with the Luftwaffe and placed under the command of General Student. Only one thing worries me and that is the attitude of the German authorities in Rome. The German embassy listens completely to the monarchy. They have become soft in the southern sun, they have become half-Italians themselves. Even Kesselring [Field Marshal Albert Kesselring, commander of German armed forces in the Mediterranean] believes what is told to him by the Italian crown prince and others around him. And I know that the Italian monarchy will betray Germany for the second time. That must be prevented by all means. Rome must not be lost or the southern front will collapse. General Student and his troops will have to especially keep an eye on that.

"Your mission to free the Duce must be kept particularly secret. I have ordered, and I give the order to you expressly, that only a total of five persons may know of this plan. General Student and you are a part of the five. In no case may the German embassy know of your order. Kesselring and his staff may not know of it under any circumstances. The three men who help you and will learn about the plan you must find yourself, but don't choose anyone from these two duty stations. General Student will brief you further."

Hitler put his arm on Skorzeny's arm and looked him directly in the eyes. "Bring me my friend Mussolini. I know you will do your best and succeed."

Skorzeny, at that moment, was affected by Hitler's personality as so many others had been in the past and would be yet in the future. He said later that Hitler had spoken with such powers of persuasion that he had no thought of danger or the impossibility of the mission to find and free a man secretly held by a hostile government. On the contrary, Skorzeny felt he definitely would succeed, because Hitler said he would.

After the conference Skorzeny went back to the teahouse to meet with General Kurt Student, commander of the XI Parachute Corps (*Fleigerkorps*), an officer who had been involved on all fronts of the war and was considered an expert in airborne operations. Later Himmler joined the conference and gave both Student and Skorzeny an hour-long lecture on the political situation in Italy as he saw it. It was known by the Germans that the Fascist Grand Council had met on July 24 and voted nineteen to seven for a no-confidence motion in the Duce and his government. When Mussolini·reported to King Victor Emmanuel at the Villa Ada at five o'clock the next day, he was put under protective arrest and his whereabouts since that time were unknown to the Germans. Himmler forbade Skorzeny to take any notes while he talked, but Skorzeny remembered clearly two salient points: Mussolini was a prisoner of King Victor Emmanuel and the king intended to hand the Duce over to the Allies as a pawn in a negotiated peace favorable to Italy.

It was midnight by the time Himmler departed and Skorzeny and Student could get down to details about the rescue mission. Student said he would immediately transfer his XI Parachute Corps to Italy from southern France by air, while Skorzeny would provide fifty commandos from Friedenthal. The commandos would leave the Staaken airfield near Berlin in Ju-52s at 7:00 A.M. on July 27 and fly to Italy. Skorzeny ordered twelve officers and twenty-five men to depart Staaken in the first transport and the remainder to follow in a second aircraft. Radl was told to select men who spoke Italian and to wear paratroop uniforms since, supposedly, they were members of Student's XI Parachute Corps. This disguise was used not to raise suspicions of Italian officers or government officials who might see them. After he had completed his arrangements, Skorzeny and Student left the Rastenburg airfield and flew nonstop to Pratica di Mare at Rome. From the airfield they were taken to the small town of Frascati where Kesselring had his headquarters. That same evening he and Student had dinner with Kesselring and cautiously quizzed the field marshal about Mussolini, while at the same time being very careful not to reveal to Kesselring the reason they were in Italy. They learned nothing. Kesselring had been unable to learn where Mussolini was being held. It was obvious to Skorzeny that if the field marshal couldn't locate Mussolini despite all his Italian contacts, he himself, a newcomer to the area, faced a difficult problem.

At the German embassy the next day, Skorzeny discovered the ambassador and his staff were just as much in the dark. They had made official inquiries about the disappearance of the Duce but the Badoglio government was evasive, saying only that Mussolini was well and comfortable. There was no shortage of rumors for Skorzeny to check out. Some vowed that Mussolini had committed suicide, others said he was in a sanatorium suffering a serious illness, while still another group stated he was in Switzerland on vacation. During the next three weeks all Skorzeny learned was that Mussolini had been taken in an ambulance from his meeting with the king to the carabinieri barracks. But there wasn't a single clue where he had been taken from there.

Mussolini's birthday on July 29 seemed to offer an opportunity to discover his whereabouts. Hitler had a deluxe edition of the works of Nietzsche prepared as a gift and gave orders to the German embassy to notify the Italian government that his personal gift from the Führer was to be delivered personally by Kesselring. The ruse failed. Badoglio said that even he did not know where the Duce was and consequently could not direct Kesselring to him. After this disappointment, Skorzeny personally doubled his efforts to locate the Duce. He visited restaurants, bars, and night clubs, always listening and watching for the smallest clue to Mussolini's whereabouts. The Italian citizens were as puzzled as the Germans, and the conversation often centered on the disappearance of the Duce. Several times Skorzeny purposely rebutted an Italian who bragged he knew where Mussolini was, in an effort to make the man angry and more careless about any secrets he might have. Once, an Italian sailor attacked Skorzeny with a knife after such an argument and only Skorzeny's past duelling experience saved him.

From a fruit vendor who delivered produce to Terracino, a small village on the Gulf of Gaeta, he learned that a "very important person" was on the nearby island of Ponza. A loose-tongued Italian naval officer in a bar told Skorzeny that his ship had transferred Mussolini from Ponza to La Spezia on the Ligurian coast and threw his wine glass at Skorzeny when the big Austrian called him a braggart trying to impress the women in the bar. When Ponza and La Spezia were checked, Skorzeny discovered that Mussolini had indeed been held at both places but had disappeared again.

As August neared its end it was more and more evident that the Badoglio government intended to surrender to the Allies. The generally deteriorating situation on all fronts and the neverending Allied air raids on Italian cities, including Rome, made such a surrender more desirable to the Italians than ever. The disappearance of several leading Italian politicians from Rome made it certain to Skorzeny that the negotiations were already underway at some secret rendezvous. It also became evident that Mussolini was to be handed over to the Allies as a part of the deal. German intelligence intercepted a letter from Badoglio showing the high priority placed on the head of the Duce. The letter was addressed to the chief of police in Rome, Carmine Senise.

Your Excellency:
This morning I sent the following message to His Excellency, Commanding General Cerica of the Carabinieri: "Inspector General Polito of the Police is responsible for the custody of the former Head of the Government, Benito Mussolini. He is personally responsible to the Government for seeing to it that the above-mentioned Mussolini neither escapes nor is released from detention. General Polito will ask Carabinieri Headquarters and the Chief of Police for whatever personnel he requires and may specify the names of the men he prefers to have with him. He is to be given everything he requests. Inspector Polito will keep me constantly informed."

Badoglio[4]

If Badoglio placed such importance on Mussolini's captivity and was willing to go to such lengths to prevent his release, Skorzeny's mission, even if he finally located the Duce, stood small chance of success.

Shortly after the Badoglio letter was intercepted, Skorzeny heard another Italian naval officer tell an Italian pilot that in his opinion Mussolini was in the Sardinia area. Try as he might, Skorzeny was unable to hear the remainder of the conversation so he didn't know whether the officer said he was actually on Sardinia or on one of the neighboring islands. Since he had no other clues at the time and was getting desperate, Skorzeny immediately investigated. Initially, when he reached the area, many of the citizens hinted that the ideal place to hold the Duce was Isola di Picco, a small island where a number of former fascists were imprisoned. That proved false, as did the rumor that Mussolini was on Caprera. Skorzeny was ready to give up his search in the Sardinia area when a young prostitute told him he should visit the city of La Maddalena if he wanted to see the great Duce! Further inquiry by Skorzeny netted the information that Mussolini had arrived at La Maddalena aboard the ship *Panthere* and had been handed over to Admiral Bruno Brivonesi, commander of the Naval base there.

La Maddalena was on the small island of Maddalena at the northern point of Sardinia and was an excellent choice for the Italians but Skorzeny wanted to confirm Mussolini's presence. One of his officers,

Robert Warger, disguised as an Italian sailor, joined a marine communications staff in the harbor of La Maddalena and through harbor tours and photographs verified that Mussolini was on the island. The Duce was held in a villa 500 meters west of the city guarded by 150 men and enclosed by a wall two meters high. In front of the villa a double guard of carabinieri patrolled day and night. A second double guard was posted at the entrance gate to the villa and a third guard was positioned in the garden inside the wall. Several telephone lines extended into the villa, making it obvious to Skorzeny that the guard commander was in direct contact with the Italian harbor command, which could provide additional troops at a moment's notice.

Skorzeny needed more information so he could formulate a plan to attack the villa. The presence of two Italian seaplanes and a sea-rescue plane, painted white with a red cross on its fuselage, worried him. It would be very easy for the Italians to evacuate Mussolini from the island, making a rescue attempt fruitless. Since he couldn't get inside the wall surrounding the villa, Skorzeny decided to make a reconnaissance flight over it and take some photographs in an effort to verify further Mussolini's presence. Later that day he took off from the Vieno Fiorito airfield in the same He-111 that had flown him to Sardinia from Italy.

"On the flight I intended to take photos with my Leica. I wanted photos of the villa grounds and the coast line," Skorzeny said. "However, just as we neared Maddalena enemy aircraft were reported in the area. I ordered the pilot to stay on course anyway and I snapped several photos from a position in the forward gun turret of the aircraft. I was still taking pictures when the plane suddenly jerked violently and started a sharp descent."[5]

Enemy aircraft had shot out one engine on the He-111 and damaged the control surfaces. Skorzeny just had time to grab the grips of the gun mount before the plane hit the water. The nose window shattered and water streamed in on top of the dazed Skorzeny. As the plane started going deeper into the water a crew member pulled him free and helped him swim a few feet away. Miraculously, the He-111 cabin had enough air inside it so that the plane nosed to the surface again, and Skorzeny was able to get his camera from the nose turret position as well as a life raft. A few minutes later the aircraft went under the water for the last time. An hour later a small Italian naval vessel picked Skorzeny and the others out of the water, but the captain of the ship never bothered to ask the big Austrian what he was doing in the area when the plane crashed.

Despite the failure of the reconnaissance flight, Skorzeny went ahead with plans to rescue the Duce. He convinced Student that a parachute attack on the villa was not practical, mainly because there was no way to get off the island fast enough after getting Mussolini. Skorzeny planned to make the rescue attempt by water, using a flotilla of speedboats, several minesweepers, and barges to carry his commandos. Hitler, notified about the pending rescue attempt, ordered both Student and Skorzeny to the Wolf's Lair again to give him the details. After listening to Skorzeny for nearly an hour, the Führer nodded.

"You have convinced me. I approve your plan. There is one thing more, however," Hitler said. "If the mission is a failure, Skorzeny, I will find myself obliged to repudiate you in public and state that you acted on your own initiative."[6]

With that warning ringing in his ears, Skorzeny returned to Italy and prepared for the mission. On August 27 Skorzeny left the harbor of Nettuno with Radl in a speedboat headed for La Maddalena. When he arrived, nothing seemed changed on the island and he was confident the operation could start as scheduled at dawn the next morning. As a precaution, however, he decided on one last personal reconnaissance on the island. Disguised as a German sailor and carrying a basket of dirty clothes, Skorzeny walked unaccosted toward the villa area. He passed directly in front of the villa where Mussolini was being held to a neighboring house where he had a fine view of the villa grounds. He was surprised to see the guards inside the wall sitting around and drinking instead of being on the alert. This puzzled him. He was still trying to unravel the puzzle when a carabinieri arrived at the terrace where he was standing. They struck up a conversation and Skorzeny, searching for information, said: "It certainly is too bad the Duce finally died from that disease he had been suffering from so long."

The carabinieri looked at him in disgust then told how that very morning he was one of the guards who had escorted Mussolini to the air-sea rescue seaplane at the dock when the Duce was taken off Maddalena. By the time the disappointed Skorzeny got back to his rendezvous with Radl, his adjutant had the same information. Mussolini definitely was no longer on Maddalena. Skorzeny ordered the rescue mission canceled and returned dejectedly to Rome.

There he found that the German position was deteriorating. More and more Italian troops were being recalled from the front lines for duty in Rome. German officials in Lisbon and Madrid reported that Italy's surrender was imminent. On September 7 an eyewitness reported to Hitler's headquarters that an American general called Taylor [General Maxwell Taylor], accompanied by a staff man, had traveled in an ambulance to the Palazzo Caprara from Gaeta where they had landed from an Italian warship. When this news was relayed to Skorzeny he knew time was fast running out on his efforts to rescue Mussolini. The American general would have made the dangerous trip only to negotiate a surrender and the Duce was part of the deal. He was correct. The very next day General Dwight D. Eisenhower, Allied commander-in-chief, announced that an armistice had been signed with Italy.

Was it too late to save Mussolini? Skorzeny, now tipped off that the Duce might be held a prisoner high in the Abruzzi mountain range east of Rome didn't think so. The report stated that on August 27 Mussolini had been flown from Maddalena to Vigna di Valle on Lake Bracciano then taken by ambulance to the village of Assergi. There he boarded a funicular railway which took him up the Gran Sasso—where he was hidden in a hotel. However, Skorzeny was suspicious of the report after what had happened at La Maddalena. He and his commandos had tortured two carabinieri officers until they admitted the Duce was on the Gran Sasso, but more evidence was needed before he attempted a rescue. Once again Skorzeny scheduled a reconnaissance flight over Mussolini's suspected prison, just as he had done at La Maddalena, but he hoped for better luck this time.

Using one of Student's aircraft, Skorzeny and Radl took off from the airport at Pratica di Mare on the same day the armistice was announced and flew to the Gran Sasso. The plane was equipped with an automatic camera, but when Skorzeny tried to use it he discovered the film was jammed and it wouldn't work. Taking his own hand camera, he crawled to the tail turret of the plane, knocked out a window, and, with Radl holding his feet, leaned out through the opening and snapped several photos of the area around the hotel and the hotel itself. The temperature at the plane's altitude was near zero and Skorzeny's hands were so cold after a few minutes he nearly dropped the camera. Wriggling his feet frantically as a signal for Radl to pull him back into the plane, Skorzeny managed to keep his grip on the camera. Confident that he had the film he needed, he ordered the pilot to return to base at low altitude where the temperature was much higher and he could get warm again. It was a lucky move because as they neared Rome a large flight of Allied fighters and bombers passed overhead. Skorzeny's plane slipped past them undetected because it was skimming the treetops.

At Frascati he discovered the German film laboratory had been bombed and was no longer in operation. He finally got his film developed at a small nearby laboratory that had come through the air raid unscathed, but the prints were only 4 × 4 inches. Examining them carefully, Skorzeny noted the heavy guard detachment in the area and saw that the funicular station was closed to the public. This verified reports from agents he had sent to try to use the funicular railway who had been turned back by Italian soldiers long before they reached it. Convinced now that the Duce was at the hotel, Skorzeny studied the terrain in the photos. It was a discouraging moment for him. If he and his commandos tried to capture the funicular railway, undoubtedly the carabinieri guarding Mussolini at the hotel would be notified and would have time either to kill him or take him off the mountain to another hiding spot. If they tried to climb the steep slope without capturing the funicular railway, they would be detected before they were halfway to the hotel and be very vulnerable to the guns from above and below. That ruled out a land attack, but an air attack seemed every bit as impossible. The rarefied air at the 3,000-foot level of the hotel presented dangerous problems for parachutists, problems that would require special equipment that was not available.

He studied the pictures closer under a magnifying glass. Suddenly he brightened.

"Look at this meadow behind the hotel," he said to Radl. "Perhaps we could land gliders in it."

It was a small triangular area on one of the photographs. Even in the small photo Radl could see rocks and small ditches but his argument that trying to land gliders in the area would be certain suicide was brushed away by Skorzeny. Determined to prove to Hitler that he could rescue Mussolini, Skorzeny ignored the warnings from Radl and later from Student and his staff officers.

"Unless you can suggest a better way," he said to the general, "I will use gliders to take the men in and we will land on the meadow."[7]

There was no better way, so Student reluctantly accepted Skorzeny's plan. Twelve gliders were ordered from France with a deadline arrival time of September 11, so the rescue operation could be launched promptly at 7:00 A.M. the next day. Student also agreed to Skorzeny's request that a battalion of parachutists from the XI Parachute Corps seize the funicular station before the gliders landed on Gran Sasso. The battalion commander designated for the mission was Major Hans Mors, one of Student's best officers. The parachutists, after capturing the funicular railway, would then cover the retreat of the commandos and the evacuation of Mussolini from Gran Sasso. Each glider would carry nine men and a pilot, and each glider task force would have a special mission. The first two groups would land and secure the meadow. Skorzeny would be in the third glider, and as soon as it landed he would head for the hotel with his men and get Mussolini before the Italians could harm the Duce. The remaining nine gliders would land and these men would secure the entire area and hold it until Mors's parachutists joined them on the Gran Sasso. Some of Student's men would be in the gliders with the commandos, too.

Skorzeny recognized one weakness in the plan. If the Italians on Gran Sasso put up a battle with his commandos and delayed Skorzeny's access to the Duce, there was an excellent chance Mussolini could be murdered prior to his release. (Skorzeny was more concerned that his mission might be a failure and he would be discredited in the eyes of the Führer than he was about Mussolini's well-being.) While he was pondering this possibility, Radl suggested taking a high-ranking Italian officer with them who might be able to convince his fellow countrymen to lay down their arms without a fight. Skorzeny was delighted. He inquired at Student's headquarters whether any of the well-known Italian officers in the area might be willing to play such a part in the mission.

"General Ferdinando Soleti is known by the Italian troops and the carabinieri on Gran Sasso," Student said, "but he will not go along with you. He is a Badoglio man."

Skorzeny grinned. "He will go."[8]

Skorzeny sent a detachment of his commandos to Rome to find Soleti and keep him under surveillance until September 12. Meanwhile he discovered the gliders he was waiting for were having trouble getting through the Allied air defense between France and Italy and would definitely not arrive in time for the mission to be launched at 7:00 A.M. Zero hour was reset for 2:00 P.M., the afternoon of September 12. This was a setback and complicated the operation—the afternoon hot air currents would make the glider landing much more hazardous. There was no alternative, however, so Student was notified. He, too, was upset since the seven-hour delay meant his parachute troops would have to attack the funicular railway station in broad daylight. The odds against success were fast multiplying.

Even more depressing that long night of September 11 was an Allied radio broadcast stating that Mussolini had just arrived in North Africa! He had been transported on an Italian ship that had slipped from the harbor of La Spezia. Skorzeny was temporarily stunned but quick calculations proved the broadcast was a hoax. He knew when the Italian ships left La Spezia and there was not enough elapsed time between the sailing and the broadcast for the ship with Mussolini aboard to reach North Africa.

On the morning of September 12, Skorzeny arrived at Pratica di Mare airport shortly after 5:00 A.M. and was told his fleet of DFS 230 assault gliders would reach Italy by noon. He checked to make certain the return flight plans were set. Three alternatives were available. First, three transport planes would land at the Aquila di Abruzzi airport several miles away and Mussolini would be taken there and flown out. This was the safest route, except for the possibility of an attack by Italian troops during the land trip from Gran Sasso to Aquila. The second idea was for a small plane to land in a field in the valley near the funicular station below the Gran Sasso. The Duce would be taken down the funicular railway, loaded into the small plane, and flown out. The third and most hazardous of the plans was for a small plane to land *on* the Gran Sasso, pick up Mussolini and take off. Skorzeny wanted to use this last idea only in an extreme emergency since there was considerable doubt whether the plane could land or take off without crashing. If Mussolini was killed in a German plane crash after the rescue, Skorzeny knew it would be the same as signing his own death warrant. Hitler would be furious.

At 8:00 A.M. Skorzeny and Radl got into his Mercedes and drove to Rome to "convince" the Italian general, Ferdinando Soleti, to go to the Gran Sasso with them. Skorzeny's investigation had revealed that a few days earlier Soleti had sent some of his own troops to the hotel where Mussolini was being held to strengthen the guard detachment. These men would definitely recognize Soleti and, presumably, not fire when they saw him. This might give the commandos time to take over the hotel without a bitter fight. Soleti, however, greeted Skorzeny and Radl with coolness and refused their "invitation" to go to the Pratica di Mare airport, stating he had more important matters to tend to in Rome. Skorzeny promptly placed him under arrest and forced him into the Mercedes at gunpoint.

By the time they returned to the airport with their prisoner, the gliders were landing. Skorzeny ordered the tow planes refueled and then took Soleti into a small building to brief him on the upcoming rescue mission. After he heard the details of the proposed Mussolini liberation plan, the Italian general was more adamant than ever, vowing that he would never take part in such an operation.

"You will ride in the third glider with me, General," he said quietly, "or the Italian army will be short one general."[9]

The commandos boarded the twelve gliders shortly before 1:00 P.M. Skorzeny forced Soleti into the third glider with a pistol in his back then ordered the Italian to sit directly in front of him. The DFS 230 glider did nothing to bolster the confidence of either Skorzeny or the general. It was a flimsy-looking combination of steel tubes and fabric with very small windows spaced at intervals along the sides of the fuselage. The windows were covered with opaque cellophane which made it impossible to see the ground clearly. Skorzeny didn't feel comfortable as he sat straddling the narrow beam that substituted for seats, waiting for the tow plane to jerk the glider down the runway, but he had no alternative. He heard the engines of the tow plane rev up for the take-off attempt then suddenly stop. Before he could get out of the glider a bomb exploded on the airfield, followed by several more. Allied bombers on the way to Rome had diverted a formation to Pratica di Mare! Fortunately for Skorzeny and his commandos, only a few scattered bombs hit the runway and none hit the gliders. At 1:30 P.M. his glider moved down the runway and moments later was airborne.

As expected, the afternoon updrafts and downdrafts buffeted the gliders unmercifully. In addition heavy cloud cover made visibility very bad for the pilot of the glider, the only occupant who could see out. Halfway to the Gran Sasso, Skorzeny's glider entered a large billowing cloud and when it came out the other side the two lead gliders and their tow planes had disappeared. Not only did this mean he would not have men covering his own landing and subsequent entry into the hotel where Mussolini was held, but he now had to do his own navigation to the Gran Sasso. Taking out a knife, he slit a hole in the fabric of the fuselage and looked out. It took him a few minutes to find a recognizable landmark—the valley of Aquila—and get the glider back on course for the meadow near the hotel. There was one cheerful note. Looking through the slit in the fuselage, Skorzeny saw Major Mors's parachutists moving toward the funicular station on schedule.

Five minutes later Skorzeny got his first close-up view of the meadow he had decided to use as a landing strip for the gliders, based on the small photographs he had taken with his Leica. He suddenly felt sick. Instead of a level smooth meadow it was a very uneven rocky section of the mountain that definitely was not suitable for glider landings. The pilot shook his head, indicating he could not possibly get the DFS 230 down in one piece. But there was no way Skorzeny was going to cancel the mission.

"Release the tow line," he ordered.[10]

The pilot's face went white and he hesitated. Skorzeny repeated his order, his bellowing voice leaving no doubts about his intentions. The tow line was released and the tow plane turned back toward Pratica di Mare and safety. The glider silently began to lose altitude, rocking violently because of the mountain air currents. With the skill he had learned from many glider landings, the pilot lined up the buffeted DFS 230 for a perfect approach to the meadow. Skorzeny, looking out the windshield, shuddered at the large rocks and uneven terrain ahead. He felt the pilot bring the nose of the glider up slowly as he put the DFS 230 into a landing attitude. At that moment a large boulder loomed directly in the landing path of the glider.

"Release the parachute," Skorzeny bellowed.

The DFS 230 had a parachute in the tail for braking once the vehicle was on the ground. But Skorzeny's glider was still several feet above the ground when the canopy of the parachute blossomed out behind. The tail immediately lifted, the nose went down and hit the ground, and the DFS 230 came to a crashing stop a few feet short of the boulder.

Skorzeny's commandos, shook up by the rough landing but not seriously injured, emerged from the glider. Soleti, who had been so reluctant to board the glider that Skorzeny had to put a gun in his back, now had a distinct change of heart. He leaped from the glider and followed Skorzeny as the big Austrian raced toward the hotel, wanting to avoid a gun battle between the Italians and the Germans.

"Don't fire until I fire," Skorzeny shouted to his commandos.[11]

He went through the first entrance to the hotel and found himself in a radio room with two confused Italian soldiers. He quickly smashed the radio with the butt of his gun. When he discovered there wasn't a stairway from the radio room to the main part of the hotel, Skorzeny went back outside and ran around the side of the building toward the front entrance. A twelve-foot-high wall blocked his path, but his commandos boosted him over it and he hurried to the main entrance to the hotel, followed by the general and his companions who had been in the same glider. Out of the corner of his eye he saw other gliders approaching the meadow with more of his commandos, and he hoped they could land successfully among the rocks.

With Soleti at his side, Skorzeny went into the hotel only to be met by several well-armed carabinieri. They raised their guns and took aim. At that moment the captain of the carabinieri, Alberto Faiola, saw Soleti, whom he knew, and ordered his men to hold their fire. That was all Skorzeny needed. He pushed his way past them and hurried up the stairs to the second floor and opened the first door he came to. Standing inside was Benito Mussolini, guarded by two Italian soldiers. Seeing Skorzeny's machine gun, they quickly held up their hands and backed against the wall. Otto Schwerdt, who later was to take part in an infamous commando operation in Denmark with Skorzeny, entered the room and took the two Italians away.

Skorzeny turned to the startled Mussolini and said, "Duce, the Führer has sent me to set you free."

Mussolini nodded and, with tears streaming down his face, embraced the huge Skorzeny. "I knew my friend Adolf Hitler would not abandon me." [12]

He put on a black overcoat over his dark blue suit and pulled his hat down to his eyes. His cheeks were hollow and unshaven and the bounding energy which was his trademark was missing. He appeared to be a tired old man awaiting further orders.

"Let's get out of here," Skorzeny said, taking the Duce by the arm and leading him toward the stairway.

By this time Skorzeny's commandos, directed by Radl, had rounded up the Italian soldiers and carabinieri and the officer in command, Police Inspector Giuseppe Gueli. Skorzeny and the inspector settled the terms of the surrender very quickly, since by this time Major Mors and a detachment of his parachutists had arrived from the valley to reinforce the commandos who had landed by glider. Once the conditions of surrender were completed, Skorzeny prepared for the evacuation of the Duce from the mountain hotel. He was already aware that the safest of the three evacuation plans was cancelled. His radio communications to Rome had been cut off for some unknown reason and he could not request Student to bring the transports to the airport near the city of Aquila to fly Mussolini to Pratica di Mare.

He immediately ordered the second plan into effect. He would escort Mussolini down the captured funicular railway to the valley below, where a Fieseler 156 Storch (Stork) short-takeoff-and-landing aircraft used for commando operations would fly him out. But this plan, too, was cancelled when the pilot seriously damaged the landing gear of the Storch when landing in the valley. That left only the third plan: try to fly the Duce off the Gran Sasso in a Storch using the rock-strewn meadow behind the hotel. It would be very risky but there was no alternative. Skorzeny had already received reports from an observation plane in the area that the Italians were rushing reinforcements to the Gran Sasso in an attempt to recapture Mussolini before he could be evacuated.

Captain Heinrich Gerlach, Student's personal pilot, was circling overhead in his Storch waiting orders. Skorzeny told him to land and pick up the Duce at once. Gerlach skillfully touched down between the wrecked gliders and rocks without damaging the Storch, taxied to a take-off position near the hotel, and motioned for Mussolini to get aboard. Skorzeny helped the Duce climb into the two-seater aircraft and then, to Gerlach's amazement, Skorzeny started to climb into the space behind the Duce's seat.

"No," Gerlach yelled. "We can't get off with three in the plane."

By this time Skorzeny was in the plane and he refused to get out. "I'm going. The Duce is my responsibility."[13]

Gerlach shook his head. The commandos had cleared a 200-yard downhill runway for him of rocks and gliders. At the end of the runway was a drop of 3,000 feet into the valley below. To add to the problems, he would be trying to get the Storch airborne with a tailwind instead of a headwind as was normal procedure. But the stubborn Austrian refused to budge from the plane. Gerlach, knowing his fuel supply was low, gave up.

"Well, for God's sake, come."[14]

Mussolini, a pilot himself, gripped the braces on the side of the fuselage as Gerlach revved the 240 horsepower engine of the Storch to full power. Suddenly he released the brakes and the plane slowly began to gain speed over the bumpy ground, jostling the passengers violently.

The terrain hampered Gerlach from reaching the proper takeoff speed although he had the throttle wide open. He reached the end of the makeshift runway lacking flying speed but he did the only thing possible—he guided the plane over the edge of the 3,000-foot drop, eased the control stick forward and dove the Storch toward the valley below in a desperate attempt to gain flying speed before they crashed. Both Skorzeny and the Duce were speechless as they watched the ground come closer and closer. Finally, when Skorzeny was certain they were going to crash, Gerlach eased back on the control stick. Slowly the nose of the Storch lifted inch by inch until they were in level flight a mere fifty feet above the trees. Gerlach's forehead was covered with perspiration, Mussolini's face was white, and Skorzeny was grinning. He had pulled off the "impossible mission."

The flight to Pratica di Mare was anticlimactic after the hair-raising takeoff from Gran Sasso. A transport plane was waiting at the airport to take Skorzeny and Mussolini to Vienna, where they checked into the Imperial Hotel. Himmler called to congratulate Skorzeny, knowing the rescue would give the SS a boost in the eyes of Hitler. As Skorzeny was getting ready to rest after Himmler's call, a full colonel came to the hotel and, on Hitler's orders, took off his own Knight's Cross to the Iron Cross and put it on Skorzeny. At that moment the Führer called.

"Today," Hitler told Skorzeny, "you have carried out a mission that will go down in history. You have given me back my old friend Mussolini. I have given you the Knight's Cross and promoted you to *Sturmbannführer* (major)." [15]

But perhaps the greatest reward Skorzeny received was permission from Hitler to visit his wife.

"You have been away from your wife too long, Skorzeny. It is not good for a man to be away from his wife's bed that length of time. Go home and enjoy yourself and make your wife happy." [16] As Eva Braun, Hitler's mistress, told him later when they met and Skorzeny told her how grateful he was for the leave time: "He understands. He understands."

4 TERRORISM VS.
MILITARY OPERATIONS

The rescue of Mussolini taught Skorzeny a valuable lesson. In many instances, greater results could be achieved by clandestine operations than by complex military operations. A political kidnapping or assassination could have a direct influence on the policy of an entire nation while a victory on the battlefield very often was countered by a defeat on another battlefield the next day. Skorzeny had an excellent teacher in Adolf Hitler when it came to terrorism. Hitler had utilized such tactics during his climb from army corporal to Führer. He was quick to grasp the importance of having a commando unit such as Skorzeny's *Jagdverbände* at his command and he wasted no time putting the unit to good use after the spectacular rescue of Mussolini.

Hitler had been receiving conflicting reports from the *Abwehr* about the political situation in France. When his army had captured the French nation in 1942 and Henri Philippe Pétain was established as a German puppet heading the government at Vichy in south-central France, Hitler thought the situation was under control. But as the Allies won victory after victory in North Africa and at the same time the Nazis refused to finalize the peace treaty they had proposed in 1942, Pétain became more and more disillusioned with Hitler. Pétain's collaboration with Hitler had made him a hated man in France and he needed to make an important move to reestablish his reputation. Pétain, according to reports from *Abwehr*, was contemplating negotiating with the Free French in North Africa to join the Allies and desert the Nazis. Hitler, his prestige at stake, ordered Skorzeny to France to kidnap Pétain in November 1943.

Leaving Radl at Friedenthal to handle the affairs of the commando headquarters, Skorzeny, Adrian Freiheer von Foelkersam, Herbert Bramfeld, and Erwin Schmiel hurried to Paris, where further orders awaited them. Or so they thought. Once again Skorzeny discovered that he was on his own, that the elite and snobbish German staff officers at the Hotel Continental in the Rue de Rivoli and the SS officers permanently stationed in their comfortable headquarters on the Champs-Elysées were much more interested in wine, women, and song than what the old Frenchman Pétain was going to do next. They laughed at Skorzeny's urgent message and tried to get him to join their social life. Finally Skorzeny took matters into his own hands. He telephoned Hitler at the Wolf's Lair and was told to requisition German troops immediately and surround the city of Vichy, blocking every entrance and exit. If Pétain tried to leave the city, Skorzeny was ordered to kidnap him and take him to Germany.

Skorzeny and his small staff, augmented by several police units and crack German troops, closed in on the spa city of Vichy. With von Foelkersam and the local police chief, Skorzeny went sightseeing in the city and gathered information enough to make a formal plan for the kidnapping of Pétain. He was delighted to learn that the entire city closed down for a siesta. Consequently, he decided that his troops would move into the city promptly at two o'clock in the afternoon during mid-siesta time on the day Hitler ordered the kidnapping. With everything at readiness, Skorzeny waited and waited. Three times his troops stopped Vichy government staff cars filled with officials trying to leave the city and turned them back. Word quickly filtered back to Pétain that he was a virtual prisoner in the city and he gave up all attempts to join the Free French in North Africa. On December 20 Skorzeny was notified to return to Germany, mission accomplished.

Although the primary aim of his assignment had been accomplished, Skorzeny was disappointed. Compared to the Mussolini rescue, the Vichy affair was very tame and he liked action. During his next operation, the plan to kidnap Marshal Tito (Josip Broz) of Yugoslavia, Skorzeny once again was frustrated by circumstances beyond his control but he was in a great deal of personal danger. Tito's guerrillas were being supplied by both the Americans and British and had reached a total strength of more than 100,000. With this large a force,

Tito was able to attack the German troops in many areas of the country and was a real annoyance to Hitler. The German troops were badly needed on other fronts but as long as Tito had them tied down, Hitler was unable to move the soldiers out of Yugoslavia. Hitler's orders were brief: "Get Tito—alive or dead."[1]

In Belgrade Skorzeny discovered much the same situation he had encountered in Rome when searching for the whereabouts of Mussolini. Half a dozen sources, including *Abwehr* agents, vowed that Tito was in half a dozen different locations. Skorzeny, completely confused by the reports he received in the capital, decided to travel to Agram, the largest city in the territory controlled by Tito. It was a dangerous trip—many of the farmers and villagers in the area traversed by Skorzeny were actually guerrillas and made a habit of ambushing Germans. The German commandant at Fruska Gora, a base on a mountain top in the area, tried to discourage Skorzeny from continuing toward Agram.

"You will never make it," he vowed. "There hasn't been a Mercedes along this road in a year. As soon as your car is spotted the word will be passed and Tito's men will be waiting for you."[2]

Skorzeny refused to turn around and, driving the Mercedes at full speed on the narrow farmland and mountain roads, reached Agram safely, much to the surprise of the Germans stationed there. At Agram he learned that Tito was using a cave near the town as his headquarters. Skorzeny immediately formulated his plan. He would "borrow" troops from the local German commanding officer, dress them in partisan clothes much like those worn by Tito's guerrillas, and make a sneak attack on the cave. Since Tito could see every road leading from Agram from his cave headquarters, Skorzeny planned to slip his men out of Agram a few at a time not to arouse any suspicion. They would gather in the woods out of sight of the sentries in the cave and then close in and kidnap, or if necessary kill, Tito.

The German general, however, held Skorzeny and his commandos in disdain. He believed in full-scale military operations for such assignments. He refused to cooperate. Before Skorzeny could contact Hitler's headquarters, the general launched an airborne attack on the cave using gliders, parachutists, and bombers. For his trouble the general obtained a full-dress uniform of Tito's and a severe reprimand from the Führer. Tito, forewarned of the attempt on his life by the bombing missions preceding the actual ground attack, escaped. Skorzeny flew back to Berlin more convinced than ever that one of his worst enemies was the German army itself.

Shortly after his return to Berlin, Skorzeny became involved in an operation that ultimately led to accusations against him by the International Military Tribunal at Nuremberg after the war. Part of his *Jagdverbände* was sent to Denmark where the resistance forces, in Hitler's words, had "become intolerable."[3] Skorzeny always denied that he was personally involved in the terrorist activities in Denmark; the Danish authorities say he was.

In December 1943 Hitler told Himmler and Joachim von Ribbentrop, his Minister for Foreign Affairs: "Terror must be fought by terror."[4]

There was a problem, however. The German occupation forces in Denmark were unable to cope with the situation. It was ironic because after the German military forces invaded the country in April 1940, Denmark was slated to have a special place in Germany's "New Order." Hitler intended to use the country that his Nazi juggernaut had captured without armed resistance as a showplace for the world to observe how well the captors would treat captives. It didn't take long, however, for the Nazis to unmask. Hitler drained the country systematically: food, gasoline, natural resources. He broke every pledge made to the country, thinking the docile Danes would knuckle under. That was a serious error.

The Danish resistance, organized carefully and slowly, began to undermine the German occupation forces. German transit systems, factories, railroad bridges, railroad lines, and rolling stock were all frequent targets. On a single night sixty factories were blown up. Despite the addition of 50,000 Nazi troops, the wave of sabotage continued unabated. Dr. Werner Best, the Nazi civilian representative in Denmark who was responsible for maintaining a pro-Nazi government, was completely frustrated. He was called to Berlin and when he returned he had a list of orders from Hitler including the declaration of a state of siege throughout Denmark, mandatory death sentences for all Danish saboteurs, and a curfew every night from 8:30 P.M. until 6:30 A.M.

Even these severe restrictions didn't slow the activities of the Danish resistance. Arrests increased from 3,250 in 1940 to 8,021 in 1943. General Kurt Daluege, Himmler's brutal troubleshooter, took over the military forces in Denmark and, in an effort to show his authority to the

Danes, demanded that the Parliament be disbanded. The committee representing the various political parties of Denmark refused and the country ended up with no government. In an act of revenge, Himmler vowed he would bring the Danes to their knees, and Daluege began arresting the 6,000 Jews who lived in Denmark and deporting them to Germany. King Christian sided with the Jews by wearing the hated yellow star and declaring: "We have no Jewish problem in Denmark."[5]

When Hitler saw that his military and security forces could not control the situation in Denmark, he turned to his clandestine units. The one man he felt he could always rely upon was Skorzeny. It is known that on the night of December 28, 1943, six men of Skorzeny's *Jagdverbände* departed Friedenthal for Copenhagen. Whether Skorzeny was with them was never proven, although he admitted to being in Denmark later that same year. When questioned at Nuremberg after the war, Skorzeny denied accompanying the commandos.

"During my absence from Friedenthal five or six people were put on special duty with the BdS Denmark [Commander of the Security Police]," Skorzeny said. "Sometime later I was requested to supply a leader, an officer to take charge. I objected for three reasons. First, there was a shortage of good officers; second, I felt this was a defense mission and I was in charge of offensive operations; and third, I would not supply an officer for a mission I would not lead myself."[6]

Allied investigators believe, however, that Skorzeny himself took over leadership of the group, although documents indicate a Lieutenant Otto Schwerdt, alias Peter, was the official commander.

The small group that left Friedenthal had passports made out in the names of commercial travelers and were equipped with revolvers with silencers and blackjacks. All were experts with explosives. They were met at Flensburg by Jacob Karstensen of the Gestapo, who was assigned to the commandos as an interpreter. The known members of the group were Schwerdt, Fritz Hummel, Ludwig Huf, Willi Glaesner, Hans Holtzer, Adolf Roemer, and Karstensen when they crossed the frontier and headed to Roeterkrug. Skorzeny's presence was never proven conclusively but facts revealed at Nuremberg indicate he was with them or was in Copenhagen waiting. In addition there was Karl Radl listed on documents recovered by Danish authorities after the war, but Skorzeny's adjutant denied being with the commandos when interrogated after his capture. He did admit being very familiar with the terrorist activities of the *Jagdverbände* members in Denmark from

December until August, but says it was because he read reports sent back to Friedenthal, not because he was with them during this period.

At Roeterkrug the commandos took the train to Copenhagen, where Huf arranged for them to stay at a flat in Florenswey 6 on the island of Amager. The following day they met with Gestapo officers to decide on terrorist activities against the Danish resistance. At this meeting Christian Damm, a Danish newspaperman, was selected as the initial victim. Damm, circumventing the strict Nazi censorship ordered by Daluege, published an underground paper that told about the concentration camps in Denmark, especially the infamous Horserod where more than 1,000 Danes were being systematically tortured. Damm also wrote scathing articles in his paper about the treatment of the Jews by the Nazis. His newspaper was smuggled out of the country to England and the facts about the treatment of the Danes by the German conquerors were broadcast throughout the world. Hitler was furious and demanded a stop to Damm's activities.

On December 30 Damm was working late in his office, finishing the final run of the latest edition of his underground newspaper. A friend of his was crossing into Sweden the following day and had made arrangements to take a copy of the newspaper with him. From Sweden the newspaper would be flown to England and the news distributed among the free world countries. Damm was bending over a small safe preparing to lock up the documents he had received from other resistance members, documents he intended to use in the next edition of his newspaper, when the door opened and three men stepped into the office. The three Skorzeny commandos, Schwerdt, Karstensen, and Glaesner, backed Damm into a corner of the room and berated the Danish publisher for his actions against the Third Reich. Schwerdt then pulled out his revolver with the silencer and shot Damm. The publisher collapsed onto the floor of the office and while he lay there writhing in pain, Schwerdt shot him again. The trio then hurried from the office thinking Damm was dead. Miraculously, he survived.

Kaj Munk, a pastor and well-known member of the Danish resistance, was not so fortunate. Most Danish churchmen stood firm against the Nazis even when the SS instigated their terrorist tactics and torture. Munk, an outstanding spiritual leader, author, and clergyman, was joined in his resistance by Pastor Ivar Lange of the Frederiksborg Church, Bishop Fuglsang-Damgaard, Primate of the Danish Lutheran State Church, and others. On New Year's Day 1944, Munk decided to preach a sermon emphasizing his sympathy for the treatment of the Jews in Denmark and the harassment of the church officials in Norway by the Nazis. He made this decision knowing full well that Damm had been seriously wounded, that the well-known Danish politician Ole Bjoern Krafft had been ambushed and that Bishop Fuglsang-Damgaard was under house arrest. His congregation was large on New Year's Day, hopeful that the next twelve months would bring them the freedom they sought. Munk's voice rang loud and clear through the sanctuary as he berated the Germans for their brutality. He was unaware that he had already been condemned to death by Skorzeny's commandos.

On January 2 Schwerdt, Karstensen, and Jacob Gfoeller, a newcomer from Friedenthal who had just joined the other commandos in Denmark, drove to Odensee where they waited until darkness fell. They then went on to Ringkoepping, where Munk resided. When he answered the knock on the door, Schwerdt never said a word. He grabbed the startled minister and shoved him toward the waiting automobile. Once Munk and the commandos were in the Mercedes, they headed toward Aarhus at full speed until they reached a point sixty kilometers from the city, where Schwerdt ordered the automobile stopped. Turning to Munk, he ordered, "Get out."[7]

The pastor slowly stepped out of the Mercedes and walked down the road without looking back. Schwerdt waited until Munk took a few steps, then shot him. The pastor dropped to the roadway and didn't move. Schwerdt quickly walked to where the pastor lay, shot him again, then leaned over and made certain Munk was dead. When he was positive his bullets had done the job, Schwerdt took a sign from his pocket and pinned it to the pastor's bullet-riddled body. It read: "Swine, you worked for Germany just the same."[8]

Witnesses who saw the Mercedes parked in front of Munk's home the night of January 2 stated that a tall man with a scar on his left cheek was sitting at the wheel of the car. Two Danish officers, Captain Carl Johann Villumsen and Captain Ole Jorgen Hald, who investigated Skorzeny after the end of the war, verified that they had information that Skorzeny had been with his commandos at Ringkoepping. This evidence resulted in a detailed interrogation of Skorzeny when he was put on trial at Nuremburg.

The murder of Munk and the attempted murder of Damm made the Danish resistance more cautious but did not halt their activities. Fritz Hummel, one of Skorzeny's men, was killed while attacking a Danish factory and the commandos narrowly escaped several ambushes. Yet, the *Jagdverbände* also continued its ruthless hunting of Danish resistance members and there were ten known assassinations. The Skorzeny commandos attacked sports gatherings, tossed bombs in restaurants where known resistance fighters ate, and made daring raids against student groups that opposed the Nazis. A large movie theatre was dynamited and several people killed because the commandos saw a known resistance fighter enter earlier. The most common type of mission was the bombing of factories. Not only were the irreplaceable machines destroyed or damaged but the workers became frightened and production fell to a low level. The commandos were careful to attack only those factories that produced goods for the Danes themselves, not factories producing war goods for Germany.

Skorzeny's headquarters at Friedenthal, whether he was there or in Denmark, received detailed reports of the activities of the commandos in Denmark. By June 1944, most of the assigned operations had been accomplished and Skorzeny's men began filtering back to Germany one by one. Skorzeny admitted at the Nuremberg interrogation that he was personally in Denmark in June, that he inspected many of the factories and buildings bombed by his commandos and was satisfied that most of the important objectives of the mission were accomplished. He needed his commandos back at Friedenthal for other special operations and convinced Himmler of this fact. The terrorist activities in Denmark were then turned over to Alfred Naujocks, a longtime Nazi troubleshooter. Naujocks masterminded the ferreting out of resistance members in Denmark until October 19 of that year, when he decided the Allies were going to win the war and he deserted to the Americans.

Skorzeny returned to Germany in late June and by the end of the month he had all of his commandos back at Friedenthal. The invasion of Europe by the American, British, and Canadian troops at Normandy on June 6 had indicated to Skorzeny that Hitler would be in need of the commandos. There would be many opportunities for special operations, and he wanted his *Jagdverbände* prepared.

When the expected call came from the Führer's headquarters, however, Hitler didn't need the commandos. He needed Skorzeny himself! The survival of Hitler and the Third Reich itself rested precariously on the shoulders of the big Austrian with the scarred face.

5 "YOU'RE IN COMMAND, SKORZENY!"

Skorzeny returned to Germany from Denmark completely unaware of the various plots to assassinate or depose Hitler. He was, however, confused about one thing. He couldn't understand why General Erich Fellgiebel, chief of communications for the German armed forces, had ignored the secret radio signals broadcast from London by the Allies to the French underground to alert the underground that the invasion was starting. It wasn't because Fellgiebel didn't know the secret signals, because Skorzeny had personally given the information to him. He had learned about the signals from the Darnand group of the French fascists with whom he worked hand in hand.

The Darnand group had alerted him that two lines of a Paul Verlaine poem, broadcast by French radio stations relaying BBC broadcasts from London, would be the signal for the invasion alert. *"Les sanglots longs des violons de l'automne"* would indicate the invasion was imminent, and *"blessent mon coeur d'une langueur monotone"* was the alert for the resistance to begin sabotage operations because the invasion would begin within forty-eight hours. However, when the signals were picked up by the Wehrmacht radio operators who had been alerted by Skorzeny, the messages were ignored by the OKW and lower echelon commanders. Even when Artur Kasche, a radio operator on duty at the Berghof, picked up the first line of the poem on June 1 and notified General Alfred Jodl, chief of the Wehrmacht Operations Staff, Jodl dismissed the warning and didn't relay it to Hitler. The same thing happened four days later, June 5, when Kasche monitored the BBC broadcasts and heard the second line of the poem, which indicated the invasion was starting. The next day American, British, and Canadian troops began landing at Normandy.[1]

Skorzeny was unaware of one of the reasons the radio signals were ignored. Many of the Wehrmacht officers were planning to assassinate Hitler and then negotiate a peace settlement with the western powers. General Erich Fellgiebel, chief of communications for the armed forces, was one of the conspirators. When the invasion alert messages were relayed to him, he made certain the messages were distributed only to certain headquarters where other assassination plotters were stationed. Yet even among the officers disillusioned with Hitler, there was a great deal of controversy about the method that should be used to strip him of his power. Some were convinced the move had to be made prior to the Allied invasion, because once the enemy overran the homeland there would be little chance of a negotiated peace with any favorable aspects for Germany. The younger officers, including Count Claus Schenk von Stauffenberg, their leader, favored killing Hitler before the invasion. Some of the older officers, such as Rommel, favored arresting Hitler, not killing him, and bringing him before a German court to answer for his crimes. Rommel was in charge of repelling the Allied invasion of Europe from the west, so when the message arrived on June 1 that the awaited line from Verlaine's poem had been picked up from a BBC broadcast, he was undecided about his next move. On the morning of June 4, he left his headquarters in France and headed for Germany by car to confer with the other conspirators as well as with Hitler at the Berghof on the Obersalzberg in Bavaria.

Skorzeny could be excused for not knowing about the assassination plot of the Wehrmacht officers since he was not intimately associated with the German armed forces commanders and their staff members. But he was also ignorant of the fact that Kaltenbrunner, abetted by the Gestapo, had a plan to dethrone Hitler by breaking up the Nazi party.[2] Kaltenbrunner and his collaborators thought they could overthrow the "stay-at-home" Nazi party leaders who were getting rich and fat while others fought and died. Hitler was not to be harmed, merely unseated from his party leadership. Kaltenbrunner decided Skorzeny was not the man to be taken into his confidence because the big Austrian was completely loyal to Hitler. So the chief of the RSHA kept the plot secret from Skorzeny.

Neither Skorzeny nor Kaltenbrunner were aware that there was yet another SS plot brewing to oust Hitler. This one was headed by Schellenberg, chief of Skorzeny's section of the RSHA. Two years earlier Schellenberg and Himmler had agreed to try to negotiate a secret peace with the Allies even if meant doublecrossing Hitler. However when Carl Lanbehn, their representative, went to Switzerland to discuss such a peace treaty with Allen Dulles of the OSS, the Gestapo learned about the trip and the reason for it. Himmler was able to convince Hitler of his loyalty to the swastika and immediately severed his connection with Schellenberg's plot. Schellenberg, whom Hitler did not suspect of being involved in the Switzerland peace feeler, continued his secret plans to overthrow Hitler and negotiate a peace treaty. At the time the Wehrmacht was putting the final touches on its own plan to assassinate the Führer, Schellenberg was in contact with American military personnel in Spain concocting an elaborate scheme to kidnap Hitler.

Hitler, at the Berghof resting early in July, was unaware of the various plots being organized against him. Skorzeny, just returned from Denmark, was awaiting orders for his commandos and overseeing his training schools. Both Kaltenbrunner and Schellenberg were working out further details of their individual clandestine plans, while Rommel was struggling to repulse the Allied invasion force at Cherbourg. One man, however, was already completing his plans. That man was Stauffenberg. One year older than Skorzeny and a man who had proven his courage just as often, Stauffenberg was organizing a plot that would test Skorzeny to the limit. Other than their age and courage, the two men were completely different. Stauffenberg was an outstanding officer in the German army, one who looked down on the SS and Nazi party members. His mother belonged to the Gneisenau family, who had established the Prussian General Staff, and the Yorck family of Napoleonic times. He was an intellectual who was very knowledgeable in the arts and often wrote poetry. In 1936 he became a member of the exclusive General Staff College because of his brilliant mind, but it wasn't until he was tested in action during the Polish and Russian campaigns that Stauffenberg was fully accepted by the other stiff-backed German officers. By January 1943, he was a lieutenant colonel in rank and an anti-Hitler conspirator by choice. Before he could really become active in the anti-Hitler movement, however, his staff car was strafed by a low-flying Spitfire in North Africa and he was nearly killed. He lost his right hand and forearm, two fingers of his left hand and his left eye.

When Stauffenberg was released from the hospital, it was generally thought he would retire from military service. He insisted on remaining on active duty, however, and was appointed chief of staff to General Friedrich Olbricht, commander of the General Army Office in Berlin. This was an ideal assignment for Stauffenberg because it enabled him to keep abreast of Hitler's plans, permitted him to attend the Führer's conferences periodically, and gave him the opportunity to enlist a powerful group of Wehrmacht officers in his assassination plan. Among those who committed themselves was Olbricht, his commander. Stauffenberg also discovered the plan Hitler had devised to put down any uprising by the millions of forced laborers in the Third Reich. The operation, named Walküre, was in Olbricht's files. It arranged for a state of emergency to be proclaimed and immediate mobilization of military forces to halt any such uprising. Stauffenberg adapted Walküre for use by the conspirators once Hitler was dead.

Once Hitler was dead! That was the key to his plan. While Skorzeny was making plans to utilize his commandos in the west, Stauffenberg was making plans to plant a time bomb near Hitler during one of his daily conferences. On July 11 Stauffenberg had his first opportunity. He was ordered to report to Hitler at the Berghof so he could brief the Führer on the availability of replacements for the troops on the western front. Ironically, as he walked toward his waiting plane at Rangsdorf airfield near Berlin that day he met Skorzeny, who was on his way to board a plane to France. The two men greeted each other and stopped to speak for a few moments. Stauffenberg asked Skorzeny if he, too, was going to Obersalzberg to confer with Hitler.

"Not today," Skorzeny replied, explaining he was going to check on some of his commandos in France.[3] Later, Skorzeny stated that the one-eyed would-be assassin was very calm and friendly.

Stauffenberg took his briefcase with the bomb inside it into the conference room but was disappointed to learn that Himmler would not be at the meeting that day. The conspirators had hoped they would kill Hitler, Göring, and Himmler at the same time, thus eliminating the top trio of the Nazi party. The takeover of the nation by the Wehrmacht would then be much easier. He excused himself, went to the nearest telephone, and called Berlin. Olbricht advised him to wait for another opportunity when all three of the party officials would be present. Stauffenberg returned to the conference, calmly gave his report on replacements, picked up his briefcase with the bomb inside, and returned to Berlin.

On July 20 Skorzeny was happy. He intended to board a train early that afternoon to go to his home city, Vienna. The trip was partially business—he had to complete some details about another attempt to kidnap Tito—and partially pleasure. He would visit his wife and daughter and see some old friends that he had not had time to visit for many long months. His lunch with a friend at the Hotel Adlon lasted much longer than he had expected. When he looked at his watch, the one Mussolini had given him, it was 12:30 P.M. He nearly upset his chair getting to his feet.

"I'll miss my train," Skorzeny explained to his luncheon companion. He handed the waiter money to cover the bill and hurried from the room.

At 12:30 P.M. Stauffenberg was also in a hurry. He had left Berlin at dawn that morning to attend another of the Führer's daily conferences, only this one was at Hitler's headquarters at Rastenburg, East Prussia. Wolf's Lair, the headquarters, had the tightest security of any area in Germany. Stauffenberg first passed through a gate at the outskirts of the Wolf's Lair, then traveled two miles through minefields and past gun emplacements to a second gate, an opening in an electrified fence that surrounded this middle area used by staff members. A mile further Stauffenberg had one final hurdle, the gate leading to the Führer's personal headquarters. Everyone, regardless of rank in the military or prestige in the Nazi party, had to have a pass to get through. Fortunately, Stauffenberg's pass satisfied the guards and they did not search his shiny yellow briefcase.

In Berlin Skorzeny reached the Anhalt Station with plenty of time to spare to catch the 1:15 P.M. train to Vienna, only to learn that because of a derailment, the train would be late. He and Karl Radl, who had joined him at the station, went to a small hotel nearby for a drink. They anticipated a long, boring afternoon waiting for the train.

At Rastenburg the Führer's meeting had been moved forward thirty minutes because Mussolini was arriving at the Wolf's Lair for a visit that afternoon. When Stauffenberg heard the news, he immediately hurried to a nearby room that had been made available for him to clean up before the conference. Once inside and certain the door was locked, he opened his briefcase and armed the bomb inside by crushing a glass capsule containing acid. He had exactly fifteen minutes before the acid would eat through the fuse wire and the bomb would explode. Closing the briefcase, Stauffenberg hurried from the room. General Field Marshal Wilhelm Keitel, chief of the OKW and Hitler's closest military advisor, was waiting and ushered him into the conference room.

"Mein Führer," the general announced, "Colonel Stauffenberg will brief you on the new divisions."[4]

It was 12:35 P.M.

Stauffenberg took the chair Hitler pointed to on his right. Only one officer separated the Führer and his would-be assassin. Stauffenberg carefully placed his briefcase under the table as near to Hitler as possible, while General Adolf Heusinger gave a report on the eastern front. Glancing at his watch, Stauffenberg's interest in the report waned. As carefully as possible he eased out of his chair while the others listened intently to Heusinger and left the room. No one paid any attention to the one-eyed officer who only attended meetings now and then. They had more important matters to hold their attention. Stauffenberg hurried from the conference building toward his car. He was hatless but he hadn't time to retrieve his hat now. His car was only halfway to the first gate when there was a loud blast as the bomb exploded.

Skorzeny and Radl were still waiting for the train to Vienna at 2:00 P.M. Skorzeny, disappointed and bored, shook his head in disgust. "I'm going to call the office. Perhaps I can get a plane to take us to Vienna."[5]

As soon as Skorzeny was in contact with his office, all thoughts about arranging a flight to Vienna vanished. Von Foelkersam, who was in charge of the office while Skorzeny was away, informed Skorzeny that there had been an attempt to kill Hitler at the Wolf's Lair.

"I don't have the details," von Foelkersam explained. "I only know there was a bomb explosion and that Hitler is still alive."[6]

Skorzeny was shocked. He immediately concluded an enemy plane had bombed the Wolf's Lair, never dreaming that a Wehrmacht officer had tried to assassinate the Führer. However, since Hitler was still alive he saw no reason to cancel his long-planned trip to Vienna.

Stauffenberg's plane was letting down to land at the Berlin airport about the time Skorzeny was recovering from his surprise. The first of many mistakes in the assassination plan occurred when Stauffenberg discovered there was no car waiting to rush him to the General Staff building on the Bendlerstrasse near the Tiergarten. This delay alarmed Olbricht. He didn't want to put the Walküre plan into effect until he talked with Stauffenberg. Consequently it was nearly 4:00 P.M. before the orders went out to the guard battalion, the Spandau garrison, and other troops that the coup d'état was underway. Stauffenberg, when he finally reached the General Staff building, put through a telephone call to General Karl Heinrich von Stülpnagel, the military governor of occupied France, and told him Hitler was dead and that the Wehrmacht was taking control of the government. Stülpnagel immediately ordered all radio and telephone lines between France and Germany cut except those of his private line at his Paris headquarters. The Wehrmacht conspirators in France and Germany had now committed themselves, believing, as Stauffenberg did, that the Führer had been killed in the explosion at the Wolf's Lair when the bomb in Stauffenberg's briefcase went off.

It was a fatal error for every officer even remotely connected with the bomb plot. Hitler was not dead, despite the fact the bomb had only been six feet away from him. He had been blown from his chair by the concussion and ended up on the floor very near the doorway. His lower thighs had more than a thousand oak splinters in them; his pants were ripped away; his forehead was bleeding from a glancing blow of a fallen timber; and his ears both pained him. But he was alive. Dr. Theodor Morell, his personal physician, took Hitler's pulse and was amazed to find it normal. In fact, once he discovered that he was not seriously injured, Hitler was elated. As he told Mussolini later that afternoon: "Duce, a few hours ago I experienced the greatest piece of good fortune I have ever known."[7] He considered his narrow escape from death a sign that he and his Third Reich were destined to be victorious.

Initially, Hitler thought a workman doing construction work at the Wolf's Lair had planted the bomb. He had his aides search for the fuse wire under the floor but they found nothing. Later in the day he learned that the explosion had occurred at floor level, not underneath, and his suspicions were aroused that someone at the conference had brought the bomb to the meeting. Martin Bormann, Hitler's ever-present right-hand man, discovered that Stauffenberg had left the building in a hurry shortly before the explosion. The German sergeant tending the telephone outside the conference room had seen him leave. The sergeant stated that the one-armed officer had no hat and was not carrying his briefcase. When shreds of the yellow briefcase were found embedded in the woodwork of the conference room, Hitler was convinced Stauffenberg was the culprit.

By this time Stauffenberg and his anti-Hitler mates had complete control of the General Staff building on the Bendlerstrasse except for what they considered one minor problem. General Friedrich Fromm, commander-in-chief of the German Reserve Army, who was headquartered at the same building, was aware of the bomb plot, and had promised to join the coup d'état as soon as Hitler was dead. But he was a very careful man, one who played both sides of the coin until he was certain he was going to win. When Stauffenberg and Olbricht, convinced Hitler was dead, launched the takeover of the government in the late afternoon of July 20, Fromm hesitated. He hesitated so long that the exasperated Stauffenberg placed him under arrest and locked him in another room of the General Staff building. Unfortunately for Stauffenberg, he did not check the room closely, did not notice there was a telephone in the room. Fromm promptly put through a call to the Wolf's Lair. When Keitel came on the line, Fromm told him rumors were prevalent in Berlin that Hitler had been killed.

"The Führer is alive," Keitel said. "There is no cause whatever for such rumors. Is Stauffenberg in Berlin?"

Fromm, frightened, lied: "No, I thought he was at the Führer's headquarters."[8]

During the time this vital telephone call was taking place, Skorzeny and Radl boarded the long-awaited train for Vienna at the Anhalt Station. It was a short ride for Skorzeny, however. At the Lichterfelde Station, the last stop in the city, Skorzeny was paged. The train didn't move until an officer on the platform was able to deliver a message to him.

"You are to return immediately. The attempt on the Führer's life was the beginning of a putsch!"[9]

The officer rushed Skorzeny back to SS headquarters where Schellenberg was waiting for him. Despite the fact that Schellenberg himself had been involved in various plots to overthrow Hitler, the officers' assassination attempt had taken him completely by surprise. He was sitting at his desk holding a large revolver. He informed Skorzeny that the Berlin situation was a complete puzzle, that the Wehrmacht conspirators were in control of the General Staff building and were issuing orders to all military units.

"I think they will be coming here after me," Schellenberg said. "Can you get someone to guard the building?"[10]

Skorzeny nodded. He called von Foelkersam and ordered a battalion to report to SS headquarters. After the battalion arrived and he was certain the SS personnel were not involved in the plot, Skorzeny visited several other military units in the city. He discovered the Armored Vehicles G.H.Q. had been alerted for action by Stauffenberg and Olbricht as had the troops at the Lichterfelde barracks. Worried about the airborne troops, he drove to General Kurt Student's home near the Wannsee on the outskirts of the city. He soon discovered that Student was not involved in the plot and, in fact, did not even believe Skorzeny's story that there was a plot in progress. A timely telephone call from Göring, however, confirmed the attempt on Hitler's life. Student quickly promised Skorzeny he would notify each of his units personally that the only orders they were to obey were those issued by him.

By the time Skorzeny arrived back at SS headquarters, there was a telephone call from the Wolf's Lair awaiting him. Keitel was on the line.

"Skorzeny, the conspirators are at the General Staff building on the Bendlerstrasse. Major Otto Remer, commander of the guard battalion of the Berlin Garrison, has been ordered to seal off the area around the Bendlerstrasse. The Führer wants you to join him there at once."[11]

Skorzeny hurried to the General Staff building but he was a few moments too late to stop Fromm, the on-again, off-again conspirator from leaving. The general was driving away as Skorzeny drove up. When he asked Remer where Fromm was going, the major shrugged and said, "He's going back to his apartment."[12]

While Skorzeny was on his way to the Bendlerstrasse from SS headquarters, Stauffenberg had discovered that Fromm had escaped from the locked room and was gathering a small group of soldiers loyal to the Führer. Stauffenberg hurried to warn Olbricht but he was too late. Fromm's men, completely unaware that the general had quickly flipped from the losers to the winners when he learned Hitler was still alive, captured Stauffenberg and Olbricht and took them to Fromm's office. The general wasted no words.

"You gentlemen, if you have any letters to write you may have a few minutes to do so."[13]

Five minutes later he told Stauffenberg and Olbricht that they had been sentenced to death in the name of the Führer. He nodded to his men who led the pair from the room. Fromm then left the building and got into his car just as Skorzeny arrived.

Who killed Stauffenberg and Olbricht? The known facts are that the pair, with others, were led to the courtyard of the General Staff building, stood up against a wall in the bright glare of the headlights from several army trucks and shot to death. The unknown fact is who killed them. Was it Fromm's men on his orders? Obviously Fromm wanted the leaders of the plot dead before they could tell Hitler that he was also in on the plan. Or was it Skorzeny on direct orders from Hitler? By this hour on July 20, Hitler was convinced that Stauffenberg had brought the bomb to the Wolf's Lair and he was enraged. It is known that Hitler talked with Skorzeny from the Wolf's Lair shortly after Keitel called and gave Skorzeny orders to go to the Bendlerstrasse. There certainly was enough evidence from Skorzeny's activities in Denmark and Italy that he was the man to accept such an assignment and carry it out successfully. At any rate, a few minutes after Skorzeny arrived at the General Staff building Stauffenberg and Olbricht were dead and the brutal roundup of the conspirators began.

Skorzeny took over the headquarters as though he owned it and within an hour he had the affairs of the high command operating smoothly once more. Hitler called again from the Wolf's Lair and told Skorzeny to issue orders to the military in the Führer's name until further notice. With Fromm in hiding and Stauffenberg and Olbricht dead, Skorzeny was in complete charge for more than thirty-six hours. He ordered reinforcements when they were requested from commanders at the front, dispatched supplies where needed, made certain the regular shipments of rations were sent to the troops, and handled the myriad of important and minor details that the high-ranking OKW generals and their staffs usually handled. Finally, on the morning of July 22, Himmler arrived to take charge until replacements for Stauffenberg, Olbricht, and Fromm were appointed by the Führer. Skorzeny went back to Friedenthal.

During the next few weeks, Skorzeny played a much more secret role in uncovering the bomb plot. He helped track down the remaining conspirators in one of the most brutal manhunts in history. Many were murdered where they were found. Others were strangled with piano wire and their bodies hung like sides of beef on meat hooks. Some, knowing Skorzeny was on their trail, killed themselves. Stülpnagel, the military governor of occupied France, shot himself but survived to hang later as did Fromm. Skorzeny went to France on the trail of Field Marshal Günther Hans von Kluge, in charge of the defense of Normandy, and Kluge was found dead near Clermont-en-Argonne. He had swallowed cyanide. Rommel was given his choice of committing suicide and maintaining his reputation as one of Germany's greatest military commanders or arrest and disgrace. He chose poison.

More than 200 persons died as a direct result of the July 20 bomb plot and the number of executions caused by Hitler's suspicions will never be known. Schellenberg and Kaltenbrunner were not touched by the bomb plot despite their own secret attempts to overthrow Hitler, nor was any member of the SS found to be involved. Skorzeny's nemesis in clandestine operations, Canaris, was caught, however, and hanged.

Skorzeny's actions during his thirty-six hours in command of the General Staff building and operations in Berlin and his ruthless tracking down and punishment of the conspirators in the weeks following the bomb plot endeared him more than ever to Hitler.

"You, Skorzeny, saved the Third Reich," the Führer told him at their next meeting. "I will always remember your great courage."[14]

Hitler did. Whenever he needed someone to attempt an "impossible" mission he always summoned Skorzeny. And Skorzeny was always ready.

6 THE HORTHY KIDNAPPING

On April 24, 1941, when the Hungarian regent Admiral Miklós Horthy visited Hitler, the Führer charmed and flattered him in every way possible. He even listened to Horthy's stories about hunting and his horses, both of which Hitler disliked very much. But Hitler was willing to be bored by the Hungarian regent because he was gratified by his support. In fact, Horthy had written him a secret letter suggesting a German attack on Russia without knowing that Hitler had plans to do just that within two months. Hitler even made certain that a prayer stool and crucifix were provided in the room of Madame Horthy, the admiral's wife, who was a devout Catholic. A large bouquet of flowers—lilies of the valley, her favorites—were placed in her room each morning.

As Hitler said later, "Horthy is a bull of a man and was, undoubtedly, the bravest man in the Austrian navy in World War I."[1]

But by March 18, 1944, when Horthy and Hitler met again, the situation had changed drastically. Horthy had refused to recognize the new Mussolini government in Italy which the Duce had set up at Hitler's insistence after Skorzeny rescued him from the Gran Sasso. He was demanding that Hitler return the nine Hungarian divisions fighting on the Russian front. Skorzeny reported his agents in Budapest had evidence that the Hungarian government was sabotaging German military trains traveling through the country. But the most critical of the accusations against Horthy was a rumor that he was trying to negotiate a peace treaty with the enemy. Hitler was furious and made immediate plans to occupy Hungary with or without the approval of Horthy, although he hoped to avoid an armed conflict with the military forces of his erstwhile loyal ally.

He invited the Hungarian regent to Klessheim Castle near Salzburg, scheduling the meeting so Horthy would be at the castle with his military leaders at the exact moment Hitler was ready to order his troops into Hungary. Hitler arranged for the talks to begin at 10:30 A.M. and to break off for lunch. At that time he would know whether Horthy intended to order his troops to resist the German invasion or not, and could inform his generals accordingly. It was a good plan but Hitler's temper and lack of tact nearly ruined the entire scenario. At about 11:00 A.M., Horthy burst from the room where he was meeting with Hitler. His face was flushed and he was talking to himself. He hurried to his quarters, slammed the door shut, and locked it. Hitler chased after him, all decorum forgotten, but Horthy wouldn't unlock the door. The Führer, frustrated by the regent's actions, ordered the invasion delayed until the matter of Horthy's allegiance was settled.

When Horthy had his special train prepared for immediate departure to Hungary, Hitler faked an air raid warning and commanded a smoke screen spread around the castle. He then forbade Horthy's special train to depart for Hungary during the air raid alert. Meanwhile he made certain all telephone communications between Klessheim Castle and Budapest were disrupted so that Horthy was a virtual prisoner. It was a long afternoon, but by 7:30 P.M. the Hungarian regent knew he was defeated. He agreed that his troops would not resist the invasion and Hitler ordered the Wehrmacht into Hungary. At 9:00 P.M. Hitler, now in good humor, escorted Horthy to his special train just as the all-clear signal sounded, on Hitler's order, to indicate the raid-that-never-was was over.

The immediate crisis was ended but Hitler's faith in Horthy was shaken. During the summer of 1944, his suspicions of Horthy's turncoat intentions increased almost daily. In August the regent replaced Hitler's handpicked pro-German head of government, Döme Sztójay, with General Geisa Lákatos, who followed Horthy's orders religiously. On September 7 Horthy told Hitler that if he did not have five more German Panzer divisions within twenty-four hours to fend off an impending Russian attack he would ask Russia for an armistice. The

Führer complied but it was his last compromise with the Hungarian regime. When he discovered for certain, as he had long suspected, that Horthy had sent a team of negotiators to Moscow to arrange peace terms, Hitler made his move. He summoned Skorzeny to his headquarters.

On September 13 at Wolf's Lair, Hitler met with Keitel, Jodl, Ribbentrop, Himmler, and Skorzeny. He came right to the point.

"We have received confidential reports that the regent of Hungary, Admiral Horthy, is trying to establish contact with the enemy in order to negotiate a separate peace. If he is successful it would spell the loss of our army in Hungary. You, Skorzeny, are going to prepare for the occupation of the Burgberg in Budapest. When I give the order, you will start the operation. In order to permit you to obtain the necessary men and weapons, I shall give you written orders which will give you extensive power."[2]

Hitler took a large sheet of Third Reich official stationery bearing the eagle with the iron cross in gilt relief in the left corner and the legend "Führer and Chancellor of the Reich" and wrote his order on it. The order stated:

Major Skorzeny of the Reserve Corps has been charged directly by myself to execute personal and confidential orders of the highest importance. I request all military and civilian services to bring all possible help to Major Skorzeny and to comply with all his wishes.[3]

Jodl gave Skorzeny a list of the forces at his command. The list included 250 men from *Jagd Verband Mitte,* 250 men from *Fallschirm Jaeger Battalion 600,* two parachute companies from KG 200, and four companies of officer candidates, approximately 700 men, from the officer's candidate school at Wiener Neustadt. From Friedenthal he selected, besides von Foelkersam and Radl, Wilhelm Gallent, Werner Hunke, Gerhard Lochner, and Ullrich Milius to help him plan and execute the mission. In addition, Hitler provided Skorzeny with an aircraft from the Führer's personal fleet.

Skorzeny, using the alias Dr. Solar Wolff, arrived in Budapest a few days later to make plans for his operation to overthrow Horthy when and if it became necessary. Dressed in an expensive civilian suit and supposedly conducting business for his firm in Cologne, Skorzeny toured the city looking for persons with information about the defenses of the Hungarians and Horthy's intentions for the German alliance. He avoided hotels where German officers stayed, not wanting to be seen associating with them, and, instead, stayed at the house of an acquaintance who was loyal to the Third Reich. He had traveled throughout Hungary before the war and was familiar with the country and the capital, especially the Burgberg, or Castle Hill, where Horthy resided in a well-guarded and luxurious government building known as the Citadel. Not only was the hill itself so well fortified that a ground assault up the steep slopes appeared suicidal, but the streets of the Burgberg were swarming with troops of the Hungarian army. With his guidebook in hand and pretending to be a tourist, Skorzeny checked for an open area where his parachutists or gliders could land. He soon discovered that an aerial assault of the Burgberg was out of the question. The only open area was surrounded by buildings housing military forces of the Hungarian government. Any aerial invaders landing there, regardless of whether they came by parachutes or gliders, would be cut down by Hungarian guns before they had a chance to attack.

Skorzeny returned to the private home where he was staying and discussed the situation with Radl and von Foelkersam. There was no doubt in his mind that if the order came from Hitler to attack the Burgberg and occupy the Citadel, he and his men faced a near impossible mission. Skorzeny was aware that Hitler had sent SS General Erich von dem Bach-Zelewski to Budapest to aid him if he was needed. Bach-Zelewski was an expert in antipartisan operations and was greatly admired by Hitler for his brutal but effective handling of the Warsaw uprising. He had brought with him giant 650-mm mortar and hours after arriving in Budapest suggested to Skorzeny that they "blow the Citadel off the Burgberg."[4] Skorzeny shook his head.

"Only as a last resort," he insisted.[5]

Bach-Zelewski had used the huge mortar to blast large sections of the city of Sebastopol on the Black Sea and to raze Warsaw. There was no question about the effectiveness of the weapon but Skorzeny feared that use of it against the Citadel on Burgberg would drive the Hungarians straight into the waiting arms of Stalin. He wanted to find a more subtle way to convince the regent to stay within the embrace of Hitler, and not order his Hungarian military forces to turn on the Wehrmacht. With the Russian 40th Army, the 7th Guards Army, and the 27th Army poised to attack Hungary from the Debrecen area, the Soviet 6th tank armies already fighting German and Hungarian troops in the Turda region, and Russian General I. M. Managarov's 53rd Army advancing from the town of Arad, any defection of Hungarian troops would be fatal to the German positions. It was a delicate situation, one that required a political operation rather than a military attack on the Hungarian government stronghold with Bach-Zelewski's 650-mm mortar.

Yet it became increasingly clear to Skorzeny that if he was to prevent Horthy from signing an armistice with the Allies he had to act promptly. On September 22 he learned that a representative of the Hungarian government, Colonel General Nadai, had flown to Naples to meet with British and American representatives concerning the occupation of Hungary by their forces prior to the takeover of the country by the Soviets. The fact that this mission failed wasn't much encouragement to Skorzeny because a few days later he learned that a special delegation of Hungarians under the leadership of General Gábor Farago was in Moscow trying for the second-best solution to the Hungarian problem—an armistice with Russia. In addition Skorzeny managed to obtain a copy of a letter sent by Hungarian prisoners-of-war in Russia to General Béla Miklós, commander of the 1st Hungarian Army. The letter pleaded with Miklós to abandon the Germans and join with the Soviet military forces in attacking the Wehrmacht troops, pointing out that Nazi Germany was being defeated militarily, would soon collapse politically, and that every other satellite except Hungary had already broken with Hitler and was fighting the German troops. Miklós was the most respected military commander in Hungary. If he threw his lot in with the Russians it would be a serious blow for the Third Reich. Decisive action was imperative immediately, Skorzeny decided. The question was—what type of action?

A conversation with Edmund Veesenmayer, Ribbentrop's aide in Budapest, gave Skorzeny his initial idea on how to handle the ticklish predicament. Veesenmayer remarked that the problems were piling up in the Hungarian-German controversy, adding that now even Horthy's son was involved. That was the first Skorzeny had heard about the son's part in the problem.

"What do you mean?" he asked Veesenmayer.

"Most people think Miki Horthy is only interested in blondes and good wine," Ribbentrop's aide explained, "but actually he does more than throw wild parties and sleep with beautiful women."

"Such as?"

"Well, right now he has been meeting with representatives of Yugoslavian partisan chief Tito talking about an armistice with Russia. Tito is acting as a go-between."

Skorzeny, aware of Miki Horthy's reputation, wasn't convinced. "I can't believe Admiral Horthy would rely on Miki. He's caused the old man too much trouble in the past."

Veesenmayer laughed. "That he has, but ever since Horthy's oldest son Istvan was killed when his plane was shot down on the Russian front, Miki has been his father's pride and joy. Besides, we have proof of the meetings. Miki met with the Yugoslavs in a villa in the suburbs of Budapest yesterday and they are scheduled to meet again on October 15."

"And the old man is proud of Miki?"

"Very much so," Veesenmayer said.[6]

Skorzeny was acquainted with Milos "Miki" Horthy, having met him in Vienna several times. The young, dark-haired, and good-looking playboy had never seemed to take either politics or the war seriously and consequently Skorzeny had never considered him as an important figure in the Hungarian crisis. But Veesenmayer's remarks had changed his opinion. If, as Veesenmayer stated, Admiral Horthy had so much confidence in Miki that he permitted him to negotiate with Tito's representatives, than perhaps Miki could also be a valuable asset to the Third Reich. If Miki Horthy was in Third Reich hands, would Admiral Horthy give up his plans to abandon Hitler to get his son back safely? Skorzeny decided it was worth a try.

Investigation showed that the meeting between Miki Horthy and Tito's representatives was scheduled for Sunday, October 15, on the second floor of a building not far from the Danube. Skorzeny made his plans carefully, fully aware that while Miki was attending the meeting as the sole representative of the Hungarian government, he would be well protected. Skorzeny arranged for two of his officers to rent an apartment on the third floor of the same building and he had several of his commandos in the apartment when the secret meeting began. Von Foelkersam was positioned with a contingent of commandos out of sight of the building, but only moments away from the front entrance. Skorzeny placed several commandos dressed in civilian clothes in a nearby park, while other commandos patrolled the street in front of the building in the uniforms of German army *Feldgendarmen* (Military Police). A few minutes after Miki's arrival, Skorzeny in the guise of "Dr.

Wolff" drove his automobile slowly down the street in front of the building where the meeting was being held, eased it into a parking spot directly in front of a Hungarian army truck, and got out. Very casually and without even glancing at the building, he walked around to the front of his car and opened the hood. The sound of the hood being opened aroused the curiosity of the Hungarian soldiers hidden in the back of the truck under a heavy canvas cover. One of the soldiers pulled a corner of the canvas back and looked out. During the seconds the canvas was open Skorzeny saw three machine guns in the truck. However, the Hungarian soldiers were convinced that Skorzeny was merely a civilian driver having trouble with his car and they pulled the canvas back over their heads.

Concealed by the hood of his car, Skorzeny glanced toward the park. Several additional Hungarian soldiers were walking back and forth in the park as though out for a morning stroll. Skorzeny noted they were heavily armed. It was obvious Miki Horthy was not going to be kidnapped without a fight. He looked at his watch. Approximately five minutes had elapsed since the meeting began, the deadline he had set for the attack. At that moment the commandos in the apartment above Horthy and the Yugoslavs were supposed to be on their way down the stairs to the secret meeting place. As Skorzeny prepared to walk toward the building, he saw the commandos disguised as military police dart through the front door of the meeting place. The Hungarian soldiers in the truck saw them, too. They opened fire with their machine guns and the last commando of the group fell face down in the foyer. At the sound of the shots, the Hungarian soldiers in the park raced toward the scene. Skorzeny put his whistle to his mouth and blew, the signal for von Foelkersam to bring his contingent of commandos to join the battle.

Skorzeny barely had time to dive behind his Mercedes before the Hungarian soldiers opened fire. He was pinned down behind the car for several minutes while machine-gun bullets pierced doors and shattered the glass of the windows. Before he was wounded, however, von Foelkersam and his force arrived and drove the Hungarian soldiers back from the truck to the entranceway of the building next to where Miki Horthy and the Yugoslavs were meeting. Skorzeny was able to escape from behind his Mercedes during the retreat of the Hungarian soldiers. As he was running toward the building where the meeting was taking place he glanced toward the entranceway where the Hungarian soldiers were taking refuge. The sight that greeted him made him stop in his tracks. Another large group of Hungarian soldiers who had evidently been hiding in the building were now struggling to get out.

"Don't let them get into the open," he called to von Foelkersam.[7] Taking a hand grenade from the commando nearest him, Skorzeny hurled it toward the doorway. It was an excellent throw because the grenade landed between two marble pillars supporting the impressive-looking entrance to the building, and when it exploded both pillars crumbled. Leaves of the portal and several slabs of marble fell on the Hungarian soldiers standing in the entrance. Those who retreated into the building were trapped inside by the debris that completely blocked the doorway. Several of the commandos also tossed grenades into the building and the resultant blasts completely trapped the Hungarian soldiers.

"Let's get upstairs," Skorzeny bellowed as he took the steps two at a time. On the first landing he met several of his commandos coming down. They had four prisoners, one of whom was Miki Horthy. The young Horthy was struggling and cursing. Skorzeny, who wanted to get away from the scene as fast as possible with as little commotion as possible, grabbed a rug from the floor and tossed it to the commandos.

"Wrap him in the rug."

The commandos threw Miki Horthy to the floor and quickly rolled him inside the rug. They then grabbed the rug and hurried down the stairs and out the door to the waiting van. The rug with Miki Horthy hidden inside was tossed into the van.

"Get him to the airport. I'll follow," Skorzeny yelled.

He trailed the van for three blocks when he suddenly saw a sizable force of Hungarian soldiers double-timing up a side street toward the scene of the kidnapping. Skorzeny knew von Foelkersam had not had time to get his commandos out of the area yet and would be trapped. Quickly he swerved his bullet-riddled Mercedes into the path of the oncoming Hungarian troops. When the officer in charge angrily came to the side of the Mercedes, Skorzeny, acting like a scared tourist, said, "You better wait here a while. Everyone back there is running around in confusion. No one seems to know what is going on. If I were you I would check closely before you walk into a trap."

The Hungarian officer hesitated, then nodded his head. He ordered his men to stay in position while he called headquarters. While the officer was at the telephone, Skorzeny turned his car around and drove off, knowing that von Foelkersam would most surely have cleared the area safely by this time. Driving full speed, he caught up to the van with Miki Horthy in it just as it pulled into the airport. He helped load the rug and the still struggling Miki Horthy into the waiting plane.

"Get him to Vienna as fast as possible," he told the pilot.

With the Miki Horthy kidnapping a success, Skorzeny sat back to wait developments. He hoped that Admiral Horthy would value the life of his son more than his desire to sign the armistice with Russia. His confidence faded, however, when he received word early the next day that security measures on the Burgberg were being tightened. The entire hill was in a state of siege and all roads leading to it were blocked off by Hungarian soldiers. At 12:00 noon Veesenmayer managed to meet with the regent, but it was a very unsatisfactory meeting. Admiral Horthy complained bitterly about the kidnapping of his son and demanded his immediate release. Then he began crying like a child and promised to call off all efforts to negotiate a peace with Russia. Yet when the old man went to the telephone to do so, he didn't speak a word. He acted so strangely that Veesenmayer became suspicious and ended the meeting abruptly. He had just rejoined Skorzeny when they learned why Admiral Horthy acted the way he did. A special radio bulletin provided an explanation by the regent himself:

> I have informed the representative of the German Reich in Hungary that we have concluded a preliminary agreement for an armistice with our enemies and for the cessation of hostilities on our part against them. I have issued the corresponding orders to the military command.[8]

Skorzeny immediately prepared to storm the Burgberg while other German officers contacted the Hungarian army commanders and countermanded Admiral Horthy's orders to surrender and attack the German troops who had been their ally. Not surprisingly the Hungarian officers were so confused by the situation that the German Army Group South had ample time to take over all operations of the Hungarian troops. Yet how long the Hungarian military forces would continue to fight side by side with the German troops was unknown. It was imperative that the regent be made to change his mind about the armistice and it was up to Skorzeny to handle the matter immediately.

Skorzeny's initial move was to send a messenger to Admiral Horthy telling him that if he resigned and legally transferred power to Ferenc

Szalasi, the Hungarian fascist leader, and agreed to leave the country, his son Miki would be returned to him and he himself would be given refuge in Austria. If he did not agree to the terms, the Citadel on the Burgberg would be attacked at 6:00 the next morning. As soon as the messenger had departed, Skorzeny and von Foelkersam began making the final plans for an attack which seemed suicidal but nevertheless had to be made. They studied a map of the hill carefully, but Skorzeny was unable to find any weak or vulnerable spots. Finally he outlined an attack which would give each of his assigned units a special role. All units would attack simultaneously at different areas around the Burgberg. The four companies of officer candidates from Wiener Neustadt would attack on the southern flank of the hill; the *Jaeger Battalion 600* would slip into the tunnel at the base of the Burgberg and fight its way up through the subterranean maze under the Citadel and the Ministry of War building; and the *Jagd Verband Mitte* would attack along the western slope. Skorzeny assigned the most dangerous task to himself and the remainder of the commandos. He would lead the group directly up the Vienna Road, the main route to the top of the Burgberg . . . and also the best fortified. He would utilize Goliath tanks to spearhead his drive up the Vienna Road. These tanks, which had just arrived from Germany that morning, were remote-controlled vehicles and were ideal for exploding mines ahead of advancing troops.

At midnight as Skorzeny was issuing orders to his units in preparation for the 6:00 A.M. attack, an officer from the Hungarian War Ministry arrived at his headquarters. The conference lasted nearly two hours but ended inconclusively. The regent would not agree to the terms of the ultimatum but wished to avoid an attack on the Burgberg. Skorzeny shook his head.

"Tell the admiral we will be at the Citadel shortly after 6:00 A.M." [9]

After the Hungarian officer departed to carry the message back to Admiral Horthy, Skorzeny established the order of march of the group going up the Vienna Road. He decided to lead the drive up the hill himself in a small truck and position the Goliaths and regular tanks behind the truck. The remainder of his commandos would follow the tanks. When von Foelkersam protested that the Goliaths should lead, Skorzeny disagreed.

"I am convinced Admiral Horthy is bluffing, that he and the Hungarian troops will not resist," he said. "I want to be in the front so I can show the Hungarian security forces that we are determined to climb the Burgberg but at the same time we are not going to fire until fired upon."

Von Foelkersam still thought the plan was too dangerous. "If the regent is not bluffing, the first Hungarian machine gun nest on the road will slaughter you and everyone in the truck."

"But if I am right," Skorzeny said, "and there is no shooting, then the regent will not lose face and can still change his mind about deserting the Third Reich."

It was a gamble but one Skorzeny felt was worth taking. At 5:45 A.M. he made one last check to be certain there was no message from Admiral Horthy. When none was reported, he got into the truck and at 6:00 A.M. exactly gave the signal for his force to start up the steep slope of the Vienna Road. They moved slowly along the road until Skorzeny saw the first barricade manned by several Hungarian soldiers. The commandos in the truck raised their rifles but Skorzeny motioned for them to keep their guns out of sight.

"We will wait and see what they intend to do," he explained.

The commando convoy approached the barricade at fifteen miles per hour but did not slow down as they neared the soldiers blocking their path. It was a tense moment but the Hungarians gave way first. Casually the soldiers moved off the road and opened the barricade. Skorzeny saluted them as the truck passed and headed on up the hill. He surmised that either his prediction that the Hungarians would not oppose the German force invading the Burgberg was correct or the Hungarians were leading the convoy into a trap on the Vienna Road. With Hungarian soldiers ahead and behind his force, such a trap could be very effective. Holding his breath while the truck moved ahead, fearing a mine might explode at any second, Skorzeny only relaxed after his convoy had passed through two more Hungarian barricades without incident.

At the top of the Burgberg, he ordered his truck driver to speed up and by the time they reached the square in front of the Citadel they were traveling at a fast rate. Suddenly the driver slammed on his brakes. Directly in front of the Citadel the Hungarian soldiers had erected a barricade of building blocks that was several feet high. There was no way for the truck to get through. Skorzeny leaned out of the truck and signaled the tank behind him.

"Break it down!"

The tank swerved past the truck and smashed directly into the barricade, going through it easily. Skorzeny's truck was right behind. Once through the barricade, however, he found himself face to face with six anti-tank guns positioned at the entrance to the Citadel. The barrels were aimed directly at his truck. Very deliberately Skorzeny stepped from the truck and walked across the terrace in front of the regent's castle. He ignored the guns and they did not fire. As he stepped inside the Citadel, he saw a Hungarian officer, revolver in hand, standing near the steps.

"Take me to the Commandant," he ordered.

The officer hesitated a second, then holstered his gun and led Skorzeny up the grand staircase of the Citadel and motioned to a doorway. Skorzeny walked in without knocking, surprising a Hungarian general inside.

"I ask that you surrender immediately, Commandant," Skorzeny said. "Otherwise I will order my men to start firing. I must know your answer at once."[10]

The general was no fool. "I surrender."

Skorzeny nodded, stepped into the hall, and gave von Foelkersam the news to relay to the commandos. Meanwhile the general gave the order to his forces not to resist. Once this matter was taken care of, Skorzeny asked the general to take him to Admiral Horthy's quarters. The general said nothing but led him down the corridor to the regent's apartment and opened the door.

It was empty.

"The regent left the Citadel a few minutes before 6:00 A.M. this morning," the general said, "and placed himself under the protection of General Pfeffer-Wildenbruch in the city."

Skorzeny was surprised but relieved. General Karl Pfeffer-Wildenbruch commanded the Waffen SS in Budapest. It was obvious Admiral Horthy had not escaped. It was also obvious that the Hungarian government seat was now controlled by Skorzeny and his commandos. Skorzeny immediately telephoned the SS headquarters in the city, verified that the regent was there, and then asked for further orders. A short time later orders arrived from Hitler at the Wolf's Lair.

"Skorzeny will take up residence in the Citadel and command the regent's residence until further notice."

From being in charge of the German military headquarters in Berlin after the assassination attempt in July to acting regent of Hungary in October was quite a feat, but Skorzeny handled it well. He made himself comfortable with the help of the regent's valet and other servants, ate well, and slept in Admiral Horthy's bed. Never a man to refuse wine, women, or song, Skorzeny enjoyed all three during his time at the Citadel. But, as always, all good things must eventually end. A few days later he received another order from Hitler: escort Admiral Horthy to the Hirschberg Castle in Bavaria.

The next morning Skorzeny reluctantly left the luxury of the Citadel, drove back down the Vienna Road, and went directly to the SS headquarters in Budapest. There he was formally introduced to Admiral Horthy, informed the ex-regent that he was going to Bavaria as the guest of the Führer and accompanied him to Hitler's private train, which had been sent for the trip. The admiral was not fooled. He knew he was a prisoner even though he was going to live in a castle. He was well aware that a pro-German government was in power in Hungary and that the Hungarian military forces were still fighting side by side with the Germans. He also knew that the man standing in front of him was the man who had saved Hungary for Hitler. Admiral Horthy sighed, looked at Skorzeny, and quietly said, "I'm ready to go when you are."

7 SKORZENY'S "AMERICAN" TERRORISTS

At Verdun, France, on the morning of December 17, 1944, the usually neatly dressed, close-shaven General George S. Patton, Jr., commander of the U.S. Third Army, was disheveled, unkempt, and excited. Looking at Eisenhower, who had convened a meeting of his front-line commanders to discuss a reported counteroffensive launched by the Germans in the Ardennes section of Belgium and Luxembourg the previous morning, Patton didn't mince any words.

"Ike, I've never seen such a goddamn foul-up! The Germans are using captured American jeeps and uniforms. They've got a whole battalion of Krauts who must have escaped from Brooklyn speaking perfect English. They're infiltrating behind our lines, raising hell, cutting wires, turning road signs around, spooking whole divisions, and shoving a bulge into our defenses."[1]

Eisenhower nodded but said nothing. He studied the map in front of him carefully.

Patton, however, wasn't finished. "The First Army captured a German officer at Liège carrying American papers. This ought to interest you, Ike. He said he was part of an assassination squad assigned to get you. His commanding officer is Otto Skorzeny!"

It was the beginning of one of the most frustrating and worrisome periods of World War II for Eisenhower, the Allied military forces, and the people of the free world. It was the beginning of Hitler's Ardennes offensive, the surprise attack by the Third Reich which showed the Western powers that the war could still be lost.

Three days after Hitler had given Skorzeny orders to go to Hungary and take control of the Burgberg and Admiral Horthy, the Führer summoned his military staff to his headquarters. The momentous conference was held at the Wolf's Lair on Saturday, September 16, while Skorzeny was prowling around Budapest disguised as "Dr. Wolff." Keitel, Jodl, and Heinz Guderian, acting chief of staff for OKW, were the ranking officers present. Göring was absent but he was represented by Werner Kreipe, chief of staff for OKL *(Oberkommando der Luftwaffe)*, who ignored Hitler's orders that no notes of the daily conferences be made so that he could provide details of the meeting to Göring. As Jodl was giving a report on the situation at the front, Hitler cut him short.

"I have just made a momentous decision," the Führer announced. "I shall go over to the counterattack, that is to say, here, out of the Ardennes, with the objective—Antwerp!"[2]

The military officers at the meeting were stunned, because the German position in September of 1944 seemed hopeless to them. Politically the Third Reich was deserted and friendless. Italy was gone and Japan had politely suggested that Germany should start peace negotiations with the Soviet Union, so the once-powerful Axis was finished. The Rumanians and Bulgarians had switched sides and Finland had broken off relations. Even if Skorzeny "saved" Hungary, the Hungarian divisions would be, in effect, canceled by the two Rumanian armies that had joined the Russians. On the eastern front the Russian summer offensive had carried to the borders of East Prussia, across the Vistula at various points and up to the northern Carpathians. On the western front the Americans had troops on German soil in the Aachen area while the British had entered Holland.

Hitler, however, saw a glimmer of hope still remaining. He recognized the fact that the speedy advance of the Americans and British in the west had resulted in long supply lines for these troops, supply lines reaching clear back to the English Channel and the Côte d'Azur. He also knew that his famous West Wall, though almost dismantled in the years since 1940, had not yet been breached, and when and if it was, there was still the Rhine to stop the enemy. And finally, as fall and winter approached, Hitler decided the Soviet offensive on the eastern front had run its course. A fanatical believer in the Clausewitzian doctrine of the offensive as the purest and only decisive form of war, he decided to take the initiative. It was his plan from beginning to end. It was his last gamble. And with so much at stake, he once again called on his master of clandestine warfare, Otto Skorzeny.

Skorzeny escorted Admiral Horthy back to Germany on October 20 and a week later was summoned to the Wolf's Lair to meet with Hitler. The official reason for the summons was for Hitler to honor Skorzeny for his action in Hungary, but the actual purpose was to brief the big Austrian on the upcoming battle. After the formalities of the meeting ended and Skorzeny had brought a rare smile to Hitler's face by relating how he had rolled young Miki Horthy in a rug and transported him to the Budapest airport, the Führer motioned for Skorzeny to join him for a private conversation. When they were alone, Hitler told him about his new plan:

"In December the German army will launch a great offensive which will be decisive to the destiny of our country. You, Skorzeny, will play an important part in it. I am going to assign you the most important mission of your life."[3]

Before he gave Skorzeny any specific orders, he explained the general outline of his plan. Telling Skorzeny that he felt the time was ripe for a great German counteroffensive, he explained that for several weeks he had been trying to decide where the weakest spot was in the western front. Hitler and his staff had been studying the choices and he showed Skorzeny the results of the study:

Operation Holland: a single-thrust attack to be launched from the Venlo area, with Antwerp as the objective.

Operation Liège-Aachen: a two-pronged attack, with the main effort driving from northern Luxembourg in a northwesterly direction, subsequently turning due north to meet the secondary attack which would be launched from the sector northwest of Aachen.

Operation Luxembourg: a two-pronged attack launched simultaneously from central Luxembourg and Metz to seize Longwy.

Operation Lorraine: also a double envelopment to be launched from Metz and Baccarat and to converge on Nancy.

Operation Alsace: an envelopment to be executed in two thrusts, one

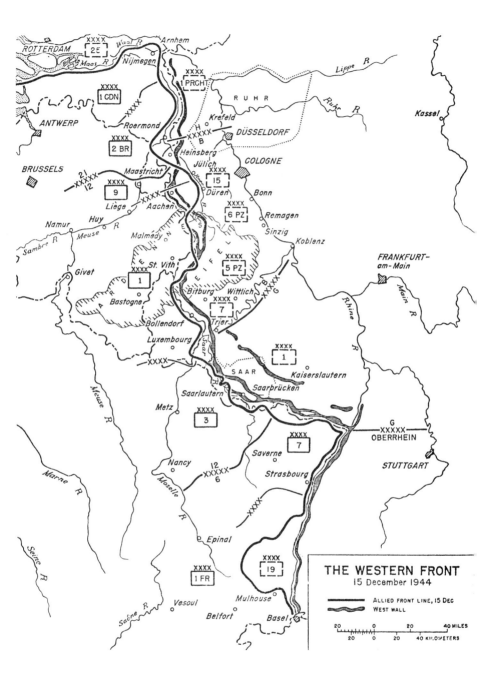

THE WESTERN FRONT
15 December 1944

━━━━━━━ ALLIED FRONT LINE, 15 DEC
〰〰〰〰〰 WEST WALL

20 0 20 40 MILES
20 0 20 40 KILOMETERS

originating east of Epinal and the other east of Montbéliard, the juncture to be made in the Vesoul area.

"I have decided on the second," Hitler stated, not bothering to explain to Skorzeny that his staff had favored the first plan, which would have meant a single thrust out of Holland. "We will start north of Luxembourg and our first objective will be to reach the Meuse River between Liège and Namur. From there we will continue on to Antwerp."

Hitler told Skorzeny that a tremendous amount of material had been accumulated, including 6,000 artillery pieces and 2,000 planes, many of them the new Me 262 jets. He explained that he was sending more than 1,300 tanks and assault guns to Field Marshal Gerd von Rundstedt, commander-in-chief of the Army West, and would deliver 1,000 more before the offensive began. Some of the tanks had been modified to spread sand on the icy roads, so the vehicles involved in the attack would have better traction. The Führer indicated that he had learned his lesson from the Russian disaster, because he emphasized to Skorzeny that all the German troops had been well outfitted with winter clothing and regular snow-removing troops had been organized. However, after all these glowing reports, of which Skorzeny, despite his deep loyalty to Hitler, was skeptical, the Führer revealed that he was hedging his bets as far as conventional warfare was concerned.

"As for you, Skorzeny, one of the most difficult tasks within the framework of the offensive will be your assignment. There are several bridges between the cities of Liège and Namur on the Meuse River and your commandos will capture one or more of these bridges before they can be destroyed. I have decided that this can be accomplished faster and with lighter losses if your men wear American uniforms."[4]

Skorzeny was shocked and concerned at Hitler's words because a few days earlier he had read in a German newspaper that commandos in British uniforms had been executed as directed by the "commando order" of the Führer. After the war Skorzeny was interrogated by Walter H. Rapp, a member of the War Crimes prosecution staff about the "commando order." (The Allies, through their intelligence agencies, had learned in 1942 that on October 18 of that year Hitler had issued a top-secret order calling for the execution of Allied commandos captured in the west. Until this time captured enemy soldiers, commandos or not, had been treated according to the rules of the Geneva Convention. This order by Hitler was known as the "commando order.")

RAPP: Now I would like to ask you the following question. When you were under the OKW did you ever hear of the so-called "commando order"?

SKORZENY: No. I first heard of the term "commando order" in prison. Late in 1944, however, I learned of it in a newspaper notice. It was not called the "commando order" but the article did state that "the commandos were removed from prison and killed." I wrote to the Wehrmacht leadership staff and asked for an explanation. I considered such an explanation very important since my missions were treated as commando missions. I admired the English commando troops and I wanted the Wehrmacht to set limits on their treatment of the enemy commandos. If two or three men were landed and they were wearing German uniforms then they should be treated as spies and executed. Commandos in English uniforms should not be executed.

RAPP: If the Führer had said that you had to wear a Turkish uniform instead of a German one, would you have done it?

SKORZENY: Yes, but it would have been clear to me that it was a spy mission.

RAPP: What about the Ardennes offensive?

SKORZENY: The mission at the Ardennes was ordered directly by Hitler and he had taken into consideration that it should be conducted according to international law.

RAPP: International law? In American uniforms?

SKORZENY: I had orders to achieve a goal in enemy uniform but we were forbidden to fight while wearing the uniforms. Hitler knew the distinction and wanted to make certain we were aware of it, too.[5]

Realizing the futility of further questioning along these lines, Rapp went on to other subjects. Skorzeny knew Hitler's contention that he and his men could rove at will behind the American front lines while wearing enemy uniforms and not be considered spies as long as they didn't fire their guns was ridiculous, but he complied with Hitler's order anyway.

Hitler assured Skorzeny that he would be provided with a large group of German soldiers fluent in the English language, all the American trucks, jeeps, and tanks that he needed for his operation, and also a large number of support troops.

"I know the time given you is very short," Hitler told Skorzeny, "but

I can count on you to do the impossible. I want you at the front when the offensive begins but I forbid you to cross the enemy lines yourself. I cannot afford to lose you."[6]

Jodl gave him further details about the mission after Skorzeny was dismissed by Hitler. Jodl was not so encouraging. He told Skorzeny that he would be provided with three days' supply of rations and munitions and that additional supplies would be brought to his troops later. In private he explained that there would be about 140 planes available instead of the 2,000 Hitler promised and suggested Skorzeny try and gather up the needed American uniforms and trucks himself. It was apparent to Skorzeny as he left the Wolf's Lair that too many promises were being made, promises that couldn't be kept.

His organization was composed of two main groups for the Ardennes offensive—a commando unit wearing American uniforms and the 150 Panzer Brigade, commandos in German uniforms. The commando unit was composed of English-speaking Germans drawn from various units in the armed forces. He received 600 initially, and from them he selected 150 of the best. Each of the commando units contained a demolition group of five or six men whose job was to blow up bridges, munition and gasoline dumps; a reconnaissance group of three or four men whose duty was to reconnoiter in depth east and west of the Meuse River to spot enemy tank, artillery, and other unit movements and to disrupt enemy forces by reversing road signs, removing minefield signs, and blocking roads; and a lead commando group of three or four men whose assignment was to cut telephone wires, wreck radio stations, and give false commands to enemy troops while behind the front lines.

The 150 Panzer Brigade was composed of two tank and one infantry combat groups, each with its own small combat staff. The 150 Panzer Brigade was to follow the well-equipped 1st Panzer Division when it launched its all-out attack on the American position. When the 1st Panzer Division reached the Hohe Venn, Skorzeny's three groups were to move forward at night and capture the bridges crossing the Meuse. They were to move fast, gambling on surprise to help achieve success, because they were not equipped for a prolonged fight with the enemy.

Skorzeny's reservations about putting his commandos in American uniforms turned to outright rage when he learned that the OKW staff had published and circulated to all military units an order, an order Allied intelligence would have a copy of within hours, which stated:

To all units of the Wehrmacht: Report until October 10, 1944 all English-speaking officers and soldiers available for special missions. These are to be directed to Friedenthal, near Berlin, in view of their incorporation in the commando units of Lieutenant-Colonel Skorzeny.[7]

He immediately wrote a scathing memo to Hitler's headquarters. It was answered personally by General Hermann Fegelein, the liaison officer between Himmler and Hitler.

"It is an incredible and incomprehensible error," Fegelein told Skorzeny, "but it is better if the Führer does not learn about it. Consequently it is impossible to cancel your mission."

Hitler set November 27 as the date for the start of the Ardennes offensive, but as that date approached it was obvious a delay was necessary. Skorzeny welcomed the extra time because he was having serious problems recruiting his commando unit. When he was interrogated after the war, Skorzeny vowed that he had only a handful of German military men who were able to speak English well enough to participate in "Operation Greif" as the behind-the-lines commando mission was designated.

"I had ten men who spoke the English language fluently, thirty or forty who spoke it fairly well, and about 150 men who managed to make themselves understood with difficulty," he said.

Yet, American soldiers of the U.S. First Army and U.S. Third Army reported many more English-speaking German soldiers encountered during the Ardennes offensive. Skorzeny, at the time of his postwar interrogation, was preparing to stand trial so he was very careful about what he revealed, stating only facts that would put himself in a better light with the Allied prosecutors. It is thought that he grossly understated the size of his commando force in hopes of acquittal. At any rate, when the Ardennes offensive began at dawn on December 16, Skorzeny had his English-speaking unit ready for acton. And he took the Americans by complete surprise.

As soon as the artillery bombardment by the German 1st Panzer Division ended and the ground units moved to the attack, Skorzeny sent four groups of commandos behind the lines. Since the U.S. First Army was unprepared for the onslaught, it quickly became disorganized and the commandos were able to infiltrate the enemy lines. They followed at the rear of the attacking panzer columns in their jeeps, and when a column got into a fire fight, the jeeps moved off the main road and slipped around the battle area on side roads until they were behind the withdrawing American troops. If there were no side roads they drove their jeeps through small trails in wooded areas until they were behind the enemy lines. Some of the commando units moved during the day, some at night. And they were successful, because with telephone wires shot out, radios failing, and outposts overrun, the Americans had only a confused and fragmentary picture of the scope and intent of Hitler's counteroffensive. Consequently, the presence of German commandos in American uniforms behind the lines went unreported initially. When Skorzeny discovered that his men were operating successfully and had not been detected, he sent many more units to join the first four.

One of his groups passed through a breach in the American lines and advanced to Huy on the banks of the Meuse River. The leader, Fritz Bussinger, checked the bridge carefully, although it was guarded by American soldiers, and then decided to walk through the town itself to get an accurate understanding of the situation. Greeting American soldiers he met and saluting all officers, he spent several hours in Huy without incident. As he was getting ready to return to his companions waiting on the outskirts of the city, an armored vehicle leading a convoy of tanks and trucks approached. The lead vehicle stopped near him and the officer in the right seat asked Bussinger the way to Marchin. He promptly pointed north, the opposite direction of Marchin and explained that the Germans had captured several of the roads leading to the city of Marchin and they would have to make a wide detour. Unaware that he was being led astray, the American officer thanked him for the information and led his convoy away . . . in the wrong direction.

Another of Skorzeny's commando units, led by Wilhelm Giel and wearing military police insignia, took over the duty of directing traffic in a small village behind the American lines. When a regiment of the 84th Infantry Division arrived, Giel and his men directed them down the wrong road. Later they listened to American broadcasts that the regiment had been missing for three days. A later investigation of the incident by U.S. officers failed to turn up a trace of any military police who had been at this particular intersection, so Skorzeny's report of the incident was verified.

An ammunition dump and a gasoline dump were both discovered by Skorzeny's commandos and destroyed. The markings of a mine field near Eupen were removed. The leader of another Skorzeny unit decided to scout the area surrounding Malmédy, but to his horror discovered he had driven directly into the outskirts of the city, which was occupied by the Americans. Deciding that since he was there he might as well do some further checking, he arrogantly drove his jeep through the city observing the enemy installations and estimating the strength of the forces defending the city. He then calmly returned to Englesdorf and told Skorzeny the city seemed lightly defended. Not once had he been stopped or questioned by the Americans, and this was fortunate because he didn't speak English well.

But after the American forces regrouped and once again became a cohesive fighting machine, Skorzeny's tactics were discovered and reported. A TWX message from Headquarters, Normandy Base Section, ETOUSA, dated December 23, to all American units, stated:

> Interrogation of prisoners of war indicates from two different SS sources that Skorzeny led small groups through lines with six vehicles presumably command cars. They were carrying forged letters of recommendation and identification papers wearing English uniforms. Interview with General Eisenhower will be attempted by the party. They will use the cover story that they have returned from the front and have vital information regarding operations and an attempt on the general's life. Possibility exists that a change of vehicles and uniforms may be made before reaching Paris for the purpose of covering their tracks. It is possible that they may have one officer with them in German uniform, claiming that they are taking him to higher headquarters for interrogation.[8]

Eisenhower's headquarters at the Trianon Palace Hotel in Versailles suddenly became the focus of the Allied powers. Because the palace had once been the headquarters for German Field Marshal Rundstedt, the American security command felt it was dangerous for Eisenhower to remain there. Undoubtedly Skorzeny had been well briefed on every detail of the building. Consequently Eisenhower was persuaded against his will to move to another building at the Versailles headquarters. Barbed wire encircled the building, tanks were positioned on all four sides, and the security force was tripled. Every time he went to another building in the headquarters complex, an entire company of soldiers surrounded him. As reports arrived at the headquarters that Skorzeny and his men were moving closer and closer, Eisenhower, although he was the Supreme Commander of the Allied military forces, was forbidden to leave his own building. It was Christmas week, which made the enforced hibernation even more galling to him, and he really exploded in anger when he discovered the security force was using another American officer as a decoy in an effort to trap Skorzeny. Lieutenant Colonel Baldwin B. Smith, a staff officer, was driven around the headquarters area daily in Eisenhower's car in hopes Skorzeny would think it was the general and make his move. He ordered the decoy operation stopped at once.

While Eisenhower was cooped up in his headquarters and Baldwin was trying to lure Skorzeny out of hiding, other American officers were having unprecedented problems caused by reports and rumors of actions by Skorzeny and his commandos dressed in American uniforms. No American trusted another unless he knew him personally. General Bruce Clark of the U.S. VIII Corps, defenders of St. Vith, was touring the area when several of his own soldiers guarding a rail intersection were not satisfied with his identification and put him in the guardhouse, where he stayed for five hours. Meanwhile his staff searched for him frantically, thinking he had been captured by the Germans. When he was finally located in the guardhouse and released, the sergeant who had ordered the general's arrest asked him for his autograph! The angry general stared at the sergeant . . . and then signed the proffered paper.

Skorzeny's commandos had spread the rumor that one of their number, fluent in the English language, was posing as Britain's Field Marshal Bernard Law Montgomery. The flamboyant and outspoken Montgomery thought he should have been the Supreme Commander of the Allied military forces not Eisenhower; he was constantly at odds with Ike, and took great delight in Ike's "imprisonment" in his own headquarters. Deciding that while Eisenhower was out of circulation would be a fine time for him to roam the combat area and increase his own prestige, Montgomery set out from his headquarters in the west and drove toward Malmédy. At the very first American security checkpoint, the egotistical Britisher told his driver to keep moving. That was a mistake. The American guards promptly shot out the tires on his command car, ordered Montgomery and his driver out of the car, and forced them into the guard shelter at gunpoint. The fuming, arguing Britisher was held there for four hours until a British colonel known to the Americans arrived and gave positive identification. Eisenhower, when he learned of the incident, was delighted and vowed that Skorzeny had done one worthwhile service.

However, the pass-identification security system set up by the American forces became very tight and Skorzeny's men gradually found themselves more and more restricted in their actions behind enemy lines. Most of their problems resulted from not knowing the intimate details of American life and manners. One group trying to return to German lines was stopped by an MP detachment and during the questioning was asked to identify Glenn Miller. Instead of naming him the most popular big-band leader in the States, the commando said Miller was the husband of Betty Grable. (He must have confused him with Harry James.)

Another commando leader, dressed in an American uniform, tried to impress the MPs at a checkpoint with his knowledge of American slang, but used a British phrase instead. Laughing when he saw an MP relieving himself at the side of the road, the commando yelled, "Keep your pecker up!" Unfortunately for him, the MP was aware that this amusing phrase had an entirely different meaning in England than the German thought. It was an English phrase meaning "Keep your chin up!" Further questioning of the commando soon revealed to the suspicious MP that the man was German. A Skorzeny group returning from the area around St. Vith had passed the questioning of the security force on the outskirts of the city and were offered a drink of wine by an American sergeant. One commando, trying to be friendly, tapped his mess kit against the bottle held up by the sergeant and said cheerfully: "Up your bottom!" instead of "Bottoms up!" The entire commando unit was captured.

The German forces were encountering so many problems in the Ardennes, that Skorzeny was forced to halt his commando operations. Nor did he fare any better with his 150 Panzer Brigade. The three groups of the brigade stayed close behind the attacking 1st Panzer Division, waiting for the division to reach the Hohe Venn. Once that objective was reached, Skorzeny was prepared to order his three combat groups to push to the Meuse River and capture the bridges spanning it. But the 1st Panzer Division never reached the Hohe Venn because the U.S. First Army regrouped and stopped the German advance. On December 20 Skorzeny contacted General Josef (Sepp) Dietrich, commander of the Sixth Panzer Army, and asked for a mission for his 150 Panzer Brigade now that the original plan had gone astray. Dietrich ordered him to attack Malmédy, which was defended by the U.S. 30th Infantry Division. Skorzeny was delighted because his behind-the-line commando groups had already reconnoitred Malmédy and reported the city was lightly defended. He also knew that the U.S. Ninth Air Force had mistakenly bombed the city three times, inflicting heavy losses on the American defenders.

Skorzeny launched his attack at 5:00 A.M. on the morning of December 21 in conjunction with a task force of the 1st Panzer Division commanded by *Obersturmbannführer* (Lieutenant Colonel) Joachim Peiper. Peiper was a man that Skorzeny would be involved with at the war crimes trials and later postwar years because of the fighting around Malmédy. Already on December 21 Peiper stood accused of killing nineteen American prisoners at Honsfeld and at least eighty-six on the road between Modersheid and Ligneuville four days earlier. Peiper was pocketed in the Stoumont-La Gleize sector by the U.S. Third Armored Division and other units such as 120th Infantry; the "Norwegians," a nickname for the 99th Infantry Battalion; and part of the 30th Division. The Americans were braced for Peiper to try to cut his way out of the pocket by the way of Stavelot. They were unaware that to the south, at his temporary headquarters located in Ligneuville, Skorzeny's notorious 150 Panzer Brigade had given up on the idea of a dash to the Meuse River when the German attack stalled and was now preparing to move on Malmédy.

The troops Skorzeny gathered at Ligneuville were a tough but motley outfit. Some were completely equipped with American uniforms and equipment; others had GI trousers and shoes but German tunics; while a third group had German uniforms. Their motorized equipment consisted of German, American, and British makes plus an assortment of hybrid vehicles that had been camouflaged to resemble American models by the addition of dummy turrets, decks, and fronts. But every man was well armed with automatic and heavy weapons. When the 150 Panzer Brigade left Ligneuville, Skorzeny was in the lead, replacing the former brigade commander, who had been killed. Von Foelkersam was his deputy.

The attack was doomed from the start. Not only had the Americans strongly reinforced the area, unbeknownst to Skorzeny, but a new weapon had been added to the American arsenal. Even Skorzeny's surprise attack by commandos trained in unorthodox tactics couldn't overcome these two obstacles. The tanks came up against B Company of the 99th Infantry Battalion as the commando unit neared Malmédy and the "Norwegians" stopped the attack in its track with mortars, anti-tank guns, machine guns, and the new weapon—POZIT, shells with proximity fuses. Nearly a hundred commandos were killed during the first minutes of the battle and they lost most of the tanks. The determined Germans, under the command of von Foelkersam, kept trying to break through the enemy defense but the "Norwegians," described in earlier German intelligence reports as the "old men," refused to give an inch. Lieutenant Colonel Harold D. Hansen, who commanded the Americans, calmly directed the defense, even when the German machine-gun crews tried to set up their pieces right in front of the railroad embankment where the "Norwegians" lay. After the crews were killed and von Foelkersam was wounded in the buttocks, the Germans retreated.

The main unit of the 150 Panzer Brigade, led by Skorzeny himself in disregard of Hitler's orders that he was not to become involved personally in the fighting, headed for Malmédy down the Stavelot-Malmédy road in the fog, and ran headlong into K Company of the 120th Infantry. The Americans, taken by surprise, retreated a short distance and Skorzeny thought his path into the city was open. First Lieutenant Kenneth R. Nelson of K Company, however, rallied the few men and blocked off the road. Fighting savagely, Nelson and his men fought off Skorzeny's commandos until a German sniper killed Nelson. Technical Sergeant John Van Der Kamp then took command and continued the fight until he was finally ordered to withdraw. Both Americans were later awarded the Distinguished Service Cross for their actions, Nelson posthumously. K Company, pursued by the men of the 150 Panzer Brigade, retreated to a nearby factory. Skorzeny immediately ordered the factory attacked, hoping to wipe out the stubborn remnants of K Company and get on with his drive to Malmédy.

This time he came up against Private First Class Francis Currey, a New Yorker, who found a bazooka in the factory and decided the Germans were not going to leave the area alive if he had anything to do with it. Using the bazooka, while small-arms, machine-gun, and artillery fire zeroed in on him, Currey knocked out the lead tank with one shot. Shifting to a new position, he spotted three Germans in the doorway of a house Skorzeny's men had taken over. He killed or wounded all three with his automatic rifle. Skorzeny couldn't believe that this "one-man army" could stop his brigade, but every time the big Austrian personally tried to challenge the private he was driven to cover by the intense fire of Currey and his companions. Currey, deciding he needed some rockets that were piled across the street from the factory, successfully ran the gauntlet of German guns and obtained them. He then advanced alone to within fifty yards of the house, took careful aim, and knocked part of one wall of the house down with a rocket. While reloading, he saw five Americans pinned down by fire from the house and three German tanks. Realizing they could not escape until the tanks and the gunners in the house were taken care of, Currey crossed the street again and procured an armful of antitank grenades from a damaged American vehicle. Firing at the tanks, he forced the German crewmen out of the tanks and into the house, which he promptly attacked from a half-track that was parked nearby. By this time reinforcements had arrived and Skorzeny decided to get his commandos out of the area and away from Currey. Currey later received the Medal of Honor for stemming the attack.

Skorzeny returned to his headquarters and reported to division GHQ that he needed more men and more equipment, knowing that he would probably get neither, because none was available. Deciding he needed a drink to make him forget Currey, Nelson, Van Der Kamp, and the other Americans who had stopped his drive on Malmédy, he headed for the nearby Hotel du Moulin. He knew there was still some cognac left by the Americans, who had used the hotel as a headquarters until they had to evacuate it during the Ardennes battle. He never made it. Hearing the whistling of an oncoming artillery shell, Skorzeny dove under a nearby truck. An instant later the shell exploded near the trailer used by the chief of staff and rocked the truck under which he was taking cover. After pulling several men from the trailer, Skorzeny and his driver leaped into his car and headed for a safer spot. Suddenly three shells burst nearby; and shrapnel slammed through the window of the car and struck Skorzeny on the forehead. Blood ran down the dazed Austrian's face. By feeling with his fingers, he discovered his right eye was cut and he had a deep laceration directly above it. Hours later, when the artillery shelling ended, he was taken to a doctor near division headquarters where, with the help of a local anaesthetic to ease the pain, several splinters of bone were removed, the laceration stitched, and the eye bandaged. He was ordered evacuated from the battle zone because of his wounds, but he only grinned at the doctor issuing the order and returned to his own headquarters.

By December 2, however, Skorzeny knew the Battle of the Bulge was over. He also knew it was a defeat for the German army. On that same day Eisenhower politely but defiantly told his security men to go to hell when they told him he was still confined to his headquarters in France because Skorzeny was threatening to assassinate him. He left his headquarters to go to the front so he could confer with Montgomery. He, too, understood that both the German attack in the Ardennes and the threat of assassination by Skorzeny were over.

Did Skorzeny try to assassinate Eisenhower? This question has never been answered satisfactorily. During his interrogation by Lieutenant Robert E. Merriam of the Historical Section, ETOUSA, in 1945, Skorzeny denied that he had ever intended to assassinate Eisenhower.

"We did not plan to capture high American officials," he stated. "This was never part of the scheme. Around the beginning of November 1944, when the unit was organized, the soldiers began to spread rumors about the employment of this special unit. Naturally we censored all the mail and at first tried to suppress these rumors. By the middle of the month, however, I began to realize that it would be impossible to stop the rumors, many of which were spread by officers of the unit. I had a meeting with von Foelkersam and decided to let the rumors go. I recall specifically that some of the men were claiming that our unit, single-handedly, was to capture Antwerp while others said we were to drive to Dunkirk and free the German troops encircled in that town. I am quite certain that the rumor about capturing General Eisenhower was started in this way."[9]

Skorzeny's explanation was not accepted unchallenged by American officials. Where was Skorzeny during the first days of the Ardennes battle? Only during the attack on Malmédy was Skorzeny's location known to the Americans. Why did so many German prisoners-of-war state unequivocally that Skorzeny intended to murder Eisenhower, if it was not true? And what were Skorzeny commandos doing so near Paris if they were not trying to stalk the general? Skorzeny, of course, was not captured during this period and his whereabouts, except during the Malmédy attack, were never ascertained. For months after the battle, American security men carried photographs of him, still wary of his intentions, still suspicious that he was on the trail of Eisenhower.

Skorzeny, however, had another man on his mind as he left Belgium on December 28 on his way back to Germany. What would Hitler say about the defeat at the Ardennes?

8 THE HIMMLER CHALLENGE

Skorzeny arrived at Hitler's headquarters on the last day of 1944. The Führer now was headquartered at Adlerhorst near Ziegenberg in the Taunus mountains, but with the loss of the Ardennes battle was preparing to move back to Berlin. Skorzeny expected to find a depressed, bitter Hitler, an angry Führer who would place the blame on everyone but himself for the defeat. When he arrived at the Adlerhorst, however, he was pleasantly surprised to find Hitler in good spirits. A small Christmas tree was still standing in the bunker, decorated with candles placed on it by his secretaries. And instead of being depressed, the Führer was still optimistic, outlining new plans to win the war. But he talked only a few minutes with Skorzeny before he ordered the commando chief to report immediately to Dr. Ludwig Stumpfegger, the tall slim SS physician who had once been Himmler's personal doctor but now was on Hitler's staff.

"You should have reported to the hospital immediately," Hitler told Skorzeny, concern in his voice. "Your wound is probably infected."[1]

Stumpfegger was horrified when he saw the soiled bandage on Skorzeny's head. He cut the bandage off, cleaned and examined the head wound, checked the eye for damage, and then carefully wrapped the wound again. He then gave him several injections to ward off further infection.

"You must be more careful in the future," Stumpfegger warned him.[2]

Skorzeny nearly laughed in the doctor's face. With the chaotic situation in Germany, how could he be "careful"? While Skorzeny was sipping a glass of cognac the physician gave him, Nicolaus von Below, Hitler's Luftwaffe adjutant, walked into the room and told him the Führer was waiting to talk with him again. Skorzeny emptied his glass and went back to Hitler's office.

After checking the bandage Stumpfegger had put on Skorzeny's head, Hitler began one of his long monologues. Skorzeny listened in amazement as Hitler vowed that hundreds of new Me-262 jet planes would knock the British and American planes out of the sky over Germany; that he had ordered Werner Baumbach, commander of the Luftwaffe bombers, to plan an immediate attack on New York; that Göring was planning a 1000-plane attack on Allied airfields the very next day. Skorzeny said nothing. He knew for certain that there was only a handful of the new jet planes; that the Luftwaffe had no bomber that could reach New York and return; and he doubted if Göring had 1,000 planes left to attack any Allied target. If he did have that many planes, why hadn't he used them during the Ardennes offensive?

Skorzeny was wrong about Göring's planned attack on the enemy airfields. On January 1, 1945, in extremely bad weather, Göring *did* launch such an attack in hopes of destroying so many Allied planes on the ground that there would be few left to support the ground troops and the decision in the Ardennes could still swing to Germany. The surprise mission was partly successful. Göring claimed that his 1,040 planes on the attack destroyed more than 500 Allied aircraft, but to his bewilderment, the enemy had several times that number remaining to support the ground forces. The Luftwaffe lost 277 planes, more than half of them shot down by their own flak, because Göring had neglected to notify the German anti-aircraft gunners at the front that such a mission was planned.

Hitler and Skorzeny talked several hours and as the commando chief took his leave of the Führer he was convinced of one fact. "It was clear to me that the last phase of the war had begun," Skorzeny said later.[3]

He returned to his headquarters at Friedenthal aware that further commando missions probably would not be assigned to him by Hitler. The situation was much too critical. It was now an all-out battle to save Berlin, to stave off total defeat if possible, although Skorzeny didn't believe it was possible. He still had faith in Hitler and was convinced that Hitler would escape from Germany before he was captured, but he didn't think the Third Reich could be saved. In fact he was already planning for the post–Third Reich years when it would be necessary for Hitler and his loyal survivors to start all over again.

At Friedenthal, von Foelkersam was pacing the headquarters, frustrated and angry. He, too, was convinced the days of the commandos were finished and he wanted a new assignment. Skorzeny tried to talk him into staying at Friedenthal longer but couldn't convince him. Skorzeny arranged for him to be assigned to the eastern front. He never saw von Foelkersam again. One by one his staff left the commando headquarters for other duties as the Allies closed in on Berlin. Some volunteered for conventional Wehrmacht units while others waited until they were ordered to the front as German manpower dwindled. The glamor and excitement of clandestine warfare was replaced with the snow-slogging, foxhole-digging life of a foot soldier. Defeatism replaced enthusiasm as the first month of 1945 passed.

Skorzeny, it was learned after the war, did not sit in his office at Friedenthal and brood about the deteriorating situation on the battlefield. As usual he was making plans and aiding others with their plans. One of the first men to contact him that January was General Reinhard Gehlen who, as chief of the Army High Command Foreign Armies East Department, was in command of all anti-Soviet espionage operations. On January 9 he made a personal report to Hitler about the situation facing the German military forces on the eastern front, warning the Führer that the Soviets were preparing to attack across the Vistula with an immense superiority in tanks, artillery, and troops. Hitler had ignored the warning and refused to move the entire Sixth SS Panzer Army from the west to the eastern front as Guderian had requested. And he belittled the report of Gehlen.

On leaving the Führer, Gehlen, now convinced that the Third Reich faced certain defeat, returned directly to his headquarters at Lossen, near Berlin, and called a meeting of his most trusted staff members. He explained that the impending Soviet attack would soon force them from their headquarters and they would be fighting for their own survival, without any time to worry about the secret files on the Soviet Union that they had compiled during the war years. Consequently he wanted all the documents in the headquarters reviewed immediately and the unimportant destroyed, the important microfilme in three copies.

While this was being accomplished, Gehlen contacted Skorzeny, with whom he had planned and executed several clandestine missions behind Russian lines. He explained to Skorzeny that he was making triplicate copies of his important files and wanted them secretly buried in three different locations in Bavaria. Knowing he could trust Skorzeny, he told him the reason.

"I know the Americans have not even considered building up an espionage network in Soviet Russia," he said. "After the war ends they will soon discover they will need such a network. I can then offer my staff and my files to the Americans and they will welcome the help. It will be good for us all, Skorzeny."[4]

The commando chief nodded. He didn't tell Gehlen that he was already involved in such secret work for other high-ranking Nazis. When the microfilmed copies of the documents were ready, he had them packed into three watertight containers to which were affixed a mechanism that would destroy the contents if any unauthorized person tried to open them. He then took the three containers into the mountains south of Berchtesgaden in Bavaria and buried them for Gehlen. This secret mission was to pay off handsomely for both Gehlen and Skorzeny in the postwar years.

During this period, when the war was winding down, Skorzeny made many other trips to various areas in Bavaria and Austria with secret cargo. Subterfuge of the highest level was used, often far surpassing that employed on his missions behind enemy lines. Skorzeny and other prominent Nazis were now spending much more time preparing for the future than fighting the war of the present, which they knew was lost. And much of their postwar planning involved the region where he had buried Gehlen's files—Bavaria. The section near the city of Berchtesgaden was known as "Hitler Territory" during the years of the Third Reich because it was there that the Führer, at the foot of the Kehlstein, had built his mountain retreat complex, the Berghof. The famous Eagle's Nest was constructed on the peak of the Kehlstein, overlooking Berchtesgaden in one direction and Salzburg the other. It was at the Berghof that Hitler relaxed with his mistress, later wife, Eva Braun, and his inner circle of associates. And it was to this area that Hitler planned to retreat and make his last stand. He was not the only one to recognize the value of the mountains surrounding Berchtesgaden as a hiding place from the advancing Allies and as a jumping-off place to Italy or Spain or South America.

As early as Christmas of 1944 many of the top Nazi officials had sent their families to the Berchtesgaden area to sit out the remainder of the war. Göring's wife and child were at his luxurious chalet in the Berghof complex and the Luftwaffe field marshal, now scorned by Hitler because the German air force had proven ineffective against the British and American bombers, was waiting for the appropriate moment to join them. Martin Bormann's wife and children were also on the Obersalzberg, where the Berghof was located. Bormann, however, remained at Hitler's side as his influence increased day by day during the last months of the Third Reich. Hated and feared by Göring, the minister of armaments and munitions, Albert Speer, Goebbels, Eva Braun, and other members of Hitler's inner circle, Bormann nevertheless was considered completely loyal to the Führer. He constantly encouraged Hitler, kept telling the Führer that because of Hitler's great intelligence and foresight the war would yet be won by the German military despite the gloomy situation in January 1945. But Bormann, too, had called Skorzeny to his office to discuss the future. Skorzeny transported a fortune in gold coins, gold bars, and other valuables that Bormann had accumulated during his years at Hitler's side to Bavaria and Austria and hid them. The gold coins were buried near the Schloss Fuschl in Salzburg in a farmer's field, while the gold was turned over to Dr. Helmut von Hummel, an aide to Bormann. Much of the Bormann gold had been made from gold fillings from the mouths of Jews who died in the death chambers. The fillings were melted into gold bars by a German company, Degussa, and forwarded to Bormann.

When the German citizens in Bavaria became curious about the trucks arriving daily in the Berchtesgaden area and the strange burials taking place, Skorzeny suggested that a few small SS hospitals should be built in the area to deceive the local townspeople. He then used ambulances marked with the Red Cross to transport his shipments of gold, jewelry, money, and other items of the Nazi treasure being hidden for postwar use. It was in this manner that Adolf Eichmann, the infamous Nazi administrator of the Jewish genocide operation during the Third Reich, managed to transport twenty-two iron boxes filled with documents and gold to the Obersalzberg. Even Skorzeny's old friend and superior Ernst Kaltenbrunner asked Skorzeny's aid in getting a few personal belongings to Bavaria, such items as:

50 kilograms of gold bars
50 cases with gold coins and gold articles, each case weighing 100 pounds
2 million American dollars

2 million Swiss francs
5 cases filled with diamonds and precious stones
1 stamp collection worth at least 5 million gold marks

Skorzeny was forced to sign a receipt for this load!

It has never been completely determined exactly what Skorzeny and his companions hid in the mountainous region around Berchtesgaden before the end of the Third Reich and probably never will be. Three decades after the collapse of Nazi Germany boxes of gold coins, valuable stamp collections, art treasures, and millions of dollars are unaccounted for. On the other hand, valuable finds are often made by accident. A farmer ploughing his field dug up two iron boxes containing 10,167 gold coins; a fisherman at Töplitzee, a known hiding place for a great many containers of Nazi treasure, hooked onto a box holding printing plates for counterfeit dollars; at least seven persons have died at Töplitzee under suspicious circumstances and many are thought to have been hunting for the treasures hidden there by Skorzeny and others.

At the war crimes trials after the war, Skorzeny was questioned by Prosecutor Walter Rapp about one report of his smuggling that had nothing to do with jewelry or gold.

RAPP: I have been asked to speak with you about a pilot by the name of Mackenson. Do you know the man?
SKORZENY: That is the famous question I was already asked before I arrived here.
RAPP: Do you know the man?
SKORZENY: No.
RAPP: Did he work for you?
SKORZENY: I can't imagine that.
RAPP: Did you only know people of higher rank?
SKORZENY: He may have been in K-200. Does he maintain that?
RAPP: Yes.
SKORZENY: It can be that he has flown me once or twice. What rank did he hold?
RAPP: Captain or major.
SKORZENY: Captain Gerlach flew me in Italy. Otherwise it was always lieutenants because they were better pilots.
RAPP: Then you deny the whole story?
SKORZENY: You simply ask me about the man. I don't know the whole story.

RAPP: The story is as follows: In the last days in Berlin between April 25 and 30, Hitler is supposed to have said to his people who were in the bunker with him that it was time to leave. Thereupon three or four Ju-52s together with ten fighters took off. This Mackenson flew one of the Ju-52s loaded with SS personnel. Eva Braun and Hitler and his immediate staff were on another Ju-52. All the planes flew to Denmark, refueled, and then flew to Spain.

SKORZENY: Ju-52s?

RAPP: Yes. Mackenson says he was shot down by an American plane. All aboard his plane died except himself. He finally was captured and interrogated and he vows that he received the orders for the flight from Otto Skorzeny. He said you could verify the action if we questioned you.

SKORZENY: It is not true. He is only trying to save his own neck.[5]

While later investigation indicates that Hitler died in the bunker with Eva Braun (although no bodies were ever shown to American or British authorities by the Russians in whose zone the bunker was located), the statement by the German pilot when he was taken prisoner is evidence that among SS personnel Skorzeny's secret missions in behalf of the Nazi hierarchy during the last days of the war were well known.

Skorzeny also had other schemes in various stages of progress during the early part of 1945. The development of an escape route for high-ranking Nazis was one. Another was his collaboration with the wealthy German industrialists who had decided the defeat of Hitler and the Third Reich was imminent and it was time for postwar planning. On August 10, 1944, representatives of such leading German firms as Krupp, Röchling, Messerschmitt, Rheinmetall-Borsig and Volkswagen-werk had met in Hotel Rotes Hause in Strasbourg to discuss their financial plight. Most of the firms had invested heavily in Reich treasury bonds—Krupp, for example, had more than 200 million marks invested—and it was obvious to the industrialists that these liens against the Third Reich were of dubious value. At Nuremberg an official of Krupp, Johannes Schröder, told about the policy discussed at the meeting.

"Under the impact of the air attacks and the war situation," he stated, "we felt that Germany had lost the war and in strictest confidence we said so among ourselves. Krupp managers were interested in saving something for the postwar era so the firm followed a new policy of secretly keeping all assets as liquid as possible. It rid itself of war bonds, cashed in claims for war damages, and collected outstanding debts from the Reich."[6]

Since Hitler was demanding that all liquid assets of the firms be made available to the Third Reich to finance the war, the industrialists were following a hazardous route. They needed someone accustomed to dangerous undertakings to help and they chose Skorzeny. Through him they were successful in transferring large amounts of money, looted property, and other assets into neutral countries. In 1946 the U.S. Treasury Department estimated that German funds had been sent by various means during the latter months of the war to Spain, Portugal, Turkey, Argentina, and several other countries. Many of the bonds and German marks were transported secretly by Skorzeny aides. Skorzeny's contacts with the wealthy industrialists at this time paid off very well during the postwar years in two ways: The industrialists were grateful and so were the officials of the countries where the huge sums of money were invested.

Despite his aid to the German industrialists who were disobeying Hitler's order that all liquid assets must go to the financing of the Third Reich war effort, Skorzeny still considered himself loyal to the Führer. He was simply looking out for his own future. He was ready to accept any assignment given him by Hitler, no questions asked. Such an assignment came on January 30, 1945 through the office of Himmler. Himmler, who already held more titles than he could have printed on his stationery, was given another one. Hitler appointed him commander-in-chief of the Upper Rhine, a new army group made up of stragglers, home-guard men, custom officials, and other soldiers not suitable for the crack panzer divisions. Himmler, always ambitious and confident of his ability to lead an army to war as well as he had led the Jews to their death, accepted the assignment with delight. He was a miserable failure, however, and his Upper Rhine army marched only one way—to the rear! Skorzeny knew about Himmler's failure as commander-in-chief of the Upper Rhine. He wasn't surprised because he knew Himmler wasn't qualified to lead an army. He *was* shocked, however, when Hitler, instead of removing Himmler from command of any ground troops, gave him another assignment. The Führer, after Himmler's failure on the western front, transferred him to the eastern front as commander-in-chief of Army Group Vistula, a shadowy force of survivors from various other military units. On the next to last day of January, Himmler gave Skorzeny his orders.

"You will form a bridgehead east of the Oder River near Schwedt," Himmler told him, "and you will maintain this bridgehead, come what might, so that my army can launch an offensive from it."[7]

Earlier in the month the Russians had launched their main offensive to capture Berlin. Two million Soviet soldiers had overrun the less than a million-man German front and cut it to ribbons. The area between the Oder and the Vistula rivers lay wide open to the Russian horde. By this time even Himmler was losing confidence in his ability to stem the Soviet tide so he promptly turned the assignment over to Skorzeny. There was one serious problem, however. Skorzeny had no troops. His commandos had been disbanded, as had the units attached to his commando unit. Never one to dodge an assignment, no matter how hopeless, Skorzeny set out to organize a force large enough to establish and hold the desired bridgehead. He was not very successful. All he could locate were Dutch, Swedish, Belgian, Norwegian, and Danish stragglers but Himmler, calling from his elegantly outfitted special train, which he had parked at Deutsch-Krone and was using as a mobile headquarters, insisted that he leave immediately with the men he had.

"I have already reported to Hitler that you have started," Himmler cried. "Go."[8]

When Skorzeny pointed out that he not only didn't have a well-organized military force but he didn't have enough artillery or ammunition, Himmler refused to listen. So at dawn the following morning Skorzeny and his ragtag army started east toward the Vistula-Oder area, directly into the path of the oncoming Soviet divisions. He didn't even have a map of Schwedt, the city of 50,000 where the SS chief expected him to establish the bridgehead. Never one to make a detour when a direct route was best, Skorzeny led his 1,000-man force straight to the city, slowed only by the refugees streaming westward. At Schwedt he selected a perimeter of defense and stationed his meager force at tactical points along it, facing the Russians on the opposite side of the Oder River. His force was a David without a slingshot facing a Goliath determined to trample it, but Skorzeny once again resorted to unorthodox tactics. He decided to corral the German soldiers moving westward through Schwedt as they retreated ahead of the Soviets and absorb them into his bridgehead force. At first the weary Wehrmacht soldiers resisted his scheme, but once they discovered Skorzeny's identity, they changed their minds and joined his group. His exploits had become widely known, and Skorzeny's reputation for achieving miracles renewed their hope that perhaps all was not yet lost. He soon had a force twice as large as the one with which he had entered Schwedt. In addition he discovered one hundred and fifty noncommissioned officers and officer cadets in the city; on Hitler's orders they were on a training exercise in the midst of the Soviet advance. They, too, became a part of his group. So did a reserve battalion of five hundred sick and wounded home defense soldiers.

While waiting for the Soviets to cross the Oder River and attack Schwedt, Skorzeny trained his nondescript force and stationed the additional men at every point along the perimeter where an attack seemed possible. The civilians, seeing that Skorzeny actually intended to defend the city, pitched in and helped dig trenches, block streets, and provide food and drink. Skorzeny at night led a few of his men across the Oder River and penetrated the Russian lines as deep as forty miles seeking information about the impending Soviet offensive. He organized other small scouting parties to scour the west side of the Oder River for additional weapons for his group. From an abandoned factory twenty-five miles south of Schwedt, they salvaged fifteen 75-mm guns to use against the T-34 and Stalin tanks. Near Frankfurt-on-the-Oder another Skorzeny patrol discovered an ammunition dump with hundreds of Mark-42 machine guns. His men also fastened some antiaircraft guns they came across in Schwedt to their trucks to use as field artillery pieces.

A few days after he had established his bridgehead perimeter, Skorzeny received a telephone call from Göring. Although Skorzeny did not know it, Göring was already planning to take Hitler's place once the Führer relinquished his position voluntarily or involuntarily. Göring asked Skorzeny about the situation in Schwedt.

"I need more men," Skorzeny told him, not convinced the obese field marshal could or would do anything about it.[9]

The next day, to Skorzeny's amazement, a battalion consisting of 600 well-trained soldiers from the Hermann Göring Division marched into Schwedt. It was a real sacrifice, since Göring had used these men to protect his country home, Karinhall. Skorzeny placed the men and some of his perimeter soldiers across the Oder River at the village of Nipperwiese with orders to resist any Russian attack as long as possible and then retreat across the river to Schwedt.

On February 17 the Soviets moved to wipe out any German units still on the east side of the Oder River. It didn't take them long to discover Skorzeny's outpost at Nipperwiese. Time and time again

Skorzeny's small bridgehead force on the east side of the river threw back the Soviets; time and time again the Soviets moved in with their tanks and ground troops. Once the Russians were within a football field's distance from the bridge across the Oder River to Schwedt, but a skilled bazooka attack by the men of the Hermann Göring Division knocked out the tanks and German snipers killed the crew members as they tried to escape from the burning T-34s. Losses were high on both sides but the Russians had many more men to lose than Skorzeny. Finally, six days after the initial attack on Nipperwiese, he ordered the men back across the bridge to the west side of the river, where his main force was stationed. It was a logical move but when the OKW in Berlin heard about it there was immediate trouble. Skorzeny was asked by radio if he had courtmartialed the commanding officer of the Nipperwiese force and if the officer had been executed. The message was so ridiculous, under the circumstances, that Skorzeny ignored it. That afternoon, however, when he returned from a scouting mission, there was another message waiting for him. This time it was from Himmler and he was asking the same question. Skorzeny radioed back: "The commanding officer was neither sentenced nor shot."

Himmler was furious. He ordered Skorzeny to his headquarters at once. When the big Austrian arrived at Prenzlau where Himmler's headquarters had been moved, he was ignored by the staff officers, an indication that Himmler was ready to punish him severely for his actions. The SS chief made him wait two hours, but Skorzeny used the time to good advantage—he drank an entire bottle of cognac. The warmth of the cognac and his anger at Himmler's question and actions made Skorzeny completely disregard the dangerous reputation of the SS chief—that Himmler could sentence a man to death with one wave of his hand, that Himmler was responsible for the mass murder of the Jews and others in the death camps, and that Himmler, next to Hitler himself, was the most ruthless of the Nazi hierarchy. When Himmler finally consented to see him, Skorzeny was ready for a showdown.

Himmler started the meeting with an angry tirade, criticizing Skorzeny for his conduct, for his insubordination, and for his lax discipline because he did not have the commanding officer of the force in Nipperwiese shot. Skorzeny waited until Himmler finished, then abruptly told the SS chief that he personally had ordered the retreat from Nipperwiese. Before Himmler could speak, Skorzeny continued:

"You sit back here where it is safe, where you have all you want to eat and drink," Skorzeny bellowed at the most-feared man in the Third Reich next to the Führer, "and you have the nerve to order a brave officer shot because he used good judgment and retreated to fight another day. All we ever received at Schwedt from you were orders. No ammunition, no food, no reinforcements, nothing."[10]

Skorzeny's outburst was timed perfectly. That very morning Guderian, convinced that Himmler was a complete failure as commander of a combat army, had proposed to Hitler that he be replaced by General Walter Wenck, an experienced officer. Guderian didn't succeed—he did later—but Himmler was frightened. He was afraid he would lose his influence with the Führer if he made a fool of himself on the eastern front. So instead of berating Skorzeny and ordering his arrest, Himmler invited him to dinner, where they discussed possible military moves along the Oder River, that would make Himmler look better in Hitler's eyes. Skorzeny, aware of Himmler's motive was quick to make suggestions, since it was more than a question of success or failure for the SS chief.

Skorzeny, using his own tactics, managed to hold the bridgehead at Schwedt until the end of February, when he suddenly received a message from Jodl in Berlin. He was ordered back to Friedenthal at once. The Führer wanted to see him.

9 WEREWOLVES AND THE ALPINE REDOUBT

Hitler arrived in Berlin from Adlerhorst shortly after 9:00 A.M. on January 16, 1945, and went straight from the Grunewald Station to the Reich Chancellery. He could no longer risk staying at his field headquarters because the enemy was closing in from all directions. He had a fear of being captured alive and was convinced by this time that Berlin was the safest spot for his headquarters. If and when Berlin was in danger of being overrun, he had planned on going to Berchtesgaden, to his beloved mountain retreat, the Berghof. It was there he had vowed to make his final stand. Unknown to the others, however, he had changed his mind.

Shortly after Hitler arrived in Berlin, Eva Braun, his mistress, left her villa in Munich and joined him. She had not seen the Führer for several weeks and was concerned about the physical change in him. "This time you will stay with me," she murmured when he greeted her. "I will take care of you. When we go to the Berghof we will go together."[1]

Hitler said nothing.

A few days later when Eva's sister Ilse was fleeing from Breslau ahead of the enemy troops, she passed through Berlin and Hitler invited her to dinner. He didn't like her because she was quick to criticize him and always blamed him for the destruction of Germany, but when Eva insisted on the invitation he agreed. Hitler and Ilse had only a mild argument about the war situation at dinner, after she graphically described the bomb damage she had seen en route to the capital. Hitler was uncharacteristically subdued.

On February 8, 1945, Hitler told Eva he wanted her to leave Berlin and go to the Berghof to make preparations for him and his staff. He suggested that she also take her younger sister, Gretl, with her. Gretl, who was married to Hermann Fegelein, Himmler's liaison officer, was pregnant. Eva protested. She didn't want to leave Hitler but he insisted. Late on the afternoon of February 8, she and Gretl left Berlin in a staff car en route to Berchtesgaden by way of Munich.

So it was a lonely, depressed Führer whom Skorzeny met with on his arrival in Berlin from the eastern front. When Hitler saw his "miracle man," however, he brightened. "Skorzeny, I have not yet thanked you for your stand on the Oder. Day after day it was the one bright spot in my reports. I have awarded you the Oak Leaves to the Knight's Cross."[2]

Hitler talked with Skorzeny for a few minutes and then excused himself, stating he was weary. "Jodl will tell you why I summoned you to Berlin."[3]

Jodl placed a map on the table in front of Skorzeny and pointed to the Rhine River. "The Americans have seized a bridge across the Rhine at Remagen. The railway bridge. The Wehrmacht failed to destroy it in time. Now it is up to your frogmen to blow it up."[4]

The Ludendorff Bridge at Remagen had been seized by the U.S. 9th Armored Division's Combat Command B under the command of General William M. Hoge. German demolition teams had set off a few charges under the span but it had failed to go down and they had had to retreat because of the oncoming Americans before they could make a second attempt. After capturing the railway bridge, Hoge had immediately contacted his commander, General John W. Leonard, who relayed the information to General Omar Bradley, commander of the Twelfth Army Group. Bradley had telephoned Eisenhower with the good news, and from his Reims headquarters Eisenhower had given Bradley the green light. "Shove over at least five divisions instantly and anything else that is necessary to make certain we can hold the bridgehead on the east side."[5]

By the time Skorzeny was examining a map of the area with Jodl in Berlin, American troops were streaming across the railway bridge. Jodl was aware of this troop movement and stressed the seriousness of the situation to Skorzeny. "There is no time to lose. The Führer is depending upon you."[6]

There was little time for proper preparation. Skorzeny briefed his "Danube Frogman Group" the next day and he explained the situation very clearly, not trying to gloss over the dangers involved in the mission.

"The water is just about freezing," he told them. "The Americans are fairly well established on the east side of the Rhine and have extended their bridgehead both north and south of the bridge and will be watching for you. I know they have already set up several searchlights in the area and will keep the bridge brightly lighted at all times. I am asking for volunteers. I am ordering no one to go."[7]

Every man stepped forward.

Skorzeny nodded. "We will leave at midnight."

The frogmen drifted down the Rhine from the north, carrying their explosives in rubber bags. Skorzeny had helped launch the frogman attack, then took a small group of SS noncoms and circled behind the Americans positioned directly east of the bridge.

"There were only six of us," Rudi Gunter, one of Skorzeny's companions that night, said. "We had synchronized our watches with the frogmen and began our surprise 'attack' exactly forty-five minutes after they entered the water. By that time Skorzeny thought the frogmen would be in the vicinity of the bridge."[8]

Unfortunately for them, the frogmen who survived the icy waters and approached the city of Remagen were trapped by the searchlights. Not one reached the bridge. The entire "Danube Frogman Group" was lost. Some were captured, some shot, and others drowned.

"We didn't know that," Gunter said, "so we made a sneak raid on the Americans on the east side of the bridge, trying to draw their attention. Just as Skorzeny gave the order for us to retreat to our jeeps before the Americans caught up with us, I was wounded in the left leg. I couldn't walk. Skorzeny never said a word. He just reached down, picked me up, and carried me on the run to the nearest jeep. We barely got out of the area alive."

Skorzeny reported back to the Reich Chancellery three days later to explain the failure of his frogmen but before he could see Hitler, German agents reported that the Ludendorff Bridge at Remagen had collapsed! Whether it collapsed because of the heavy American traffic over it or because of the aftereffects of previous efforts by German troops to destroy it before the capture by Americans was never determined. Skorzeny was ready to admit that his frogmen didn't deserve the credit, but upon his arrival at the bunker he was ignored by all except a few staff officers. Finally Jodl explained why Hitler couldn't see him. "Eva Braun returned to Berlin today."[9]

Later Traudl Junge, Hitler's secretary, explained to him what had happened a few hours before Skorzeny arrived at the bunker underneath the Reich Chancellery, where Hitler and his inner circle were forced to spend most of their time. "Eva arrived shortly before noon," Junge said, "and she went directly to Hitler's study. Hitler was sitting on the blue-and-white sofa when she entered and for a moment he just stared at her. He tried to bawl her out for coming back to Berlin instead of going to the Berghof where it was much safer. Despite his attempt to sound severe, he was delighted to see her. He looked at me and said, 'Who else would come back!'"[10]

Skorzeny never did see Hitler again. Late that evening Jodl told him that the Führer was still talking with Eva and that it would be best if Skorzeny went back to Friedenthal to await further orders. Skorzeny inquired when Hitler intended to go to Berchtesgaden, where he would be out of the path of the advancing Russian troops who were moving closer and closer to Berlin. Jodl hesitated. Finally he admitted that he did not know. The Führer was now wavering about leaving Berlin as he had previously planned to do. Jodl said that Hans Baur, Hitler's personal pilot, still had aircraft standing by to fly Hitler and his staff out of Berlin, but so far the Führer had refused to leave.

Skorzeny was shocked. "Tell him time is running out."[11]

Jodl nodded but said nothing.

Skorzeny was shocked because in September 1944 he had received orders from Himmler to assist Gruppenführer Hans Prützmann in a special assignment. Prützmann had met with Skorzeny at Friedenthal and outlined his assignment. He had been ordered by Himmler to build up an organization to work behind enemy lines as the Allies moved deeper and deeper into Germany. It was to be an organization of guerrilla fighters similar to the underground resistance movement that had fought against the Germans in Poland, France, Italy, and the Balkans. The new group was to be called Werewolf. Skorzeny was asked to help train and equip the organization. At that time, however, he was still involved with his commando missions and emphasized to Prützmann that his help would be severely limited.

At a second meeting with Skorzeny in October 1944, Prützmann reported that his Werewolf units were progressing very well and that Himmler and Hitler were both delighted. The guerrillas were organized into groups of three to six men, each group directed by a Wehrmacht officer from the district in which the group was assigned to operate. Rations for sixty days, two small arms and 15 to 20 pounds of explosives were issued to each Werewolf member and each district unit had established its own underground headquarters.

"This can be done in forest areas," Skorzeny agreed, "but not in inhabited sections because the danger of betrayal is too great."[12]

Between October 1944 and March of 1945 Skorzeny trained 400 Werewolf recruits at the commando school in Neutrelitz. The courses lasted five to eight days and included instruction in shooting, sabotage without equipment, and fundamental facts about explosives. Meanwhile Prützmann continued to organize more and more Werewolf groups in a desperate effort to have one group for each district of the Third Reich. He also conferred with German industrialists about planting saboteurs in factories to make certain the plants were destroyed before any enemy takeover. By March Skorzeny thought that the Werewolves were ready to terrorize all of Germany and to make the problem of occupying the country by the enemy forces so difficult that the conquering armies would be glad to get out. Prützmann had given Skorzeny this information during a meeting in Prützmann's headquarters, a special train in a brickyard near Königswusterhausen. He had also told the commando chief that Hitler had ordered the Werewolves to prepare to fight indefinitely and, if necessary, to retreat to the mountains south of Berchtesgaden where the SS units were going to make a final stand at the Alpine Redoubt.

It all sounded good, but when Skorzeny left the Reich Chancellery bunker after Jodl told him he was not certain Hitler was going to Berchtesgaden after all, he decided to do some investigating on his own. He checked on the Werewolf unit assigned to occupy Weimar and he soon discovered Prützmann had definitely exaggerated the efficiency of his organization. Some of the members had been forced to "volunteer" and had no heart for such activity; no provisions had been made for the Weimar group to contact higher echelons by radio; the establishment of liaison was very haphazard; arms provided were inadequate; and the group had only a vague idea about its assignment. Skorzeny returned to Friedenthal convinced that the Prützmann guerrilla movement would die young. The only hope for a final stand was in the Alpine Redoubt, the mountainous area around Berchtesgaden where he had buried much of the Nazi treasure and secret documents in earlier weeks.

The question of the Alpine Redoubt and the fear of a Nazi suicide stand in the Bavarian mountains was a real puzzle to the advancing American military forces. An OSS confidential report, supplied to Eisenhower in early April 1945, sounded ominous although the intelligence agents involved admitted that some of the information in the report was questionable.

> Most reports at hand agree on the general area of the Alpine Redoubt in South Germany and Austria. With Berchtesgaden as the headquarters, the Redoubt would extend northeast to the mountains of the Salzkammergut, south to the Brenner Pass or to Bozen, west to Vorarlberg. One report speaks of four centers of resistance within this region: Salzburg-Berchtesgaden; the area of Kufstein; Jenbach on the Inn River; and Kitzbühel. The area is mainly in western Austria with a small part of the mountains of southern Bavaria included.
>
> There is also good evidence of the intention to hold numerous outworks of this bastion but whether it is expected that the Wehrmacht or the SS will take care of this is unclear. The regions mentioned include the Black Forest, the Taunus-Spessart-Rhoen chains, the Boehmerwald, and the Silesian mountains.[13]

The report went on to say that the withdrawal of government and Nazi party offices and files toward central and southern Germany gave support to the rumor that Hitler intended to fight to the end in the Bavarian-Austrian mountain area. Skorzeny's training schools at Sonthofen and Bad Tölz were suspected of training Werewolves and resistance fighters who would fight on at the Alpine Redoubt. Allied agents noted that the SS was gathering in the mountain area and strong attempts were being made to convince the people of Bavaria and Austria to struggle to the end with appeals to regional patriotism. "The consensus of evidence is that the SS, not the Wehrmacht, is to control the military side of the resistance as well as the political, sabotage, and intelligence activities. Otto Skorzeny, with the special units he trained, appears to be the most likely head of sabotage and subversive activities planned for the Alpine Redoubt."[14]

Other agents learned through interrogation of German prisoners that

Skorzeny had convinced Hitler that part of the *Hitler-Jugend,* the male branch of the German youth movement, and part of its female counterpart should join the resistance movement in the mountains. Many of these youngsters had already been trained under the security police for this work. They appeared to be especially adept to act as couriers and to gather small-scale intelligence.

Skorzeny did everything possible to recruit SS units for the final battle at the Alpine Redoubt, rallying those of his commando units he could locate and contacting Radl, who did the same. He also tried to convince the OKW that the Wehrmacht should make its final retreat toward Berchtesgaden when possible so the regular army units could join in the resistance. When he received little response to his suggestion, he visited all the local army headquarters and asked the commanders of these units to join him with their men in the Alpine Redoubt. Some were eager and agreed, while others, anxious to end the fighting, refused.

About this time Skorzeny disappeared from his regular haunts around Friedenthal. Even his closest associates were unaware of his whereabouts. It wasn't until after the war that it was learned that Skorzeny had been on another secret mission for Hitler at this time. The mission, using the code name *5K Immergruen,*[15] was to set up a government in Austria under the leadership of Kaltenbrunner in which the Bishop of Salzburg would play an important role. For that purpose Skorzeny delivered a large cache of gold and valuables to the church in Melk.

Nor did Skorzeny limit his travels at that time to Austria. An Italian, Moscato DiGela, with German identification papers was arrested in April 1945 as he tried to enter Italy. While being interrogated at St. Joseph's Prison in Grenoble he admitted he had been recruited by Skorzeny to spy for Germany. He was to return to Italy and gather as much information as possible regarding American and British installations and plans. He was also to secure similar information from the Italian Ministry of War. Information which he secured was to be transmitted back to Germany by a German agent in the French Embassy in Rome. At the end of six years he was to return and join the French army as a German agent. Skorzeny was already making long-range postwar plans.

The American intelligence agents questioning the Italian asked if he knew where Skorzeny was at that time. They were almost certain he was in the Alpine Redoubt making final plans for the resistance battle but they received a surprise.

"Otto Skorzeny is in Paris. I saw him on April 5 standing in front of the Ambassador Hotel."[16]

Questioned further, the Italian gave an accurate description of Skorzeny and related some information about him which the Americans did not know. It was obvious he was well acquainted with Hitler's commando chief.

If Skorzeny was traveling in Austria and France at this time, did that mean that the rumor about the Alpine Redoubt and the planned suicide stand by the SS and possibly the Wehrmacht was false? It was important to find out because Allied headquarters was allotting military forces and supplies to counteract such a stand, military forces and supplies that were sorely needed in other battle zones. For many weeks Eisenhower had been receiving reports about the Alpine Redoubt which indicated that forces fanatically devoted to Hitler were going to withdraw into the mountains of southern Bavaria, western Austria, and northern Italy. Many on his staff expected these Germans to block the mountain passes and hold out indefinitely. Eisenhower wasn't completely convinced, however. He wanted more information, but time was running out for a clear-cut decision. If he ignored the rumor and Skorzeny and his supporters did establish such a resistance movement, the Germans could force the American troops to fight a long and costly guerrilla war in an area much more familiar to Skorzeny than to the Americans. If Hitler's commando chief could hold out long enough, he might even force the Allies to offer surrender terms better than the planned unconditional surrender. Before he made his final decision, Eisenhower contacted London.

The intelligence summary of the situation by British agents arrived at Eisenhower's headquarters within a few hours. The London report stated that the concept of a war to the end and the area chosen for it were both completely in line with the attitude of the Nazi party leaders. The combination of military defensibility, homeland love, and melodramatic setting of the suspected Alpine Redoubt was exactly what would appeal to Hitler's Wagnerian tastes. The report admitted that the British had no firm evidence how long Skorzeny expected to carry out the resistance in the mountains, but based on information learned from various sources, the stay-behind Nazis intended to lie low for a year or two and then start operations. This remark only increased Eisenhower's concern, as did the remarks that the last-ditch stand seemed to be almost completely an SS operation. The Wehrmacht was not playing a very large part in the plans for an Alpine Redoubt. He knew the SS was much more fanatical and would stop at nothing to accomplish its aims.

After studying all the evidence presented to him by American and British agents, Eisenhower decided that facts clearly indicated the Nazis intended to make the try. He was determined not to give them an opportunity to carry it out. The U.S. Third Division, under the command of Major General John W. "Iron Mike" O'Daniel, was assigned the task of moving into the Berchtesgaden area where Hitler's mountain retreat, the Berghof, was located and the city designated as the headquarters for the Nazis manning the Alpine Redoubt. At the same time the XXI and VI Corps of the Seventh Army were ordered to advance toward Innsbruck and the Brenner Pass, another section of the Alpine Redoubt. It was a change in overall strategy but Eisenhower considered it worthwhile. He didn't want Skorzeny and his resistance fighters to get a foothold in the mountains.

Eisenhower had never forgotten that Skorzeny was the man who had ruined his 1944 Christmas by threatening to capture or assassinate him during the Ardennes offensive. He was still chafing over his enforced confinement in his headquarters and was determined that Skorzeny would not escape this time. He ordered an all-out effort to capture Hitler's commando chief, and "Wanted" posters[17] resembling those used by the Federal Bureau of Investigation for the ten most-wanted criminals were printed. A photograph of Skorzeny was placed in the center of the poster. At the top of the photograph was printed "spy," at the right "assassin," and to the left "saboteur." Underneath was a detailed physical description:

Name: Otto Skorzeny
Rank: SS Obersturmbannführer
  (Lieutenant Colonel)
Age: 37
Height: About 6' 4"
Weight: About 220 lbs.

Complexion: Dark
Hair: Dark and wavy
Ears: Large, close to head
Chin: Protruding
Moustache: Hitler-type, may be
  clean-shaven
Scars: Sabre scar from left
  cheekbone to corner
  of mouth

The comments at the bottom of the "Wanted" poster indicated the opinion Eisenhower and Americans and British in general had of Skorzeny:

> This man is extremely clever and very dangerous. He may be in American or British uniform or civilian clothes. He usually wears a signet ring on third finger of left hand. Any information concerning this man should be furnished to the nearest G-2 office without delay.

Several thousand posters were printed and distributed throughout the western-front battle area.

The object of all this attention was still moving throughout the German zones of Germany and Austria at will. Skorzeny had acquired an *Unterkumftzug* (headquarters train) from the Reichsbahn so he could move around frequently without the necessity of packing and repacking every time. He usually positioned the train on a siding in a wooded area or near an abandoned factory to avoid detection by attacking Allied aircraft. But the area still under Nazi control was dwindling fast and Skorzeny decided to visit his home city of Vienna one last time before he moved into the mountains around Berchtesgaden for the final stand. Instead of going in his headquarters train, Skorzeny requisitioned a staff car and drove by himself to Vienna. According to reports received at Hitler's bunker from Baldur von Schirach, *Gauleiter* (district leader) of Vienna, the city was still in German hands and was in no immediate danger of capture. Consequently, when Skorzeny arrived and discovered burning buildings, deserted streets, and not a sign of a German garrison he was shocked. Street barricades were unmanned. When he stopped at one of the barricades to move it so he could drive past, two elderly policemen stepped from the darkness and explained to the puzzled Skorzeny that there were more Russian soldiers in Vienna than German. Fortunately, the Russians were still on the outer ring of the city. Obviously, he had driven through their lines without incident but now he hurried to Schirach's headquarters. Schirach was calmly eating dinner in a room lit by candles, still confident that Vienna was secure.

"I haven't seen a single German soldier," Skorzeny told him. "The street barricades are unmanned. The Russians can walk into Vienna and take control of the city at any time."[18]

Schirach laughed at the warning. He explained to Skorzeny that he had two divisions of German soldiers at his disposal and that a third division was on its way from the Danube to reinforce them. Skorzeny knew no troops were available and told Schirach so. Finally he convinced Schirach the situation was serious and that he should contact Hitler's headquarters in Berlin. Reluctantly, Schirach telephoned the bunker on his private line, which had not yet been destroyed, and described to Jodl the situation in the city as described by Skorzeny. He asked Jodl to declare Vienna an open city for the sake of the 90,000 war-wounded in hospitals in the city. Jodl conferred with Hitler and the reply even shocked a Nazi diehard such as Skorzeny.

"As the situation of the city appears to be hopeless, army trucks are to take Hitler's collection of antique weapons from Vienna to the Obersalzberg at once!" [19]

Skorzeny, aware that Vienna was lost, quickly drove to his mother's home, only to discover she had left the city a few days earlier. At his factory he found two longtime employees having tea and waiting for the Russians. He offered to take them out of the city in his car but they refused to leave their families. After one final look at his own home, Skorzeny turned his Mercedes toward Berchtesgaden and the Alpine Redoubt.

At Berchtesgaden, Salzburg, Kitzbühel, and the other cities where Himmler, at Hitler's orders, was supposed to have stationed strong contingents of SS units and large supplies of arms and food, there was nothing. Although Skorzeny didn't know it at the time, Himmler was too busy trying to arrange a secret surrender agreement with the Allies through the Swedish internationalist Count Folke Bernadotte to think about Hitler's Alpine Redoubt plan. For many of the top-level Nazi officials it was every man for himself. Göring had left the Berlin bunker April 20 to go to Berchtesgaden, but not to join any last-ditch fight in the mountains. He merely retired to his estate on Obersalzberg near Hitler's Berghof to await the end, confident that the Americans would treat him more like a hero than a vanquished enemy. Ribbentrop, Speer, and many of the other members of the Nazi hierarchy suddenly found "urgent" business that required them to leave the Berlin bunker, business that had to do with their postwar plans. Soon after Skorzeny arrived in Berchtesgaden, for instance, he received a message from Dr. Walther Funk, president of the Reichsbank, wanting to know if he could place the state treasure and himself under the protection of Skorzeny on the Obersalzberg. Skorzeny denied after the war that he replied to Funk's request but subsequent postwar activities of the Austrian indicates that he probably did strike a deal with Funk.

While Skorzeny had discovered that the Alpine Redoubt was only a figment of Hitler's imagination, the American forces advancing on Berchtesgaden hadn't. They were expecting to be confronted by fanatical SS units, Werewolf groups, commandos, and scattered military forces in the mountains. O'Daniel's Third Division, rushing to Berchtesgaden, managed to capture two bridges across the Sallach River before they were destroyed by the Germans, and the general quickly ordered his troops at Piding to use the bridges to enter Bad Reichenhall. The Americans surprised 3,000 German soldiers in Bad Reichenhall and took them prisoners. O'Daniel was surprised to discover they were regular German army troops, not SS units as he had been told to expect in the Alpine Redoubt.

From Bad Reichenhall to Berchtesgaden was a straight path and by late afternoon of May 4 the first American soldiers entered the city. The Berghof was quickly located and the Nazi flag ripped from the pole in front of Hitler's mountain retreat. Approximately 2,000 Wehrmacht soldiers were captured in Berchtesgaden, the supposed central headquarters for Hitler's Alpine Redoubt. Where were the Werewolf units? Where were the SS garrisons? Where was Skorzeny?

The first two questions were answered on May 6 by an official message to O'Daniel from Allied headquarters:

> Effective immediately all troops will stand fast on present positions. German Army Group G in this sector has surrendered. No firing on Germans unless fired upon. Notify French units in the vicinity. Full details, to be broadcast, will be issued by SHAEF.

There were no Werewolf units, no SS garrisons prepared for a final suicide resistance. But the third question was still unanswered. Where was Skorzeny?

THE ALLIES
AND SKORZENY

II

"I cannot leave a forwarding address but I'll return later."

10 THE CAPTURE

Late April 1945 was a confusing time for Skorzeny. He was not certain whether Hitler was going to leave Berlin or not. At least this was the claim he made during the postwar years, although there is evidence that he had orders to plan on flying the Führer to South America. Twenty-eight years after the war he indicated to a visitor at his Madrid office that Hitler *could* have escaped from the bunker in Berlin as late as April 30 and perhaps had done just that despite the official conclusion that the Führer had shot himself.

"It was entirely possible for the Führer to leave the bunker by a subterranean passage under the Reich Chancellery," Skorzeny explained, "climb to street level on the Hermann Göring Strasse, cut across the Tiergarten at the Zoo Station area near the Adolf Hitler Platz, and follow the railway lines to the Reichssportfeld. He could then have crossed the Scharndorfestrasse, traversed the Piechelsdorf Bridge, and walked to the Havel. He then could have been picked up by a seaplane that would have landed on the river."[1]

Allied investigations into the death of Adolf Hitler had revealed that a seaplane *had* landed on the Havel River on either the night of April 29 or 30, taxied across the water for a few minutes, and then took off. Had Skorzeny pulled another "miracle" and rescued Hitler just as he had rescued Mussolini earlier? If he did there is no evidence to prove the rescue, because Adolf Hitler has never been seen alive since 1945. But, on the other hand, there is little evidence to prove that Hitler died in the bunker as the United States and Russia finally agreed he did in

1955, ten long years after the Führer's supposed death. The reason the decision was delayed so long was that the Russians, in whose zone the bunker was located, were never able to provide a body, a burial place, or any other factual verification of Hitler's death.

Nor has anyone ever proven where Skorzeny was the night of April 30, 1945. It is known that on May 2, 1945, he was in his special train on a siding near Radstadt, Austria, and in contact with Kaltenbrunner who was hiding out in Bad Aussee, southeast of Salzburg. He was also in touch with Wilhelm Spacil, the chief of Amt II, the department handling economic matters for the SS. Spacil visited Skorzeny's train several times and on May 7 Karl Radl, Skorzeny's longtime adjutant, drove to Spacil's headquarters at Wald. Spacil testified after his capture that he gave Radl 50,000 francs worth of gold coins, 10,000 Swedish crowns, 5,000 dollars, 5,000 Swiss francs, and 5 million reichsmark to take to Skorzeny.[2] The next day Skorzeny, Radl, and a few SS officers who had also taken refuge in the headquarters train went up into the mountains near Radstadt. Since the money was never recovered by Allied investigators, it is thought Skorzeny and his companions hid it in the mountains for future use.

The commando chief established a mini-headquarters in a chalet stocked with food and drink and waited for the Americans to come and arrest him. He was aware of the "Wanted" posters distributed throughout the area with his photograph and description on them, so he anticipated that within a day or so he would be taken prisoner. Surprisingly, he was ignored. When he talked to neighboring mountain dwellers he was told that the Americans had arrested several men in the area in the mistaken belief they were Skorzeny and that more than a hundred U.S. soldiers were scouring the mountains nearby looking for him. Skorzeny decided that in order to save his fellow countrymen any undue hardship on his account he would notify the Americans just where he was located. He wrote a short note giving his location and asked a farmer to deliver it to the commanding officer of the American military detachment in the village of Annaberg. There was no reply, no American troops came knocking on his door. The Americans, basing their judgment on Skórzeny's past actions, figured it was a ruse to throw them off his trail. Skorzeny sent a second letter and it, too, was ignored.

A few days later Skorzeny took matters into his own hands. He went to Annaberg personally, walked into the building used by the Americans as a temporary headquarters, and tried to surrender. The only occupants of the building were a captain from the U.S. 15th Infantry Regiment and two visiting French officers. Skorzeny stood near the trio listening to the American tell the two Frenchmen about his last visit to Paris while he was on leave and the beautiful women he had slept with. Finally Skorzeny interrupted the captain.

"I am *Obersturmbannführer* Otto Skorzeny," he announced, drawing himself up to his full height. "I am ready to surrender and to surrender 300 members of my *Jagdverbände* scattered throughout this area."[3]

The captain looked at him and smiled, not even recognizing the name. "Well, I can see you are too tall to be Adolf Hitler and not fat enough for Göring. But right now I don't have time to handle the surrender of every SS officer who walks in here. Just be patient. Your turn will come."

While the amazed Skorzeny stood and watched, the American captain and the two Frenchmen walked out of the headquarters!

He returned to his mountain chalet. The next two days he considered escaping into Spain, since the Americans in the area appeared to have little or no interest in him. A Luftwaffe friend had access to a small airplane and volunteered to fly him across the border. It was a tempting offer, one Skorzeny would have quickly accepted if he had not felt responsible for his men. Instead, he and Radl returned to Annaberg on May 16 and Skorzeny convinced the unimpressed American captain to provide a jeep to drive them to Salzburg where he could discuss the surrender with higher-ranking American officers. The drive north from Annaberg to Salzburg gave Skorzeny an opportunity to see the changes in the Bavarian area since the end of the war. Occupation troops were everywhere, controlling the small cities as well as the larger ones. The American sergeant driving the jeep was a drawling Texan who was very friendly and didn't harbor any bitterness against Germans. He waved and whistled at all the attractive young women, stopped the jeep at one small village to help an old woman catch a chicken running loose in her yard, and tossed some candy to several young boys playing soccer in a pasture. Between Bischofshofen and Berchtesgaden he became involved in a conversation with Skorzeny. When Skorzeny, whose name meant nothing to the sergeant, explained that he had rescued Mussolini, the American became more interested.

"Then you must be the guy that led those Germans wearing our uniforms behind our lines during the Battle of the Bulge?"[4]

Skorzeny admitted he was the man, feeling apprehensive about the sergeant's reaction to his confession. He had nothing to worry about from him, however.

"Well, I'll be damned!" He looked at Skorzeny as he pulled the jeep to a stop in front of a *weinhaus* in Berchtesgaden. "Buddy, I'm going to get you a bottle of wine so you'll enjoy the rest of the trip to Salzburg. When they get their hands on you at divisional headquarters they're going to string you up real fast."

He left Skorzeny and Radl unguarded in the jeep while he purchased the wine, giving them an opportunity to escape, but Skorzeny refused. He was determined to surrender his men and make certain that any charges against them by Allied forces because of their commando tactics were explained accurately, so they wouldn't be falsely accused of crimes they didn't commit.

At Salzburg, feeling warm from the wine and more confident that his name would be recognized and he could finally negotiate the surrender, Skorzeny presented himself to an American major of the 30th Infantry Regiment. The major was no more impressed than the captain in Annaberg had been, and was ready to dismiss Skorzeny when Lieutenant John McLean standing nearby suggested he take Skorzeny to Werfen, where the S-2 of the 30th Infantry Regiment was located. The major shrugged and gave him permission.

At Werfen Skorzeny was taken into a villa used by the intelligence section and told to wait while the lieutenant conferred with the officer in charge. Skorzeny was wondering what his next move would be if he was ignored here as he had been every place else he tried to surrender, when suddenly his situation changed dramatically. American soldiers appeared at the doors of the room carrying machine guns and he saw the barrels of other machine guns protruding into the room from the open windows. He was covered from all directions. An American soldier walked over to him and jerked his pistol from its holster, the same gun that the other Americans he had contacted had completely ignored! He was searched carefully, including all openings in his body that could conceal poison, handcuffed and ordered into another jeep. An American military policeman sat beside him in the back seat of the jeep, a pistol pressed against Skorzeny's side. Armored cars bracketed the jeep, their guns trained on Skorzeny. *Someone* had recognized the name Otto Skorzeny!

He was taken back to Salzburg, where the 307th Counter Intelligence Corps (CIC) was located, for preliminary interrogation. He immediately insisted that his men be taken into custody and gave the American officers a complete list of the men and their locations: forty men near Altenmarktthal; fifty near Hochfilsen; ten near Annaberg; fifty near Lofer; twenty near Mauterndorf; and forty near Bad Aussee. Others were scattered around the area, including several of the officers who had fought with Skorzeny. All were quickly apprehended by American military units and imprisoned.

During this preliminary interrogation at Salzburg in May, less than a month after the end of the Third Reich and the war, Skorzeny emphasized his desire to continue the fight against Russia and communism. He volunteered to his American captors that he had an excellent knowledge of the Soviet industrial complexes in the Urals from his activities in that area. He also was knowledgeable, he insisted, about the Ukrainian resistance movement sponsored by the Germans during the war. The American agent who interrogated him commented on the report he submitted, "Despite the short time allotted for the interrogation of Skorzeny, it is believed he is sincere in his desire to give all possible information. At the present time Skorzeny still feels his responsibility as a SS officer toward his subordinates. He also seriously considers the eventuality of a Western bloc against communism. This consideration certainly was primordial in his voluntary surrender in the hope that he might be given an active part in this undertaking. Due to his Austrian ancestry, he is clear-minded and pliable but politically short-sighted to the point of naiveté."[5]

It was the American agent who was naive politically at that time, not Skorzeny. The United States and Russia had emerged from the war as the world's two most powerful nations and in peace, as in war, were considered allies. Skorzeny's prediction that the Americans could not trust the Soviets sounded like a repetition of Hitler's propaganda on the subject as his Third Reich was collapsing. In May 1945 the problems that the U.S. would encounter with Russia as the victors began the monumental task of restoring Europe, problems that would lead to the Cold War, had not yet surfaced. It was peaceful in Werfen and Salzburg, and Skorzeny's warning was shrugged off as "political naiveté."

Now that Skorzeny had been captured, the attention he received became overwhelming. A cablegram was sent to the occupational forces throughout Europe stating: "Captured Lieutenant Colonel Otto Skorzeny, Head of RSHA AMT VI Sabotage."[6] It was an open invitation to everyone, military or civilian, who wanted to accuse Hitler's commando chief of war crimes and to the media, to whom the huge, scar-faced adventurer was an outstanding subject for newspapers, magazines, radio, films, and other outlets. One of the first organizations to take advantage of the opportunity to bask in the glory of the capture of Skorzeny was the U.S. military itself. A secret order authorized by Eisenhower directed that priority be given a request by G-2 to send a sound crew "for a movie interview of German saboteur Colonel Skorzeny."[7] The film was shown to military units and the public at every opportunity.

Reporters from the United States flocked to Salzburg to meet the big Austrian who had tried to kill Eisenhower. Skorzeny, using their eagerness as leverage, insisted that he would not appear before them handcuffed. After a call to Colonel Henry Gordon Sheen, Eisenhower's chief of counterintelligence, the handcuffs were removed and he was ushered into a room where the reporters and other media representatives were waiting. The question asked first and most often was why did he try to kill Eisenhower? Skorzeny insisted that he had not tried but if he had set his mind to the rumored attempt he would have succeeded. The reporters, of course, did not believe him nor did United States intelligence and counterintelligence officers. Skorzeny could not be shaken, however, and after an hour the press conference was ended. As *The New York Times* reported the following day: "Handsome despite the scar that stretched from ear to chin, Skorzeny smilingly disclaimed credit for leading the mission to murder members of the Supreme Command." The *Christian Science Monitor* was not so gentle, stating that Skorzeny had "an aggressive personality to go with his physical equipment and a mind adapted to subversive activity."

Another question put to Skorzeny by both reporters and intelligence interrogators was the report he flew Hitler out of Berlin on April 30. Again Skorzeny smiled and denied the accusation. These two questions were asked repeatedly by the military officers of Great Britain, France, Russia, and the United States, prosecutors at the war crimes trial, reporters, and even by fellow SS prisoners. Skorzeny's answer, always given with a smile, was a denial of the charge, but he was not believed. The mystery surrounding the end of Hitler added to the legend and even today there are a great many persons around the world who think that Skorzeny actually did help Hitler escape from the bunker in Berlin.

Late in May Skorzeny was transferred to a prison at Wiesbaden and put in the same cell as Kaltenbrunner. Hidden microphones were placed in strategic spots in the cell by the Americans in hopes that Skorzeny and his companion would discuss in private some of their Third Reich activities. It was a waste of time. Skorzeny had used hidden microphones and all the other secret surveillance equipment available to the Americans on his own missions as commando chief. All the Wiesbaden authorities recorded were stories about the practical jokes the two Germans had pulled and the women they had chased during their university days. Also picked up on the hidden microphones were the sounds of scraping boots, a technique Skorzeny knew would irritate the listeners.

Yet he was cooperative in many other ways. Once again, the Americans decided to film his interrogation but the filming went very badly. The two interrogators stuttered and stammered in front of the camera, forgetting their questions and, in general, making fools of themselves. Skorzeny, calm as usual, suggested they shut the camera off temporarily and rehearse the interrogation. After an hour's rehearsal the scene was shot without a hitch. The interrogators were so pleased with their performance when they saw the final cut that they provided Skorzeny with American cigarettes as long as he stayed at Wiesbaden.

On September 10 Skorzeny was escorted to an aircraft and flown to Nuremberg, where the first war crimes trials were scheduled to be held. At Nuremberg he was reunited, usually from a distance at first but later at much closer range, with Karl Dönitz, the admiral who had been commander-in-chief of the German navy and had succeeded Hitler during the last days of the Third Reich; Heinz Guderian of the OKA; Robert Ley, head of the German Labor Front; Schirach, whom he had last seen in Vienna shortly before the end of the war; Rudolf Hess, the infamous Hitler associate who had made the mysterious flight to England in 1941; Albert Speer, minister of munitions and armaments; Albert Kesselring, the field marshal of the Luftwaffe who was commander-in-chief of the German forces in Italy and later on the western front; and others. Kesselring even took Skorzeny to the cell of Admiral Horthy, the Hungarian regent Skorzeny had removed from Budapest in 1944 and who had been freed from the castle in which Skorzeny had imprisoned him. Horthy was going to appear as a witness at the Nuremberg trials and was permitted special privileges, one of which was all the American cigarettes he desired. He smoked continuously while he tried to convince Skorzeny he, Horthy, had always been loyal to Hitler. Skorzeny wasn't offered a smoke, however.

A few weeks after his arrival at the Nuremberg Court Prison, Skorzeny was transferred to the so-called "witness wing," a part of the prison where living conditions were more tolerable than at Wiesbaden. He was held on the ground floor with seventy other prisoners, while several women prisoners were incarcerated on the second floor. A wide light shaft ran vertically through the center of the building so Skorzeny could talk with the women internees at times and before long managed to get several of them to do his washing and mending. In turn, when the American guards insolently urinated in front of the women prisoners in the exercise yard, it was Skorzeny who had the practice stopped. He was the only prisoner with the courage to complain to the American officer in charge of the exercise yard. His fellow prisoners thought Skorzeny would be severely disciplined, but instead the American officer ordered the guards to use the latrine provided for such purposes.

Skorzeny soon discovered, however, that his commando activities were under investigation as war crimes, and there was a possibility he would be tried by an American tribunal. He was questioned time and time again about his activities in Denmark, the wearing of American uniforms by his commandos during the Ardennes offensive, and his part in the battle around Malmédy during which SS officer Joachim Peiper, who had been under Skorzeny's command, was now accused of herding approximately one hundred captured Americans into a field and murdering them. "Wild Bill" Donovan, head of the OSS, Skorzeny's nearest equivalent on the American side, traveled to Nuremberg personally to question him. "Blood brothers" turned informers were placed in his cell to try to gain his confidence and obtain information that could be used against him during a trail. Skorzeny discovered that Erich Kordt, one of Ribbentrop's aides, had defected to the Americans, and when Kordt tried to become friendly with him, threatened to strangle the German traitor. Kordt later testified at the war crimes trials against Ribbentrop, but not against Skorzeny. Other informers were used by the Americans, but it soon became apparent that dealing with Hitler's commando chief was different from dealing with the average prisoner.

In May of 1946 he was moved to the prison at Dachau. The trial of the major German war criminals had started in November of 1945 at the Palace of Justice in Nuremberg. Through the prison grapevine Skorzeny had learned that it was not going well for the Germans. The International Military Tribunal made up of prominent jurists from the four major powers and the American, British, French, and Russian prosecutors were carefully and meticulously telling the world about the Third Reich activities of Göring, Hess, Ribbentrop, Keitel, Kaltenbrunner, Dönitz, and other top Nazi officials. It was a shocking story that made guilty verdicts a certainty for most of the defendants. Skorzeny was glad to leave Nuremberg, glad not to have to watch the prisoners on trial become more depressed each day. He was also delighted that his close friend and longtime adjutant, Karl Radl, was transferred to Dachau with him. Radl was the one man he could trust.

Shortly after his arrival at Dachau the armed guard around his cell was doubled and through the window of the prison he saw American troops stationed along the wall of the former concentration camp. Later that day he learned that the Americans had received a report that Skorzeny was on the loose and with a group of SS officers and commandos was going to free all German prisoners at Dachau. When Eisenhower's headquarters was notified that Skorzeny was himself a prisoner at Dachau and certainly not in a position to lead a raid on the prison, American authorities were not convinced. Despite his already long months of imprisonment and interrogation, Eisenhower's staff insisted that the man imprisoned at Dachau must be an imposter, that Skorzeny was still free and that the European command intelligence corps was continually receiving reports that he was conducting subversive activities in Germany. Finally, after an investigation, Thomas H. Buckley, a special agent for the 970th Counter Intelligence Corps detachment at Munich reported: "Otto Skorzeny is still interned at War Crimes Enclosure 29, Dachau. Major Scott, Screening Section, states Skorzeny is to be tried at Camp Dachau and there is no possibility that he will be removed from there for some time. In the event of his removal, CIC will be notified."[8]

Skorzeny realized that he was not going to be automatically exonerated by the Americans after their intensive interrogation and investigation of his commando activities. It was a disappointment because he had felt certain that once he gave his captors the details of his operations they would quickly determine no charges were applicable. Colonel Albert Rosenfeld, the American chief prosecutor, summoned him to his office, under heavy guard, and read the indictments to him.

Skorzeny was charged with improper use of military insignia; wrongfully encouraging, aiding, and participating in the killing and illtreatment of American prisoners; stealing of U.S. uniforms; and stealing Red Cross parcels from prisoners of war. Skorzeny, shocked at the charges, remained cool during the following press conference, but back in his cell he began preparations for his defense, knowing that he was in a fight for his life.

Skorzeny wasn't the only one preparing for his trial. The Americans needed more information to back up the charges against Skorzeny and in desperation called in the Counter Intelligence Corps to help. Also, American, British, French, and Russian authorities had received reports that there was a possible underground organization of former members of Skorzeny's commandos determined to free Skorzeny as well as other SS prisoners. Consequently, in an effort to learn more about Skorzeny's activities, past and present, Karl Alberts, an undercover agent of Counter Intelligence Corps Region V, was planted in Dachau with Skorzeny. The agent soon became friends with Franz Konrad, a former SS Hauptsturmführer who had been in charge of the liquidation of the Warsaw ghetto, and Konrad introduced the agent to Skorzeny. When Skorzeny was transferred to the camp hospital to have his gall bladder removed, the agent spent a great deal of time at his bedside and eventually they became good friends. He listened to Skorzeny tell about his personal anxieties, problems, hopes, and fears.

The agent succeeded in convincing Skorzeny that in a few days he, Alberts, would be out of prison and if there were any messages Skorzeny wanted to send to anyone on the outside he would be glad to deliver them. Two days later Skorzeny gave the agent two notes and requested that the agent deliver them personally. One was to Frau Ursula Bartel, who lived at the village of Hofheim, near Murnau, and asked her to give Skorzeny's "belongings" to the agent so he could deliver them to his wife. The second note was to SS Sturmführer Werner Ditter, a prisoner at Dachau whom Skorzeny could not contact directly because of his hospitalization. The agent, telling Skorzeny he had to be careful whom he contacted, inquired why Skorzeny wanted him to take a note to another prisoner. Skorzeny quietly told him that Ditter, another SS prisoner at Dachau by the name of Nikolau, and the prisoner-doctor of the camp, a Dr. Hennings, were in charge of maintaining contact with those on the outside of the prison. Ditter was in a position to move around camp freely since he was the camp barber and periodically was permitted a visit to the city of Dachau. And in Dachau, Skorzeny told the agent, the fiancée of Dr. Henning, Fraulein Andree (Andy) Frey, would take messages from the prisoners and make certain they were delivered.

In addition, Skorzeny told the agent that several boxes containing his personal documents, valuables, money, and other items were deposited with various persons in Austria. The breakdown of these deposits, as listed by the agent were: a box with Frau Tussi who lived at Unter-Tavern; two boxes at Dr. Staffa's at Ramsau; one box with Dr. Porsche, inventor of the Volkswagen, who lived on his estate near Zell am See; one box and one rucksack with Frau Brandstetters in Graham; and one box with Fraulein Schruffe at Neunkirchen. He confided that he also had hidden a box containing correspondence between the former Hungarian regent Horthy and Hitler and very valuable jewels in Austria, but he would not disclose the location.

American military authorities, notified of Skorzeny's statements by the CIC agent at Dachau, became aware that the rumors about Skorzeny's preparations for the postwar years were true. It was decided that the information gathered by the agent warranted further investigation to learn more about Skorzeny's plans if and when he was released from prison and to obtain documents that would help convict him at his forthcoming trial for war crimes. The CIC agent who had been in contact with Skorzeny in Dachau, Karl Alberts, was using the name of Peter Holtmann at the prison. Holtmann and special agents Robert E. O'Neil and Ben J. W. Gorby visited the city of Dachau and, while the other two agents stayed out of sight, Holtmann contacted Fraulein Frey. His report indicated there definitely was an underground network at work at the prison in Dachau, one that was well organized and dangerous to the occupation forces.

As Holtmann became more friendly with Fraulein Frey he discovered that she was in permanent contact with prisoners interned at the Dachau prison and that she used members of the Polish guards as couriers. She didn't hesitate to tell him that she had shot two Poles in a field near the prison when they threatened to blackmail her. Holtmann quizzed her about the escape plans of the prisoners, using her network, and obtained a great deal of information about how and where the forged identification papers were procured, other persons involved in the network, and planned routes of escape. He immediately forwarded this information to Region V headquarters in Regensburg and the American military authorities at Dachau were notified.

Holtmann then visited Frau Bartel, to whom one of Skorzeny's notes was addressed. Frau Bartel lived in a room at a farmhouse in Hofheim. She, too, was very friendly after she saw Skorzeny's note and gave Holtmann five parcels to take to Skorzeny. Copies of all the documents in the parcels were made and a detailed inventory of every parcel was kept by the agent before he visited Frau Emmi Skorzeny at Franking in the Braunau district. Frau Skorzeny, after accepting the parcels and making certain she could "trust" Holtmann, confirmed that she was in constant touch with Fraulein Frey at Dachau. She told the agent that she knew her husband planned to escape and asked Holtmann to warn Skorzeny not to come to Austria. The agent also learned that several former SS officers were guarding the home where Frau Skorzeny lived and that she was well taken care of financially.

After the other boxes belonging to Skorzeny were picked up by American soldiers, two facts became evident: there definitely was an SS underground network in operation that was financed by money and valuables hidden by Skorzeny and his fellow officers and men during the latter months of the Third Reich in preparation for the postwar years; and, Skorzeny had a large following of dedicated commandos and SS officers who were still devoted to the principles of Hitler's Third Reich. Yet, the American authorities were not overly worried. They were convinced that Skorzeny would be found guilty at his upcoming war crimes trial and be put behind bars. This would bring an abrupt end to his grandiose plans for the future.

11 THE TRIAL

In August 1947, twenty-seven months after the end of the Third Reich, Skorzeny and eight other German prisoners were brought to trial in a converted wooden barracks at Dachau. Between the time the indictment had been read to Skorzeny by Rosenfeld and the actual start of the trial, the situation had changed drastically. The trial before the International Military Tribunal at Nuremberg which had started in November 1945 finally ended in October 1946 and the verdicts reached regarding the actions of the twenty-one high-ranking Nazis was not encouraging for Skorzeny and the others waiting their turn. Eleven were sentenced to death by hanging, three were given imprisonment for life, four were sentenced to terms of ten to twenty years, and only three were acquitted. Kaltenbrunner, Skorzeny's former superior officer, was hanged on October 16, 1946, as was Keitel, from whom Skorzeny had received many of his orders at the Führer's headquarters. Jodl, too, died at the end of a rope. Göring, who had sent troops to help Skorzeny at the Oder River bridgehead, beat the gallows by taking poison two hours before his scheduled hanging. Himmler had committed suicide even before he could be brought to trial. And in addition to sentences handed out to the men on trial, the IMT had judged the Gestapo, the SD, and the SS as criminal in nature. When Skorzeny heard the verdicts through the prison grapevine at Dachau, any doubts he had that he was in a fight for his life at his own trial immediately vanished.

The IMT trial had taken so long and the court made up of the four major powers was so unwieldy, that the Allied Control Council established military tribunals in each of the four zones into which Germany had been divided for the purpose of trying the remainder of the Nazis. Skorzeny, in the American zone, was scheduled to be tried by an American tribunal. And since two of the main charges against him—the wearing of American uniforms during the Battle of the Bulge and murdering American prisoners of war—involved the U.S. military forces, Skorzeny faced a court determined to see him punished. When he discovered that the chief lawyer appointed to defend him and the other eight prisoners was Colonel Robert Durst of the U.S. Army, his hopes of a fair trial faded. After his initial meeting with Durst, he was very discouraged. The American military lawyer was abrupt and unfriendly when he interviewed Skorzeny and as much as told him he thought he was guilty. Skorzeny was convinced after this first meeting that Durst hated all Germans. The second and third meetings were no better. Meanwhile, six German lawyers volunteered to defend Skorzeny and his companions, and a straw vote by the nine German prisoners gave an overwhelming majority vote of confidence to the German lawyers instead of the American. Skorzeny, however, didn't vote. Durst had made him so angry he wanted to strangle the American but there was something about the man's attitude that intrigued Skorzeny and made him want to trust Durst even against his own will.

With the beginning of the trial fast approaching, a decision had to be made by the prisoners about their legal representation. On the morning of the day the final decision had to be made, Durst again walked into Skorzeny's cell. He looked just as stern and unfriendly as before as he faced the taller Austrian. Looking him square in the eye, Durst said, in his usual harsh voice, "Skorzeny, I think you are innocent. Now that I am convinced of that I am determined to get you free of all charges."[1] He turned and walked out.

Skorzeny believed him but he had a difficult time convincing the other eight prisoners that they should put their lives in the hands of an enemy lawyer instead of fellow Germans. Finally, because they knew that Skorzeny, based on his reputation, had the toughest battle to face in the courtroom, they capitulated and agreed to permit Durst to handle the defense. Durst brought in two assistants, Lieutenant Colonel Donald McClure and Major L. I. Horowitz, to aid in the preparation for the trial. Meanwhile, three of the six German lawyers refused to work with Durst and left Dachau.

Another crisis arose a couple of days later when Durst proposed that Skorzeny give the evidence for all the prisoners on trial rather than have each of the nine Germans take the witness stand. Durst felt that he could present the defense arguments more clearly and concisely if he was working with one defendant. But the other prisoners recognized the danger. Skorzeny was more liable to be found guilty than any of the others. After all, didn't the Americans consider him "the most dangerous man in Europe?" To place their fate in the same witness chair with Skorzeny didn't seem to be a good bet. However, Durst patiently explained to them that the main challenge at stake in the trial was not individual actions but overall techniques permitted or not permitted in war. He stated he was convinced that none of the nine was guilty of murdering prisoners of war or stealing Red Cross parcels, two of the charges made against them. But he felt the prosecution was going to zero in on the wearing of American uniforms by Skorzeny's commandos during the Ardennes offensive. In that case, Skorzeny was the man to present the defense on the witness stand. This time the eight prisoners were much harder to convince that Durst was correct than they had been earlier when Skorzeny convinced them Durst, and not the German lawyers, should handle their case. To place their lives on the line and depend upon an enemy lawyer and a man whom the Americans considered to have attempted to kill Eisenhower, to keep them from hanging was almost too much. But with the same persuasive power that had inspired his commandos to face seemingly insurmountable odds during the war, Skorzeny persuaded the other prisoners that, while it was a gamble, it was the best opportunity they had to win.

The trial began the morning of August 18. Skorzeny, who had spent nearly a month in solitary confinement during his twenty-seven months as a prisoner and the remainder of the time in a small cell with one or two other prisoners, suddenly found himself in a large room with several hundred spectators, military policemen, and the American tribunal staring at him. Press representatives from around the globe crowded into the room, knowing that Hitler's commando chief was always good copy. Standing in front of the nine U.S. colonels who made up the tribunal was Rosenfeld, the chief prosecutor who had read the indictment to Skorzeny shortly after he had arrived as a prisoner at Dachau. He was smiling as he called the first prosecution witness. "Karl Radl, take the stand, please!"[2]

Skorzeny didn't believe he had heard correctly. Radl, his trusted adjutant, the man with whom he had faced death many times, a prosecution witness? But his ears had not deceived him. Radl, his face red and his eyes downcast, walked to the witness stand and without once looking at Skorzeny testified that he had been at Friedenthal when the orders were given by Skorzeny for his commandos to obtain American uniforms and papers so they could operate behind the lines during the Ardennes offensive. Other than this, Radl gave very little testimony, but Skorzeny was hurt that his close friend would testify against him at all. Werner Hunke, who had accompanied Skorzeny to Budapest to overthrow the Hungarian regent and had been involved in other commando missions, had refused to testify for the prosecution, although he was offered immunity if he did. Skorzeny also learned that Gottlob Berger, the SS general who specialized in security problems and was scheduled to stand trial for the wartime murder of Jews, had also given his American interrogators information about the American uniforms.

"He was allotted a task during that unfortunate offensive in 1944 about which I had a row with him," Berger said. "He forced his way into one of our P.W. camps and compelled the commandant at the point of a pistol to hand over British and American uniforms. The Führer had ordered this but I objected strongly. I told Himmler that Skorzeny should be punished."[3]

Fortunately for Skorzeny, the Americans were skeptical of Berger's testimony and he was not chosen as a prosecution witness. Two years later he was sentenced to twenty-five years in prison for his treatment of the Jews during the war.

Skorzeny had not recovered from the shock of hearing Radl testify against him when he discovered Rosenfeld had another surprise awaiting him. The American prosecutor summoned a German captain who had been the supply officer at Friedenthal during the Ardennes offensive. The captain accused Skorzeny of distributing poison bullets to his commandos to use against the Americans during the December battle! Even Durst was upset and looked quizzically at the big Austrian during the captain's testimony. This was a serious charge, one that would even take precedent over the wearing of American uniforms.

"How could you tell the poison ammunition from the regular ammunition?" Rosenfeld asked the supply officer.

"The poison bullets had a red ring around them."[4]

At that point in the testimony the tribunal adjourned for the day. Durst immediately asked Skorzeny to explain what he knew about the poison ammunition. Skorzeny had a ready answer. Months before the Ardennes offensive his commandos had captured two Russian agents who had infiltrated the German lines on the eastern front, intent on assassinating Skorzeny. Their guns were found to be loaded with unusual-looking ammunition and after a laboratory analysis it was discovered the bullets contained a lethal poison. This was verified when Skorzeny shot a stray dog with one of the bullets and the dog died within seconds. Skorzeny had asked German specialists to make him fifty rounds of the ammunition, but not for use on the battlefield, he insisted. He gave one bullet to each of his commandos and told them to place it in the last chamber of their guns. If they were trapped and did not want to fall into enemy hands, the poison bullet would be a quick and deadly alternative.

Durst shook his head. "I believe you but I don't think the tribunal will. We have a problem, no question about it."[5]

Suddenly Skorzeny grabbed the American lawyer's arm. "Perhaps he was referring to our waterproof ammunition, instead of the poison bullets. They had a red ring around them, too. And I did issue the waterproof ammunition to my men before the Ardennes offensive."

"But how can we prove it?" Durst asked. "The first subject on tomorrow morning's agenda will be the poison bullets."

Skorzeny grinned. "Leave it to me."

Within minutes after being escorted back to his cell, Skorzeny had contacted his prison network. He smuggled a message to Henning, the prisoner-doctor in the camp, telling him he needed at least one of the waterproof bullets with the red ring around it by the following morning. Henning got the message to his fiancée, Fraulein Frey, in the city, and through her SS friends she managed to get the bullet. It was delivered to Skorzeny in a piece of bread given to him the next morning for breakfast. Just before the trial opened that day he handed the bullet to the surprised Durst.

The supply officer was called to the witness stand once again and Rosenfeld had him elaborate on the use of the poison ammunition and repeat several times for the benefit of the tribunal and the press how he identified the bullets by the red ring around the case. When he turned the witness over to Durst for cross-examination, Rosenfeld smiled, confident that he had proven that "the most dangerous man in Europe" had used poison bullets. Durst started out by questioning the supply officer about prosecution testimony he had given earlier at Nuremberg during the International Military Tribunal trial, testimony that had later been proven false. The supply officer admitted he had done so, but when Durst tried to shake his testimony about Skorzeny's use of poison bullets, the captain merely grinned and insisted he was telling the truth. At that point Durst took the waterproof bullet with the red ring around the case from his pocket and held it in the palm of his hand.

"Is this the type of bullet you are speaking of?" he asked.

The supply officer nodded. "That is the bullet. Yes."

But the American lawyer as well as Skorzeny noticed the German captain was nervous. It only took Durst a few minutes to get him to admit that the bullet in the lawyer's hand was a waterproof bullet distributed to the commandos by Skorzeny and that the poison bullets were entirely different in appearance. He confessed he had lied.

It was a battle won but the war continued. Rosenfeld, not discouraged by his defeat, sought victory by pressing harder than ever but he had problems. When he charged that Skorzeny had stolen Red Cross parcels before the Ardennes offensive to obtain American uniforms and equipment, the prosecution witness, an American infantry officer, testified the Red Cross parcels had arrived but were late. There was no evidence they had been stolen. Rosenfeld dropped that accusation quickly. But Skorzeny was worried about the section of the indictment accusing him of "wrongfully encouraging, aiding, and participating in the killing and ill-treatment of American prisoners." He knew the charge was false and had no idea why he had even been indicted for such a thing. Several times before the trial Skorzeny had been questioned about the actions of SS officer Joachim Peiper in the attack on Malmédy during the Ardennes offensive. He had repeated over and over that he had not been with Peiper; they had both attacked the city with their respective units but from different directions. He didn't think that Peiper, as rumored, had murdered over a hundred American prisoners during the fight for Malmédy, but even if he had, Skorzeny had no knowledge of the incident. He thought he had convinced his interrogators of this fact but now it was obvious that he had not.

Rosenfeld, however, took Skorzeny by surprise again when he suddenly announced to the tribunal that the charge of ill-treatment and killing of prisoners was dropped. He had a good reason for dropping the charge, one that Skorzeny had not learned about through his network or the grapevine. Peiper had been tried a month earlier, and on July 16 had been found guilty and condemned to death. During his trial Peiper had testified that Skorzeny had no part in the disputed incident, so Rosenfeld knew he couldn't prove the charge.

As soon as Rosenfeld announced the charge was withdrawn, Durst petitioned the tribunal to release Skorzeny and his eight associates. The American lawyer argued that without the charge that Skorzeny had mistreated and killed prisoners there was no substance to the indictment against him. They were determined to try Skorzeny for ordering his men to wear American uniforms during the Ardennes offensive, basing their decision on a part of the rules of war handed down by the Hague Convention of 1907. As Durst explained to Skorzeny as he prepared him for the witness stand to give his side of the question, there were no definite guidelines set down at the Hague Convention, only generalities. Basically the members of the convention stated that soldiers could confront the enemy in disguise as long as they discarded the disguises before the fighting started. There were no clearcut rules how long before the fighting started the disguise had to be discarded or how. Skorzeny swore to Durst that he definitely had told his commandos not to fight while wearing American uniforms and that Hitler had warned him of the Hague Convention rules. He also told the American lawyer that his men had obeyed his orders because they knew the difference between being considered commandos and spies if they were captured. Spies in American uniforms had no defense. Commandos who wore their regular German uniforms underneath the American uniforms and doffed the American uniforms before resisting or attacking did have a defense based on the Hague Convention rules, in Skorzeny's opinion.

Durst wasn't so sure. "It will depend upon how the tribunal interprets the rule. We need a better approach."[6]

Skorzeny agreed. "My plan was merely an adaptation of one used quite often by you Americans and the British. I can testify about the numerous occasions your soldiers wore our uniforms."

The American lawyer concurred in that decision but as he told Skorzeny, "I'm not certain that we won't antagonize the tribunal by bringing up such actions. But we'll do it. If one side can do it, then the other side can, too. I just wish we had factual evidence to present about such incidents."

Skorzeny agreed that he had no documentation to present, that it would be up to American authorities to search out the documentation to prove or disprove his testimony. Would the Americans do so?

Durst shrugged his shoulders. "We can only hope."

Skorzeny was on the witness stand for two days. He told the tribunal he had given his commandos orders they definitely were not to fight while in American uniforms; that they did not fire a bullet while in the disguise; that he and his men had abided by the Hague Convention rule; and that if he was guilty of the charge then the Americans and British were guilty because they, too, had followed the same procedure many times. The last statement aroused the interest of the tribunal, but Skorzeny couldn't tell whether they were surprised or angry. He was asked to be more specific about such incidents involving Americans, British, or any other Allied unts.

"British officers were captured in Hungary wearing German uniforms," he said, adding, "and they were not shot. Many Polish resistance fighters wore German uniforms as did underground fighters in Yugoslavia and Italy."

But what about Americans, he was asked?

Skorzeny had purposely not mentioned the Americans because he was being tried before a tribunal composed of American officers. Now, however, he didn't hold back.

"Hitler told me that American soldiers in German uniforms were caught near Aachen and it was this incident which gave him the idea for us to wear American uniforms during the Ardennes offensive," he told the tribunal.

When asked to document the charge, Skorzeny admitted he couldn't because all German records had either been destroyed or captured. Durst, using his skill as a trial lawyer, made a very eloquent argument before the tribunal that two wars had been fought since the Hague Convention of 1907 and, just as weapons changed, so did operational procedures. What was frowned upon in 1907 was, in many instances, common practice in 1944 both in war and civilian life. Both sides had used the enemy uniform technique during World War II.

The tribunal was unconvinced. They had concrete evidence that the man on trial, standing before them in the court, had ordered his men to wear American uniforms. Skorzeny admitted it. But where was the evidence, the documentation that American, British, and other military units fighting for the Western powers had done so? Rumors were not acceptable as evidence in a court of law. Both Durst and Skorzeny were depressed as the day's session ended. The next day would bring the trial to a conclusion. The tribunal had other prisoners to try. Weeks or months could not and would not be spent searching for evidence that might verify Skorzeny's statements, evidence that probably did not exist any longer, if it ever had. Skorzeny had no further defense. He had explained the facts of the operation as clearly as he could and used every skill at his command to justify his actions. He didn't have any more to say.

He didn't sleep that night, and the following morning when he walked from his cell to the barracks where the trial was being conducted, he was tired and discouraged. He was surprised to find that Durst was smiling and in good spirits. He didn't seem worried at all. Skorzeny didn't like it. Had he made a mistake in permitting the American lawyer to handle his defense instead of the German lawyers who had volunteered to defend him? He quickly put that thought out of his mind, however, when he remembered the excellent and skilled arguments Durst had presented in his behalf during the trial. No one could have done better.

When the trial convened, Durst was asked by the tribunal if he had any further witnesses or evidence to present. Instead of answering in the negative as Skorzeny expected, Durst got to his feet and stated that he had one more witness. "Wing Commander Forrest Yeo-Thomas, will you please take the stand?"

Skorzeny watched as a slim, handsome officer wearing a British Royal Air Force uniform walked to the witness stand. He was unaware that Yeo-Thomas, known as The White Rabbit, was a British agent who had worked with French resistance groups throughout the war. His exploits were well known to German intelligence but at the time of Skorzeny's trial in 1947 Skorzeny had never heard of Yeo-Thomas. He didn't know that the British agent, after nearly two years in occupied France with periodic return trips to London to report on his underground activities, had been captured and imprisoned at Buchenwald concentration camp. Nor did he know that Yeo-Thomas had accomplished the impossible— he had escaped from Buchenwald! Now as he watched the British agent take the oath before the witness chair, Skorzeny recognized the ludicrous position he was in. A German, he was being defended by an American military lawyer before a tribunal composed of American military officers and the witness in his behalf was a stranger wearing a British uniform.

Durst immediately began questioning Yeo-Thomas. After asking him whether he had ever met Skorzeny prior to the trial and making certain the tribunal heard the witness answer in the negative, Durst inquired whether Yeo-Thomas understood the charge against Skorzeny.

"I've been told he is accused of ordering his men to wear American uniforms during the Ardennes offensive. I don't know if he did or not, but I want to go on record as saying that if he did there was nothing wrong with the order."[7]

Skorzeny was delighted. Rosenfeld was incredulous.

"Could you explain further?" Durst asked.

Yeo-Thomas didn't hesitate. "We did the same many times. Once I ordered my men to wear German uniforms when we planned to storm a prison to release a comrade. That was at Rennes. We stole a German car and several documents."

"How did you obtain the uniforms?"

Yeo-Thomas grinned. "By hook or by crook."

"Were you armed?" Durst inquired.

"How else could we get rid of the guards at the prison?"

Skorzeny sat up straighter and leaned forward in his chair. He didn't want to miss a word of the testimony.

"You mean you planned to kill if necessary?"

The British agent nodded. "Of course."

Yeo-Thomas explained that the very night of the prison attack he was arrested by the Gestapo, but his men went through with the operation and it was a success. Under the skillful questioning of Durst, the British agent testified that the British Secret Service often wore German uniforms, were always armed, and, when trapped, used their guns without hesitation. He also explained that German soldiers were sometimes ambushed so that their papers and uniforms could be obtained by the British agents, and the same two items were often taken from German prisoners.

Durst, who had obtained Yeo-Thomas as a witness when the British agent volunteered his testimony, nodded and ended his questioning. As Yeo-Thomas stepped down from the witness chair, Skorzeny and the other prisoners stood at attention in a gesture of appreciation.

The verdict was no longer in doubt. The tribunal had to acquit the Germans or admit that the victors fought under one set of rules, the losers another. "Acquitted on all counts" was the official verdict announced a short time later by Colonel Andrew G. Gardner, president of the tribunal.

The *Stars and Stripes* headlined the verdict in its September 11 issue:

SKORZENY CASE MAY ALTER WAR LAW

NUREMBERG: Otto Skorzeny, who kept generals and American soldiers guessing, now has international lawyers puzzled. War crimes counsel said the acquittal of Skorzeny and his comrades by a Dachau military court might lead to the rewriting of the rules of war.

The article quoted Rosenfeld as saying "the verdict will have legal consequences" and other international lawyers agreed.

As Skorzeny walked from the courtroom after his acquittal, Rosenfeld joined the journalists standing nearby and remarked, "I still think Skorzeny is the most dangerous man in Europe."

No one disputed him.

12 ESCAPE

There was no question in the mind of Rosenfeld that Skorzeny had been found not guilty of the charge only because of the camaraderie of a fellow behind-the-lines agent. Rosenfeld was not alone in this conclusion, either. There were too many rumors about the man, too many intelligence reports pertaining to him, and too many countries interested in Skorzeny for him to be an ordinary German soldier falsely accused of war crimes.

"He's an unregenerate bastard and we'll have to keep close tabs on him," Colonel George Whitmer of the French intelligence branch muttered to a companion as he leafed through several reports.[1] Whitmer was in Dachau as an observer at the Skorzeny trial, hoping that he could obtain evidence enough to bring charges later against Skorzeny for his wartime actions in Paris and other French cities.

Despite his acquittal by the American tribunal at Dachau, Skorzeny's troubles were not over. Both Denmark and Czechoslovakia demanded the American authorities turn him over to stand trial for war crimes in those countries. After further investigation, Denmark decided that Alfred Naujocks was the prime leader of German activities against the Danish underground, and the charges against Skorzeny were dropped. Since the Russians controlled Czechoslovakia by this time, the Americans concluded that they wanted Skorzeny because of his commando tactics in the Ukraine—tactics which, as far as was known, did not involve war crimes—and refused to extradite him. So Skorzeny stayed in Dachau, but more as a "guest" than a prisoner. The United States wasn't quite sure what to do with him.

Finally, while trying to decide on the next move, the U.S. Army Historical Division asked Skorzeny to write his personal account of the Mussolini rescue. It would be an interesting addition to their files and at the same time keep him busy. Skorzeny was moved back to the Oberursel interrogation camp, but when the U.S. officials wanted to put him back in the same small cell he had been in previously, Skorzeny rebelled. He promptly wrote a letter to the Office of the Chief Historian:

Sir: I herewith state that in case I am to be further detained by the U.S. authorities, I am interested in some historical work. It must be understood, however, that I cannot write for your organization under the present uncertain and undignified conditions in which I find myself at the present moment. My position must be clarified first, and circumstances now involving me can be cleared up within a few days. It is my wish that I be discharged to my home in Vienna so as to join my family there. I should be very pleased to write for the Historical Division in my home.[2]

The first reaction at the Historical Division headquarters was to ask who the hell Skorzeny thought he was, making such demands. But when the letter was forwarded to CIC, as was customary in the case of Skorzeny, there was a different reaction. While a discharge was out of the question, it was decided that Skorzeny should be given a parole. Not because he demanded special treatment, but because there was still considerable suspicion among U.S. officials that Skorzeny might have evacuated Hitler from the inferno of the Berlin bunker during the final hours of the Third Reich, and that the Führer was still alive. These suspicions had been newly aroused when an undercover CIC agent, Walter Hirschfeld, had a long conversation with Hans Fegelein and his wife. They were the parents of Hermann Fegelein, Himmler's liaison officer with Hitler and the husband of Gretl Braun, the sister of Hitler's mistress Eva Braun. Hirschfeld, disguised as an SS officer who had played a leading role in the counterfeit money scheme of the Nazis, contacted the elder Fegelein at his home at 20 Johann-Sebastian Bachstrasse in Munich. The CIC agent had several long conversations with Fegelein and gained his confidence. During one of the final talks, Fegelein said, "You need not worry that your work was in vain. You will receive thanks one day. *The Man* will call for you himself and give you the commendation."³

Hirschfeld, taken back, asked, *"The man,* our Führer? But he is supposed to be dead."

"I think I can say with certainty that the Führer is alive. I have received word through a special courier. My son hinted that the Führer lives."

The CIC agent notified his headquarters. There was an immediate reaction. Not only was the elder Fegelein insinuating that his son, whom U.S. officials thought had been executed at Hitler's orders on April 28, was still alive, but the Führer, too. Hirschfeld was ordered back to Fegelein's home to hold further conversations. In order to consolidate his friendship with the elder Fegelein, the CIC agent handed over to him 15,000 reichsmarks, which he explained was surplus cash he had received for jewelry he had buried as the war drew to an end. The money actually had been obtained from secret SS funds found by American authorities. Fegelein, confident that Hirschfeld was a former SS officer, was more receptive to the CIC agent's questions.

"Do you really believe the Führer is still alive?"

"Yes, I am positive of it, for my son Hermann sent me a courier after the capitulation."

"Was he still in Germany?"

Fegelein nodded. "Yes, at that time he was still in Germany. The courier told me that my son wanted me to know that he and the Führer were safe and well."

Hirschfeld shook his head. "But that all sounds unreal. Even many SS officers state the Führer is dead and his body burned."

When Fegelein couldn't be shaken from his belief that both his son and Hitler were still alive, the CIC decided to give Skorzeny a leave of absence to visit his family in Vienna . . . and keep him under constant surveillance. If Hitler was still alive and in Germany, there was a possibility Skorzeny might try to contact him.

The agents shadowing him were encouraged when Skorzeny went directly from the Oberursel interrogation camp into the city and to the home of Hanna Reitsch, the much-decorated woman pilot who had been a close friend of Hitler's. Investigation immediately after her surrender in 1945 had revealed that she had been in the Berlin bunker with Hitler from April 26 until April 28, and she, too, had been questioned about flying the Führer out of Berlin. She, like Skorzeny, had denied the allegation. But when Skorzeny visited her as soon as he was given a leave of absence, suspicions were aroused again. Unfortunately, the two merely talked for a while about their personal situations and then parted.

Skorzeny then went to Munich and Vienna, visiting his wife and daughter and several old friends. While in Austria he stayed out of the public eye, since he was still sought there for the part he had played in the *Anschluss* in 1938 when the Nazis seized power. Back in Germany, he spent the remainder of his leave of absence in the mountains around Berchtesgaden resting and meeting former SS officers. Even these meetings, however, were innocent get-togethers of old friends as far as the CIC agents could determine. Promptly on January 15 when he was due back at Oberursel, Skorzeny reported at the gate. A few days later, his work for the Historical Division delayed, he was back at Dachau.

The CIC's interest in Skorzeny increased during the first part of 1948 in direct proportion to the increase in the ever-growing conflict with the Soviet Union over postwar policies in Europe. The hope that the United States and Russia could cooperate as well during peacetime as wartime soon faded. The Potsdam Conference in 1945 had divided the defeated European territory among the United States, Britain, France, and Russia. It soon became evident that Russia, intent on establishing a much broader zone for herself, wanted to control the Dardanelles and the Mediterranean and to have a dominant role in managing the industrial Ruhr. Russia spent a great deal of time and money trying to influence the war-weakened nations of France and Italy through their Communist parties. In Poland, which Russia occupied after the war, the Soviet military ousted the London government-in-exile and organized a Communist regime under Boleslav Bierut. The United States under President Harry Truman slowly came to the realization that the Soviet Union intended to dominate all of Europe if possible, that Moscow, instead of disarming as the United States, France, and Britain had done immediately after the war, was increasing her military strength on the continent. The Soviet takeover of Czechoslovakia and establishment of the Berlin blockade—which forced the United States to initiate the Berlin airlift—inflamed anti-Soviet feeling throughout the United States.

At the same time that the U.S. officials were becoming aware of Soviet aggression intentions, they also realized that U.S. military forces in Europe, because of rapid postwar disarmament, would not be able to defend the Western zones of occupation if the Russians decided to attack. And because of this realization by the U.S. officials, Skorzeny and other Nazis who had faced the Russians during World War II and were intimately acquainted with Soviet tactics, as well as knowledgeable about counterintelligence methods successfully used by the Wehrmacht and RSHA, became invaluable. Reinhard Gehlen, who had been in command of all anti-Soviet espionage operations and who, in late 1944, had predicted his staff and files would eventually be welcomed by the Americans after the war, became affiliated with the newly formed Central Intelligence Agency of the United States. And Skorzeny? Documents declassified three decades after his imprisonment indicate that both the Soviet Union and the United States sought his services.

The first hint that the Russians were trying to contact Skorzeny came from the commando chief himself while he was still in Dachau. On January 28, 1948, Skorzeny wrote a memorandum to the camp commander in which he said, "During my confinement I have openly and overtly been offered the opportunity of collaborating with communist and Soviet circles. These offers were made both by German and by Soviet parties."[4]

Skorzeny was interrogated about these contacts. He stated that while detained in Nuremberg as a witness in November and December 1945 he became acquainted with a certain Lieutenant Bingel of the *Abwehr*, also a prisoner, who stated that upon his release he was going to immigrate to the USSR. Bingel had told him the Soviets were interested in making use of a man such as Skorzeny although he did not state for what purpose. Some days later, while passing through a hallway on his way to interrogation, Skorzeny had been approached by a Soviet officer who whispered hurriedly that he would like to have a long conversation with him. Nothing further developed because Skorzeny avoided the Soviet officer afterward.

When he was moved to Regensburg in August 1946, Skorzeny discovered that many of the SS officers detained there were pro-Soviet. They suggested to him that he could find employment with the Soviets, although no specific proposals were made. Then in Dachau in May 1947, another prisoner whom Skorzeny believed to be a Polish officer stated to him that the Soviets were vitally interested in establishing contact with him. Skorzeny refused. A few days later the Polish prisoner escaped. Skorzeny was convinced that the Soviets wanted him both because he was an engineer and because his name would be an attraction to young former members of the SS to jump on the Soviet bandwagon.

The CIC gradually began to ignore the rumors that Skorzeny might have flown Hitler out of Berlin, and concentrated on enlisting him against persistent Soviet aggravation. But because of official U.S. policy and public opinion it was necessary to try to get Skorzeny's aid without attracting attention. The CIC tried to make contact with him while he was in Dachau but as a report about agent August Beurer's efforts indicates, in wasn't easy.

> The undercover agent reports that Beurer was apparently able to sneak a letter written by the undercover agent and addressed to Otto Skorzeny into Camp Dachau with the help of Polish guard personnel. However the letter was twice returned because it is impossible to come close to Skorzeny. There was no chance to come near him in daytime. The only possibility to at least attempt to come near Skorzeny was through night letters and he will now make another attempt to sneak the letter through the guards to Skorzeny at night.[5]

When the contact was finally made, Skorzeny indicated his willingness to cooperate with U.S. intelligence agencies but his imprisonment impeded such cooperation. The German Ministry for Reconstruction and Political Liberation was determined to put Skorzeny on trial before a denazification court and the U.S. government could not officially oppose such a trial without placing itself in an embarrassing situation. Consequently, when he was transferred from Dachau to the German internment camp at Darmstadt, there was nothing the American intelligence officers could do. However, it was believed at that time that Skorzeny would quickly be classified as a "simple fellow-traveler" of Hitler and be released. Since the American tribunal had already cleared him, it was very unlikely that the German court would do otherwise. But for some reason never determined, his case encountered a series of postponements, seven in a row.

In midsummer the CIC became apprehensive because Czechoslovakia was once again pressing for Skorzeny's extradition to stand trial for war crimes. This time the Czechs were working through the war crimes commission of the United Nations, of which it was a member, and it appeared the demand would be successful. With the newly formed CIA also wanting to use Skorzeny as an agent, the need for quick action was imperative. Both the CIA and the CIC notified Skorzeny that the decision on the extradition request could be delayed for a few weeks by using the excuse of overload of paperwork, but after that length of time his situation would be perilous.

Skorzeny took the hint. He contacted his SS friends outside the prison and a plan was quickly prepared to get him out of the German internment camp. Correspondence was handled by the head of the internment camp censoring office, Lieselotte Schröter, who had become a very close friend of Skorzeny. She had an apartment in the camp where she kept Skorzeny's incoming and outgoing letters and he visited often to pick up or drop off mail. Once she was surprised by the camp commandant, Joachim Kosmetschke, as she was distributing uncensored mail to Skorzeny, and he quickly relieved her of her duties. Eight days later, through the efforts of the CIC and CIA, she was reinstated and the flow of uncensored mail continued.

Skorzeny also had the help of a personal courier to set up his escape plans. "Bunker Jacob," whose real name was Jacob Gröschner, was closely connected with the U.S. intelligence services after he appeared at Passau early in 1948 to report that he had been recruited by the Soviet Union to handle several missions in West Germany. The former SS officer stated that the Soviets wanted him to kidnap Otto Skorzeny, assassinate Land President (Governor) Arnold of Westphalia and bomb the bi-zone headquarters of the Allies in Frankfurt. Gröschner was detained at Dachau for questioning and soon was cooperating with the CIC, gathering information for them, and keeping in contact with Skorzeny, a longtime friend of his. When he was released from Dachau, he went directly to Darmstadt, where he picked up a letter from Skorzeny given to him by Frau Schröter. Gröschner then delivered the letter to an SS contact in Hannover, where the final plans for Skorzeny's escape attempt was made.

While his SS associates in Hannover were putting the final details of the escape plan together, Skorzeny was assigned to a work force which each day went into the city to clean up the rubble. Until he had been warned by the CIC and the CIA that the Czechs would probably be successful in having him extradited from Germany to Czechoslovakia to stand trial, he had always insisted he would stay at the internment camp until cleared by the denazification court. Now, however, he told his guards that he was withdrawing his promise not to try to escape. When the camp commander heard about his remarks he summoned

Skorzeny to his office and he told Kosmetschke the same thing.

"If the opportunity arises," he told the camp commander, "I intend to leave."[6]

Kosmetschke laughed at him but he ordered the security tightened around the internment camp. The camp commander was certain Skorzeny could not escape but he didn't count on the commando chief's patience, experience, and the outside help promised him. Kosmetschke wasn't even suspicious when "Bunker Jacob" visited Darmstadt and was permitted to have a meeting with Skorzeny in his cell at the formal request of the CIC. It was during this meeting that "Bunker Jacob" gave Skorzeny the plan set up by the SS to get him out of the internment camp.

On July 27 a car carrying three German civilians, all former SS officers, left Hannover headed for Darmstadt. At Würzburg the three Germans stopped long enough to put American military license plates on their car and to change into the khaki uniforms and white helmets of U.S. army military policemen. Where did they get the uniforms? Skorzeny in later years laughed at the question. "They weren't stolen. They were provided by the Americans."[7]

Several hours later the car stopped at the front gate of the Darmstadt internment camp and the three Germans disguised as a U.S. captain and two enlisted soldiers, all wearing the insignia of the military police, entered the gate guardhouse.

"We are here to take prisoner Otto Skorzeny to Nüremberg for his scheduled hearing tomorrow," the captain told the guard on duty.[8]

The guard, intimidated by the American military uniforms and believing he was doing his duty, glanced at the forged documents and promptly turned Skorzeny over to the trio. Flanked by the "military police," Skorzeny walked out the gate and disappeared from the camp forever.

Skorzeny's escape was not announced by the Germans for two days. His cell was searched in an effort to determine who had helped him, but all the Germans found was the letter Skorzeny had left behind addressed to the chairman of the denazification tribunal.

Very Honorable Mr. Freudell:
Since you have probably learned of my escape out of the camp from the German leader of the Internment Camp Darmstadt, I consider it my duty to explain the reasons for my step to you, Mr. Chairman.

First, I wish to reassure you that I always appreciated your personal objectivity and your personal wish for a just decision. That you had to deal according to the law and allow the full measure of the law to fall upon me, I, as a person brought up with a sense of duty and respect for law, fully understand. Nevertheless, the postponement from month to month of my trial has made me realize that outside elements have entered the scene, thereby destroying the impartiality of the tribunal. In spite of my belief in your personal will for justice I feel that it will be impossible for the court to carry through its freedom for a just decision and that the court must and will bow to stronger outside elements.

After the capitulation of the German army, Mr. Chairman, I, as a soldier, which is all that I was, freely gave myself up with a trust in the justice of the victors without making any effort to avoid my responsibility. For over two years I tried, under the surely not-light circumstances of my internment, to clear myself and restore the honor of my name to the world. The American military tribunal in Dachau cleared me and my comrades of all charges and therewith declared to the public that I had acted and fought purely as a decent soldier and had only done my duty to my Fatherland. In spite of this official release I was kept under arrest. The American authorities were so liberal as to offer me, an Austrian citizen under the law, the choice to go to either a DP camp or a German internment camp. I chose the latter because I wished to rehabilitate myself before a German court after this release from an American court. I did that at the time in the hope of finding only justice before a German court and prepared myself for months for these proceedings. However, I will not allow myself to fall under a one-sided, outside-influenced decision and thus lose the honor which was restored to me by the American court.

Only for these reasons have I withdrawn myself from further German court proceedings. If I'm given the opportunity to come before a German court which stands only under the law and is strong enough to resist the hate exerted from outside sources as is worthy of the old German justice traditions, I will immediately place myself at the service of this court. As a German who loves his Fatherland and fought for it as did every German man, I have only one wish: to live in honor in this Fatherland.

Yours sincerely,
Otto Skorzeny[9]

German authorities were embarrassed by Skorzeny's escape but they were confident that he would soon be recaptured. His huge physique and scarred face made him easily identifiable, while his reputation made him well known in all parts of Germany. Another reason they were confident that he would not be free long was that less than a month before his escape there had been a currency reform in West Germany and the procedure required to exchange the old currency for the new made it impossible to get money without being noticed. And they were certain Skorzeny, because of his profligate habits, would need money. But as the days and weeks passed and he was not found, hopes that Skorzeny would soon be back in Darmstadt faded. The German Minister of Reconstruction and Political Liberation, Gottlob Binder, was accused of permitting Frau Schröter to continue to deliver and send uncensored mail at the internment camp for Skorzeny even after she was caught doing so by the camp commander. As Ludwig Kiel, a member of the government, stated, "When Skorzeny became a fugitive and the most pressing suspicion, yes the certainty, that Frau Schröter helped him with the flight was known, she was still returned to her post by orders from your office. Herr Minister, I deplore it in the extreme that through your silence you allow your name and the name of your party to be used as a cover for intrigues of this sort by friends of the Nazis."[10]

Binder remained silent. Kiel, an antifascist, was furious but could do nothing.

Rumors were rampant about Skorzeny's whereabouts. Communists vowed that the American authorities had flown him to the United States where he was employed as a flying instructor. They even gave details. According to the Soviet sympathizers he was in the state of Georgia demonstrating to the CIA an experimental apparatus he had developed in 1943–1944 for picking up persons from the ground with a low-flying aircraft! Others were certain he was in France. A certain Fraulein Rudad living near Rosenheim in Bavaria reported to the American authorities that Skorzeny was living near her and intended to cross into Austria soon. A thorough investigation of the area failed to turn him up. About that time another woman, Fraulein Rienbold, claimed that Skorzeny had been living in Flensburg but had escaped to Argentina. And the press in Brazil reported that Allied intelligence in Germany had intercepted a letter from Skorzeny postmarked São Paulo. The report proved false.

Only one fact was certain: Skorzeny had left no forwarding address.

13 THE PHANTOM
COMMANDO

In 1948, when Skorzeny escaped from the German internment camp at Darmstadt, it appeared to be an isolated incident. Some
believed that the Americans had helped him get away because he was
of value to their intelligence agencies. Others thought the Germans had
permitted him to escape to avoid the embarrassment of a denazification
trial of a Nazi hero who had already been cleared by an American
tribunal of any involvement in war crimes. And there were still others
who were convinced that he had escaped on his own, using the skill he
had practiced as Hitler's commando chief during the Third Reich.
However, three decades later, after secret documents pertaining to the
immediate postwar years in Europe were declassified, a much more
complex and complete view of the overall situation is revealed.

These documents indicate that the Western powers decided to join
Russia in a winner-take-all manpower game. At first Russia, France, the
United States, and Great Britain were mainly interested in making
certain that the Nazi officials, supporters, and military commanders
received the punishment due them for the war crimes. Gradually,
however, each country became aware that certain Nazis could be
important to its postwar interests. All four countries waged a secret war
to obtain the services of the rocket experts at Peenemünde who had
developed the V-1 and V-2 for Hitler. The United States was successful
in getting such experts as Wernher von Braun and Walter Dornberger

to move to the States. Braun was instrumental in developing the U.S. rocket program for the exploration of space and Dornberger became prominent in the aerospace industry. Russia, too, obtained many scientists, including nuclear experts. But as the Cold War developed between Russia and the Western powers, both sides began seeking Nazis who could help politically and militarily and aid in gathering intelligence from the other side of the Iron Curtain.

The Western powers selected three men: Reinhard Gehlen, Hjalmar Schacht, and Otto Skorzeny. Gehlen, Hitler's foremost spymaster, was needed because his organization was still intact and could obtain the necessary intelligence from sources in Russia. Schacht, the financial genius of the Third Reich, was sought for his knowledge of hidden Nazi assets, his contacts around the world, and his talents as a financier. Skorzeny, the adventurer, was the ideal man to combat the covert aggression of the Soviet Union. That all three men had been very close to Hitler and the Nazi hierarchy was forgotten during the hectic, worrisome years immediately after World War II. Present needs far outweighed past deeds.

Skorzeny was still being shifted from prison to prison when the United States first went after Hitler's superspy Reinhard Gehlen. U.S. General Edwin Luther Sibert, G-2 to General Omar Bradley, was the officer who "found" Gehlen. When he discovered that a delegation of Russian officers had visited Flensburg looking for Gehlen, Sibert decided that if the German was that important he wanted to see him too. He found Gehlen in an American prisoner-of-war camp, ignored by U.S. personnel. An excellent and skilled interrogator, Sibert learned that Gehlen had hidden away documents and files which dealt with his espionage work on the eastern front during World War II. Sibert also discovered that Gehlen's network of agents in Russia was still intact. He immediately reported his "find" to Walter Bedell "Beetle" Smith, Eisenhower's chief of staff, who, in turn, passed the information on to Washington. In a few weeks Gehlen was out of prison and in the United States conferring with military intelligence officials. In 1946 he returned to Germany, set up headquarters south of Munich at Pullach, and became the Soviet intelligence-gathering arm of the U.S. military. In 1947, when the CIA was established, Gehlen's organization worked with the CIA in the silent conspiracy until 1956, when Gehlen became the chief intelligence officer for the new West German government. One of the first items on Gehlen's agenda when he returned from his stay in the United States was to get his friend and Third Reich cohort Otto Skorzeny out of prison. It took a while but he was successful.

The second member of the silent conspiracy was Hjalmar Schacht, "The Banker with the Standup Collar." Schacht was a financial genius who became a very close friend of Hitler before Hitler came to power. In 1932, when he was fifty-five years old, Schacht signed a petition presented to President Paul von Hindenburg favoring the seating of Hitler as chancellor. Hitler never forgot the financier's support when he had needed it most and during the Third Reich Schacht held such posts as Reich economic minister, Reich minister without portfolio, and president of the Reichsbank. His contacts around the world with financiers enabled Schacht to play an important role in the Nazi hierarchy, although Hitler became suspicious of the older man after the assassination attempt on the Führer's life on July 20, 1944. He thought Schacht had had prior knowledge of the plan and hadn't told him. Schacht was imprisoned in Ravensbrück, Flossenbürg, and Dachau concentration camps during the next ten months, until he was arrested by the Americans in 1945. At the IMT trial in Nüremberg, he was acquitted. Later he was brought to trial by a German denazification court at Baden-Württemberg, found to be a "Nazi chief offender" and sentenced to eight years in prison. On September 2, 1948, a few days more than a month after Skorzeny escaped from Darmstadt, Schacht was released from prison. He immediately sought to locate the commando chief. He needed him to help recover the hidden assets of the Nazi treasure.

The third member of the silent conspiracy remained at large as far as the world knew. Private citizens and even intelligence and military personnel not in on the silent conspiracy filed report after report about Skorzeny's suspected whereabouts and could not understand why the commando chief was not apprehended. Years later, a California citizen wrote a scathing letter to Senator Sheridan Downey after reports that Skorzeny was seen in Argentina. "I wish to stress that after preliminary investigations concerning the extradition of Otto Skorzeny, I had no further news from you. Please wake up the State Department and let us have some action in this matter."[1]

The State Department's reply to Senator Downey's query about Skorzeny summed up the situation very well at the time without revealing any of the confidential information about the silent conspiracy. It stated, in part:

Unfortunately, Otto Skorzeny's precise whereabouts are not yet known. To give some idea of the confusion regarding this point, it may be useful to cite the record of rumors regarding Skorzeny's whereabouts which have appeared since July 27, 1948, the date on which he escaped from the prison camp at Darmstadt where he was being held by the German officials for trial before a German denazification court. On September 22, 1948 it was rumored that he had gone underground in Brazil. On November 7, 1948 there was a report that he had reached the United States via Spain. On January 25, 1949 there was a rumor that he was living in the British zone of Germany under an assumed name. On April 26, 1949 it was alleged that he had arrived in South America, together with his wife. On June 2, 1949 another rumor had it that he was in Argentina or en route to that country. On June 23, 1949 another rumor suggested that he was attempting to proceed to Syria from Germany. On July 16, 1949 Swedish press reports alleged that he was in Sweden. These reports were followed on July 18 by rumors that he had proceeded to Sweden from Denmark and was attempting to go to Argentina. Late in August, further rumors once more suggested that he had reached Argentina and it was evidently in response to this rumor that your constituent first wrote you.

There has since been nothing to confirm Skorzeny's rumored presence in Argentina, but on February 14, 1950, the New York *Herald Tribune* carried an item reported by *Tribune* correspondent William J. Humphries, from Paris, that the Paris newspaper *Ce Soir* had carried the day before a photograph, allegedly of Skorzeny, just taken on the street in Paris. The French newspaper also alleged that Skorzeny was about to go to Italy.[2]

The photograph of Skorzeny in the French newspaper was the first verification of his whereabouts since his escape. But where had he been between July 27, 1948, and February 13, 1950? Were any of the rumors listed in the State Department's letter true? Was he in the United States at any time during this period? Was he working for the CIA or some other American intelligence organization? Top secret documents of the various U.S. intelligence agencies declassified thirty years later are masterpieces of deception. The letters exchanged between agencies are polite and detailed, but actually tell nothing of substance. Only by studying the queries and answers three decades later, with the advantage of knowing what happened during this period and the effect on world history, can the rumor of the exchanges be appreciated.

When the Assistant Chief of Staff, G-2, U.S. Army, Europe, queried the 66th Counter Intelligence Corps Group about the advisability of using Skorzeny as a source of intelligence about Soviet activities in Europe, one paragraph of the reply deserves an award for doubletalk: "In view of his past, as well as the notoriety received by Skorzeny in the press during the past years, it is felt that any open sponsorship or support of Skorzeny by the U.S. government, or any influence exerted by the U.S. government on behalf of Skorzeny, would probably expose the U.S. government to extreme international embarrassment. Furthermore, the possibility exists that Skorzeny has been and is being utilized by U.S. intelligence."[3]

The adjutant of the 66th Counter Intelligence Corps Group not only knew the "possibility existed" but was an actuality because they had observed a U.S. Military Attache Office captain from Madrid meet with Skorzeny near Tegernsee, Bavaria, a few days earlier to discuss intelligence matters!

In another query to the 66th Counter Intelligence Corps Group, the answer to whether Skorzeny was providing the group with information or not was deftly sidestepped. "Skorzeny is not a source or contact of our organization. We casually follow his international travels and record them when we come across them, but we are not in direct or indirect contact with him, and are not attempting to penetrate his circle, at least in Germany."[4]

The recipient of the letter scribbled in ink at the bottom of the typewritten message, "How's that again?"

A letter from Bernard A. Tormey, a colonel of an artillery unit of the U.S. Army, to the director of the intelligence division of Headquarters, European Command of the U.S. Army was more explicit. When he received a report that Skorzeny could provide the United States with some intelligence about Russian activities in Tormey's area, he wrote: "It is requested that this headquarters be notified whether Skorzeny is connected with an intelligence agency or not."[5]

The colonel's letter wasn't answered.

The U.S. intelligence agencies were able to deny their association with Skorzeny because he actually was working with Reinhard Gehlen's espionage and counterintelligence organization as a part of the silent conspiracy between the United States and the Nazi spy chief who had served Hitler so well and was now employed by the CIA. And Gehlen was busy! His agents had managed to photograph the first Soviet jet fighter, the Mig-15, at the Schönwalde airfield near Berlin, obtain samples of the fuel used in the jet and even a piece of the metal from which the fuselage and wings were constructed. His group, known as the Gehlen Org, located a training base in East Germany used by the Soviets to train East German "police" in the use of heavy artillery, tanks, and automatic weapons, and destroyed it. During the latter months of the Berlin airlift, the gigantic air operation required when Russia blocked the ground routes through East Germany to West Berlin, airfields at both ends of the airlift were well-protected from Soviet saboteurs by Gehlen's agents who kept them under surveillance at all times. Skorzeny was an important cog in the well-oiled spy machinery set up by Gehlen in behalf of the United States. In fact, that was why he was in Paris when his picture was taken in 1950. France had a large Communist party and Skorzeny was gathering information about its activities when he was spotted by the press photographer.

He had first stayed in the tiny state of Andorra because several former SS agents were living there. Later he moved to Paris, traveling under the assumed names of Schneider and Steiner, and established residence at St. Germain-en-Laye. Despite being well known in Paris from Third Reich days, Skorzeny went undetected by the public until February 13, 1950, when his photograph and that of his companion, a short brunette woman, was published in *Ce Soir*. There was an immediate outcry of indignation from the Communists, Jews and French citizens who had suffered under the Nazi occupation, French soldiers who had fought the Germans, and citizens who couldn't believe an escaped Nazi could reside in their country without being arrested. At about the same time that his photograph appeared in the Paris newspaper, it was revealed Skorzeny had sold his memoirs about his Third Reich activities. A few weeks later his manuscript was published in Germany and France. When the French newspaper *Le Figaro* printed a condensation of the Skorzeny memoirs, the Communist party reacted violently. Thousands of party members and sympathizers marched on the headquarters building of the newspaper, driving the officials of *Le Figaro* out the rear door.

The Paris police prefect was overwhelmed with inquiries demanding to know why Skorzeny was not arrested. "What effort have you made to detain the SS Obersturmbannführer?" "How is it possible that Skorzeny resided in France for months but was not reported to the police?" The prefect had a stock answer for everyone. He insisted that he could not arrest Skorzeny because Skorzeny had been cleared by an American tribunal and was not on any nation's list of wanted war criminals. But those wanting Skorzeny apprehended immediately pointed out that this was not true, that he was listed by the U.N. War Crimes Commission as a wanted war criminal and had been so listed since February 1948. His name was listed under Case No. 20-e-4095/48-11, which stated, in part:

> Skorzeny, Otto, German citizen, former commanding officer of the Special Duty Detachment in Vizovice. Date and place of alleged crime: April 1945 in Ploština. Number and description of the crimes: murder, looting, wanton destruction of property. Short statement of facts: the defendant Otto Skorzeny took part in a punitive action against assumed members of the underground movement in April 1945 in the village of Ploština where twenty-seven persons were killed, all of their possessions plundered and their farms burned.[7]

There had been a massacre of Czech guerrilla fighters at Ploština during the closing days of the war by the retreating SS, a last desperate frenzy of violence by the defeated elite. However, Skorzeny was not at the scene. Records proved that he was still in the Berlin area at the time, making a final effort to slow down the Russian advance.

Despite proof that Skorzeny's name *was* listed as a war criminal on the U.N. list, no effort was made to arrest him. However, Skorzeny decided he had worn out his welcome in France and disappeared from his residence in St. Germain-en-Laye. He went back to Germany, the country that supposedly was hunting him. According to a report of the U.S. 7970th Counter Intelligence Corps officer not aware of Skorzeny's association with Gehlen and the CIA, Skorzeny "had aid from Americans" on the trip—a report that undoubtedly was true.

The North Koreans had moved into South Korea on June 26, 1950, and many Allied officials thought it was a prelude to a Soviet attack on Western Europe. The United States, France, and Great Britain had only seven undermanned divisions with which to hold West Germany from falling under the influence of the Soviets, while the Russians had twenty-two divisions ready, plus the new East German army. For the Western nations facing the Communists in Asia and in Europe, German industrial might and Prussian military prowess both became invaluable. However, there were several embarrassing problems. Many of the German industrialists were in prison or still awaiting trial in an internment camp. Most of the prominent SS officers and men were on the run or in prison, too. How could the munition plants be rebuilt and manned by the former owners without the United States being ridiculed by the rest of the world? The Germans had been threatened with death or long years in prison for exactly the same thing that the United States now wanted them to do . . . except this time there would be no slave labor.

And the German military manpower? That was the reason for Skorzeny's trip to Germany. As one Communist reported: "Skorzeny went to Germany in 1950 to hire as many of his experienced SS men as possible to help the Americans."[8] He first went to the Munich area, to the village of Sutten, where he moved in with a family by the name of Scholm. It was a perfect hideout for Skorzeny who stayed there for nine months, using the alias of Rolf Steinbauer, while contacting his SS acquaintances in Bavaria.

Once again it was a photographer who forced Skorzeny's hand. The Munich newspaper *Die Abendzeitung*, getting a tip that Skorzeny was living in Sutten, sent a photographer to the village, and he secretly snapped a picture of Skorzeny. The newspaper printed it the next day with the caption: "Are Skorzeny and Steinbauer one and the same person?" Strangely enough no police went to investigate, but journalists did, and Skorzeny promptly left Sutten to take up residence in Munich at No. 31 Blumen Strasse. Rudolph J. Geiser, Special Agent of the U.S. Counter Intelligence Corps, made a reconnaissance of the building and reported:

> Skorzeny, using the alias of Rolf Steinbauer, is living at No. 31 Blumen Strasse, Munich, together with a former girl friend of his by the name of Louise Preiss. The building in question is a 3½ story brick construction located at the corner of Blumen Strasse and Angertor Strasse. The ground floor of said building contains the storage rooms for a printing concern located next door. The first and second floors are occupied by the Reparations Office, Munich branch. The third floor contains the offices of the construction firm of Macher & Preiss and also the living quarters of Preiss. A check of all door bells and name plates on the various doors failed to reveal the name Steinbauer. Judging from the appearance of the building, it can be considered as an ideal hideout, especially since the building is in a fairly inconspicuous locality.[9]

Skorzeny was there all right. So was Hermann Lauterbacher, former deputy Reich leader of the Hitler Youth, who was working with the Gehlen Org and the Americans. After arranging with Lauterbacher to recruit SS officers in the Munich area, Skorzeny moved on. He spent some time in West Berlin, a feat in itself since security measures were extremely strict in the divided city at the time. While in Berlin he stayed with Hilde Weissner, an actress whom he knew very well during the war. Later, after he had completed his business with SS contacts in West Berlin, he and the actress went to Hamburg and once again Skorzeny recruited a large number of his former SS comrades. British intelligence spotted Skorzeny in Hamburg and, not knowing of his mission for the Gehlen Org, prepared to arrest him and return him to Darmstadt. It took several discreet hints from the CIA to "lay off" before the tenacious English agents looked the other way.

Skorzeny next turned up in Düsseldorf. The local police, unaware of the true relationship between Hitler's commando chief, the Bonn government and the CIA, and Gehlen Org, reported that Skorzeny was using the office of Karl Uhrmeister, owner of the firm *Gesundheitstechnick* (Health Technician) as a front for some mysterious activities. He was still using the alias of Rolf Steinbauer and visited the office of Uhrmeister located at Grafenberger Allee 32-34, commonly known as the Eos-House, at various intervals. He appeared at the office at the beginning of each month and stayed for several days, handling correspondence and making long-distance telephone calls. According to the local police, an investigation verified that the Uhrmeister firm was a plumbing shop which did very little actual business. The office staff consisted of Uhrmeister, his wife, and two female secretaries. The two secretaries had been obliged to sign, on three separate occasions, statements to the effect that all business transactions were to be kept secret and not disclosed to outsiders. The interior of the office, according to the report, resembled a bank vault with the usual security arrangements and installations of steel cabinets, barred windows, and steel safes. At the close of business hours, all correspondence and files were locked in the safes. The local police report closed with the statement that "the firm of Uhrmeister's is for all purposes a front for clandestine activities." [10]

This report was submitted to the German administration of the Northrhine-Westphalia area with the certainty that Skorzeny would immediately be arrested and the local police would bask in the glory of their security achievement. However, the German authorities, more knowledgeable about the situation, stonewalled the local police. They explained they would have to check with the British occupation authorities regarding what action should be taken against Skorzeny, since Düsseldorf was in the British sector. The British immediately stated that officially they had no reason for Skorzeny's arrest, but the Germans could do as they wanted. After much consultation between Düsseldorf and Bonn, it was decided to detain Skorzeny under the charge of false identity in order to satisfy the critics. Strict orders were issued by the German authorities that "no records of the case should be kept in written form and that all communications should be on a personal, oral basis only."[11]

Skorzeny, tipped off that he might be detained temporarily by the German authorities, probably by the CIA through the Gehlen Org, left Düsseldorf and went to Salzburg, Austria, just across the German border from Berchtesgaden. He stayed with Lothar Rafael at Hollbrunn 16 in the city. During his stay in Salzburg, Skorzeny was in direct contact with Raoul Konitz and Erich Werner, both former *Abwehr* members under Canaris.

Skorzeny's time was not all spent on activities undertaken for the Gehlen Org and the U.S. authorities, however. He had a second important reason for visiting Salzburg. He wanted to divorce his wife Emmi. Skorzeny hired Dr. Friedrich Steinbach of Salzburg to handle the divorce details while he was in Austria rounding up the SS officers and men. With that detail taken care of, Skorzeny headed for Spain. There were two persons he especially wanted to see there. One was a beautiful aristocrat, the second was Hjalmar Schacht, the financial genius of the Third Reich.

Marshal Philippe Pétain, center, *with Göring*, right. *Pétain was once the proposed target of a Skorzeny kidnapping plan.* (National Archives)

General Dwight D. Eisenhower in a jeep at the front. Skorzeny ruined Ike's 1944 Christmas. (National Archives)

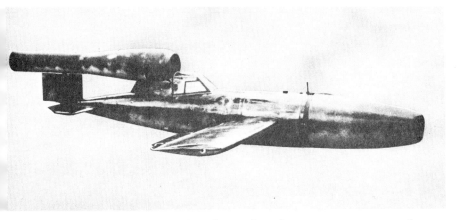

A V-1 modified so it could be flown by a pilot. This was a joint project of Hanna Reitsch and Skorzeny. (National Archives)

Benito Mussolini immediately after Skorzeny rescued him from the Gran Sasso. (National Archives)

Miklós "Miki" Horthy, second from left, *with Hitler. Skorzeny later kidnapped Horthy and held him hostage during a Budapest commando operation.* (National Archives)

Bormann, Hitler, and Ernst Kaltenbrunner, left to right. *Kaltenbrunner was head of the Reich Main Security Office and supposedly Skorzeny's superior, but he seldom knew what Skorzeny was doing.* (National Archives)

Evita Perón arriving for a visit in Spain. She and Skorzeny were close friends during the post-war years. (National Archives)

Evita Perón attending one of her many official functions as wife of Juan Perón, dictator of Argentina. The Peróns were pro-Nazis and benefited from Bormann treasure. (National Archives)

Benito Mussolini, Hitler, and the King of Italy, Victor Emmanuel III, left to right. When the King of Italy had Mussolini imprisoned in 1943, Skorzeny rescued him in one of the most dramatic incidents of the war. (National Archives)

Tito (Josif Broz). Skorzeny was ordered to kidnap or kill him during the war but the mission was not successful. (Library of Congress)

Mussolini with Skorzeny's commandos at the time of his rescue. (Library of Congress)

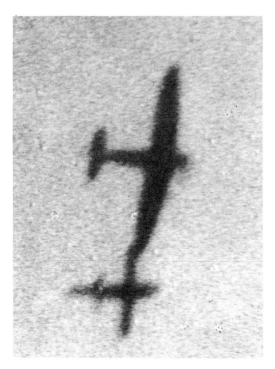

A Spitfire pilot tipping a V-1 off course by using his plane's wing tip. Skorzeny's piloted V-1s could have avoided such tactics. (Imperial War Museum)

The Berghof, Hitler's mountain retreat near Berchtesgaden. Skorzeny often visited Hitler at the Berghof. (Herzegger)

American Flying Fortress captured by the Germans. Skorzeny planned to use such captured planes on surprise attacks against the Allies. (United States Air Force)

Eva Braun, Hitler's mistress and wife for a day. She liked Skorzeny and held long conversations with him while he was waiting to see Hitler. (National Archives)

Skorzeny and his commandos would often mingle with civilians on public transportation to escape detection. (John Kiser)

The "Wanted" poster distributed throughout Europe by the Allies. (USAISC)

A b s c h r i f t !

Technische Hochschule in W i e n .
_____

Herrn   Otto S K O R Z E N Y
geboren am   12. Juni 1908   in   Wien
hat am   11. Dezember 1931 an der Technischen Hochschule in Wien
            vor dem Prüfungsausschuss für Maschinenbau

                    die zweite Staatsprüfung

                      s e h r   g u t

                      bestanden.

Er ist auf Grund des Erlasses des Herrn Reichsministers für Wissen-
schaft, Erziehung und Volksbildung vom 30. November 1938 = WJ 5020/38,
WU, WR, Z IIa berechtigt, den akademischen Grad

            D I P L O M = I N G E N I E U R

    im Gebiete des Deutschen Reiches zu führen.

    W i e n , den 26. April 1940.

        Der Rektor der Technischen Hochschule in Wien

                gez. H a n s

                (Siegel)

P.d.R.d.A.:

H-Obersturmführer (Ing.)

Skorzeny's diploma when he graduated from engineering school. (BDC)

THE MAN WHO KIDNAPPED MUSSOLINI, KEY BRAIN OF A HUNDRED EXPLOITS ...

Skorzeny turns up— and poses a picture

Scarfaced OTTO SKORZENY
" At last I can drop the mask "—and with hair slicked back, he permits a picture for the first time in seven years.

Right: *Handwritten autobiography composed by Skorzeny.* (BDC)

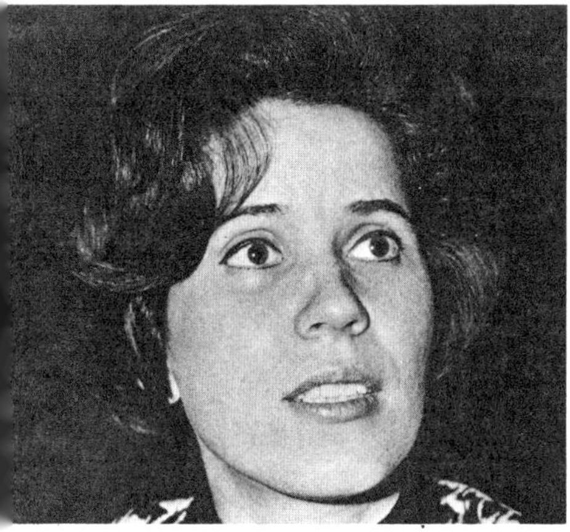

Beate Klarsfeld, a postwar Nazi hunter. (Betsy Nolan Public Relations)

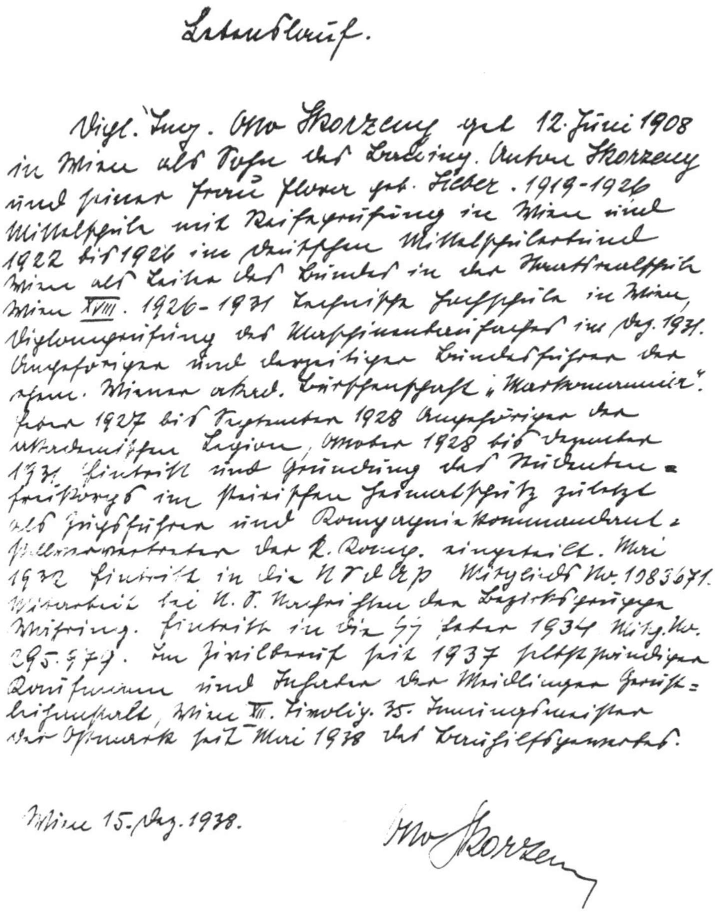

Lebenslauf.

Dipl. Ing. Otto Skorzeny geb. 12. Juni 1908 in Wien als Sohn des Dipl. Ing. Anton Skorzeny und seiner Frau Flora geb. Lieber. 1919-1926 Mittelschule mit Reifeprüfung in Wien und 1922 bis 1926 im Deutschen Mittelschülerbund Wien als Leiter des Bundes in der Staatsrealschule Wien XVIII. 1926-1931 Technische Hochschule in Wien, Diplomprüfung des Maschinenbaufaches im Dez. 1931. Angehöriger und derzeitiger Bundesführer der schlag. Wiener akad. Burschenschaft „Markomannia". Jänner 1927 bis September 1928 Angehöriger der Akademischen Legion, Oktober 1928 bis Dezember 1931 Eintritt und Gründung des Studenten-freikorps im steirischen Heimatschutz zuletzt als Zugsführer und Kompagniekommandant-stellvertreter der 2. Komp. eingeteilt. Mai 1932 Eintritt in die NSDAP Mitglieds Nr. 1083671. Mitarbeit bei N.S. Nachrichten der Bezirksgruppe Währing. Eintritt in die SS Jänner 1934 Mitg. Nr. 295.979. Im Zivilberuf seit 1937 selbständiger Kaufmann und Inhaber der Meidlinger Gerüst-leihanstalt, Wien XII. Tivolig. 35. [illegible] der Ostmark seit 1. Mai 1938 des [illegible].

Wien 15. Dez. 1938.

Otto Skorzeny

THE WORLD AND SKORZENY

III

"You would be astonished to know all the names of kings, presidents, and dictators I have known."

14 THE FRANCO CONNECTION

Skorzeny was welcome in Spain. When he left his residence on Calle de Alcalá to walk to his favorite restaurant, Horcher's in the Calle de Alfonso, photographers and journalists didn't worry him. The authorities were well aware he was in the country and Spanish citizens were accustomed to Germans. When his photograph or an article about his living in the country appeared in one of the newspapers, it was passed over lightly by government officials and average citizens alike. He was a regular guest at Horcher's. The owner, Otto Horcher, had operated a gourmet restaurant on Berlin's Kurfürstendamm during the Third Reich that had been a gathering place for the Nazi hierarchy. When the average German citizen had been required to observe one-meal Sundays and bread was rationed, Göring, Himmler, Canaris, Kaltenbrunner, Ribbentrop, Schacht, Skorzeny, and other Nazis had been served lavish meals at Horcher's. In addition, many foreign visitors had eaten at the restaurant, not knowing that cameras and listening devices were installed at strategic locations. Not only did Horcher supply all the food the Nazis wanted to eat, he also provided the conversations of the foreign guests to them. In 1946 he moved to Madrid and opened another restaurant, an ideal place for Skorzeny to meet Hjalmar Schacht and other Germans. He also used it as a letter drop when secrecy was needed.

Since the First World War Spain had been an important center for

German clandestine activity. At that time, Canaris had become very well acquainted with Francisco Franco who was then a young colonial officer stationed in Spanish Morocco. Canaris had been in Spain conducting a secret mission for the German navy, and during the latter stages of World War I conspired with his new-found friend Franco to incite the North African rulers against Germany's enemies, France and England. During the time between the two World Wars, Canaris managed to obtain much-needed copper, lead, mercury, and tungsten from Spain for the German war plants and, in turn, Hitler helped Franco during the Spanish Civil War by providing military aid. When Franco became the absolute ruler of Spain in 1939, he didn't forget the help the Nazis had provided or his friendship with Canaris. He made it possible for the Nazis to transform Spain into a stronghold of German espionage. Spain was an ideal spot for radio reception and the Nazis established a sending and receiving network that reached all the way to Africa. More than a hundred agents were based in the German embassy in Madrid to receive, send, and decipher messages. Meteorological bases were constructed in Spain, the Canary Islands, and Spanish possessions in North and South Africa. The Nazis also operated an excellent courier service to South America from Madrid. When Skorzeny took over part of the responsibilities formerly shouldered by Canaris after Canaris became involved in the Hitler assassination attempt in 1944, the files of the contact men and agents in the Spanish network were transferred to him. Consequently, after the Third Reich ended, he was familiar with the Germans and German contacts in Spain.

After the end of the Third Reich, the Madrid Nazi colony grew fast as diehard Nazis fled Germany. It was estimated at 16,000 by 1950.

One of the persons awaiting Skorzeny's arrival in Madrid was Hjalmar Schacht. Schacht was well aware of Skorzeny's activities after the escape from Darmstadt, because Gehlen and Skorzeny kept him posted. Now he needed Skorzeny's help for his own escort mission. Schacht had a distinct advantage over many of Hitler's former associates; he knew what the German industrialists and professional men had done before and during the Third Reich and he also knew what their American and British counterparts had done in the same period. And neither record was a shining example of legitimate business practices. At the IMT trial in Nuremberg, Schacht was helped indirectly because he had dealt with prominent Americans such as John Foster Dulles during the early years of Hitler's influence. There were many American businessmen who didn't want their financial connections with Rhine and Ruhr industrialists to become public knowledge. Perhaps as a consequence, Schacht was judged innocent of any war crimes at the IMT trial and eventually, through appeals, was freed by the German denazification court. In a short time he was again involved with Nazi finances, only now he was trying to get the "hidden" funds released in behalf of German and American-British interests.

In Munich, not far from where Gehlen had established his headquarters, was a German-Spanish society headed by Prince Dr. Adalbert of Bavaria. It was composed of German businessmen who had supplies of material, large sums of money, and manufacturing companies in Spain fronted by Spanish owners. When it became evident that the Third Reich was going to collapse, these Germans had transferred as much of their wealth to neutral Spain as possible, without the knowledge of Hitler. Schacht had been the expert in this act of corporate camouflage. His skill was unequalled in the field of financial legerdemain and he made it a practice to keep even the most complicated details of the secret transactions in his head and not on paper. Consequently; when it came time to unravel the corporate tangle, Schacht was needed . . . and the Western powers wanted the former German industrial might reestablished as quickly as possible because of the Cold War and later the Korean conflict. Since many of the members of the Munich German-Spanish society were not free to travel, Schacht went to Spain.

When Skorzeny arrived in Madrid, his first contact was with Schacht. Skorzeny soon was handling the Spanish interests of Klöckner AG, the Wolff trust, the Feldmühle Paper Company, the Messerschmitt works, Krupp conglomerate, the H.S. Lucht Company, and others. He asked Léon Degrelle, who had been Belgium's leading Nazi collaborator to aid him in handling German interests in Spain. Hitler once said that if he had a son he would want him to be just like Degrelle. Like Skorzeny, Degrelle was an escapee. Though a Belgian court had sentenced him to death for high treason, he had avoided the hangman by escaping to Spain, where the Franco regime protected him. As the battle line in Korea went from Inchon toward the Yalu and back again to the south as China entered the war, Britain, France, and the United States ignored the restrictions imposed upon German industry as far as war production was concerned and urged the barons to go all out. U.S. High Commissioner John J. McCloy declared an amnesty for 101 prisoners, among whom were Alfried Krupp, the munitions baron, and other German industrialists who could help the West during this critical period. Skorzeny, Schacht, Degrelle, and others working with them soon were able to provide the desperately needed help. Eleven months after Krupp's release, for instance, 13½ million tons of steel were produced in Germany, and up from the 11 million limit set by surrender terms, and within three more years production was up to 18 million tons. Machine tools stored in Spain were taken from their hiding place and put back into service. Also, tool steel that had been smuggled out of Germany during the latter years of the war was made available to the West by Skorzeny and his associates. And Schacht, using his financial creativity, made certain there was plenty of money available to rebuild the bomb-damaged plants and pay the necessary wages as, one by one, the Ruhr factories went back into operation.

However, U.S. intelligence units, both military and civilian, knew that Otto Skorzeny, Reinhard Gehlen, and Hjalmar Schacht, the most prominent members of the silent conspiracy, had divided interests. Their aid to the West was appreciated, perhaps saved much of Europe from falling under Soviet influence when the United States, Great Britain, and France were weak militarily during the immediate postwar years. But it didn't take long to realize that the trio needed watching, that they were as interested in their own personal welfare as that of the West. Gehlen wanted to be the head of intelligence for the new West German government as soon as the Germans were permitted to establish their own rule independent of the Western powers. With this in mind, Hitler's superspy kept German interests dominant over CIA interests and in many instances caused serious problems for Washington. Schacht made certain that the "hidden" funds he managed to release by untangling the corporate camouflage established during the Third Reich went for the benefit of Germany. If, indirectly, this meant helping the West, fine. In many instances, however, millions of dollars or their equivalents in foreign currency, part of the missing Nazi treasure, went to help former Nazis and to help in establishing a pro-Nazi West German government.

Skorzeny was interested in a personal fortune, his SS comrades, placing former Nazis in any new West German government that was formed, and beautiful women. However, he tried to project a different public image. "Believe me," Skorzeny told an interviewer, "for some years it has not been pleasant to be known as Mussolini's rescuer. Here in Spain I feel at last I can drop the mask. There is no reason for secrecy. I am not ashamed of what we did and how we did it. I work fifteen hours a day trying to build up various engineering enterprises. I am working for the future."[1]

A United States Air Force intelligence officer who became friendly with Skorzeny in Madrid at this time reported that "a customary greeting from Skorzeny is not unlike being welcomed by a huge bear or engulfed by a huge St. Bernard dog. Skorzeny likes good Scotch whisky and mixes only a little plain water with it. The woman with whom he is living appears to be the business head of the house. He even stops discussing a matter at her bidding."[2]

The woman was Countess Ilse von Finkenstein, a niece of Hjalmar Schacht, whom Skorzeny married in Madrid after his divorce from his first wife was completed. Her real name was Ilse Lüthje, and she was a Bavarian whose estates were confiscated after the war by the Soviets. They lived in a large villa on Lopez de Hoyos in Madrid after their marriage in 1954 and entertained lavishly. Her first husband had had wide business interests in Germany during the Third Reich, including the Otto Wolff iron and steel complex. After her marriage to Skorzeny, the countess continued to be active in business affairs. When she was observed visiting the Madrid office of Victor Oswald with Frank Gallati, a Britisher known to be interested in exporting armaments and other materials to Egypt, U.S. intelligence officers began an immediate investigation. Their report indicated she was acting in behalf of her husband and her uncle in a sale of arms to Egypt, but the details were never verified. Not long after this meeting, however, Skorzeny arranged a German sale of railway stock and tools to Spanish interests, a sale that totaled more than $5 million.

Skorzeny was involved in other deals, some successful, some not, which were designed to increase his personal fortune. Julian P. Fromer, American consul in Bilbao, heard about Skorzeny's business tactics from a friend while they were vacationing at the fishing village of Lequetio. Skorzeny was also spending part of the summer at Lequetio, where his huge figure, tanned to a dark brown, stood out conspicuously. One day when Skorzeny was swimming nearby, Fromer's friend asked, "Do you know Skorzeny is involved in Spanish arms sales to Egypt?"

Fromer shook his head. "A rumor?"

"No rumor. The son of Castor de Uriarte who is owner of the

Marquina arms firm of Esperanza y Cia confided to me that Skorzeny appeared at the factory and told his father that unless he was 'cut in' on the arms contract between Esperanza and the Egyptian government, he [Skorzeny] would use his influence with General Naguib to have the order canceled."

"What happened?" Fromer asked.

His friend shrugged his shoulders. "Esperanza is still selling arms to Egypt. Others have told me that it was well known that Skorzeny was making lots of money arranging the sale of Spanish arms to Egypt."[3]

When Fromer checked with the British consulate about the rumored Skorzeny involvement in an arms sale to Egypt, the vice-consul said he had heard the same rumor, and intelligence reports from British agents indicated that Skorzeny was training Spaniards to carry out anti-British sabotage in the eventuality of an outbreak of all-out Anglo-Egyptian hostilities. Skorzeny was kept under constant surveillance by British intelligence, he said.

In another incident that convinced American officials they were involved with a very dangerous ally was discovered accidently by a U.S. artillery officer. The officer's wife had been a model in the United States. When she had an opportunity to model clothes for a German designer named Eberhard Horst, after she had accompanied her husband overseas, she quickly accepted. Through Horst she and her husband met Alfred Ellenhausen, who visited their home several times. On one of his visits, he mentioned Otto Skorzeny. The artillery officer immediately recognized the name and asked if Ellenhausen knew him.

"Very well," Ellenhausen said. "I will see him again next week in Madrid. We have a matter of 200 M-46 tanks and 800,000 liters of gasoline to discuss."

The officer was skeptical. "Where would you keep something like that out of sight?"

"Switzerland. When we sell them they will be shipped from there."

The artillery officer notified the G-2 division of the U.S. Army, Europe, and an investigation was begun at once. While it was verified that Skorzeny and the man called Ellenhausen, which was probably an alias, were definitely involved in international arms sales, the ultimate destination of the tanks and gasoline in Switzerland was never determined. Not officially. But Skorzeny's financial fortunes increased by leaps and bounds during this period.

Several times Skorzeny was accused of contacting American military personnel in Germany from his Madrid office in an effort to purchase stolen weapons. One American soldier stationed at Bad Nauheim admitted being involved with Skorzeny in an arms deal, but he backed out before robbing a warehouse because the promised money wasn't delivered on time. Three others managed to steal an air-to-air, heat-seeking missile from a storage area and disappeared. Skorzeny was thought to be involved but it was never proven. Even the Federal Bureau of Investigation under J. Edgar Hoover, although a domestic intelligence organization, took an interest in Skorzeny's actions. Hoover's informant was "a person residing in the United States who, to our knowledge, is not connected with any agency of the U.S. government."[4] The informant, who had personal contact with Skorzeny in Madrid, stated that Skorzeny said he could obtain steel through his friendship with a former prince of the German House of Hesse and that he was a good friend of Willy Messerschmitt, the former German aircraft manufacturer, who was ready and willing to make valuable technical contributions to interested parties anyplace in the world. Skorzeny also had mentioned that he had been approached near the end of the Third Reich by several leading German bankers who asked him to fly $14 million worth of gold out of the country to a neutral nation. He insisted that he had decided to remain in Germany to "face trial as a Nazi, believing that his future is in Germany and that it is his destiny some day to be president of Germany."

It was not the first time U.S. intelligence had been told there was a possibility Skorzeny had smuggled a fortune out of Germany during the last days of the Third Reich. A short time before the FBI informant's report, the U.S. Department of State had received an airgram from the World Jewish Congress stating that "Skorzeny succeeded in smuggling out of Germany over two million marks."[5] Sir William Stephenson, an outstanding British intelligence agent during the war, and Ernest Cuneo, an international lawyer who had been associated with the OSS, began an investigation of Nazi "dirty money," believing it was in Spain and South America primarily. They soon discovered certain U.S. officials and British authorities wanted to curb the search. Why? Unofficially, intelligence agents became convinced that bankers and industrialists in the West would be embarrassed if the truth was discovered, that Schacht's corporate camouflage concealed American and British secrets as well as German.

An even more surprising action that illustrated Skorzeny's ever-growing influence in Europe, the Mideast, and South America was the request of the Austrian authorities for extradition of Skorzeny from Spain for war crimes. When the Spanish newspaper *Joint Weeka* announced that the Austrian government had requested Skorzeny be arrested, the U.S. embassy in Madrid sent an officer to talk with Dr. Karl Grüber, the Austrian ambassador to Spain. Grüber stated that this affair had been a source of constant embarrassment to him and his government since there had never been any request for Skorzeny's extradition. He suggested that the "error" had come about because the Austrian government had requested the arrest of a notorious swindler by the name of Torko who was wanted by the Austrian police on charges of fraudulent export operations.

"At the time Torko was arrested," Grüber said, "some Spanish newspapers confused Torko with Skorzeny."

Just why, since the names and the accusations were entirely different, the Austrian ambassador couldn't or wouldn't explain.

"To make matters worse," Grüber complained, "Skorzeny, rather than keeping quiet, held a press conference denying the war crime charges which resulted in additional publicity. I admit there was an investigation into Skorzeny's alleged complicity in the murder of three members of the Austrian resistance in April 1945, but the investigation, although carried on for several years, was too inconclusive to ask for Skorzeny's extradition and therefore at this time no action is planned against him."[6]

Grüber didn't mention that nearly five years earlier the Vienna district court had closed its case against Skorzeny and had granted him an official Austrian passport. Austria had also refused to grant Czechoslovakia permission to transport Skorzeny through the country even if the Czechs were successful in extraditing him for war crimes . . . which they were not! Nor did he say anything about the business arrangement between Skorzeny's Madrid office and *VÖEST*, the United Austrian Iron and Steel works. Skorzeny was the company's secret representative in Spain and South America!

When it became known publicly that Skorzeny was associated with *VÖEST*, many Austrians wanted to know how Skorzeny, suspected of war crimes and an intimate of Hitler during the Third Reich, had obtained such a position. The vice-chancellor of Austria, Dr. Bruno

Pittermann, was asked if he considered it appropriate that the foreign representative of a leading national industry was one of the most prominent figures of the Third Reich. His answer was to give the opinion of the board of directors of *VÖEST:* "Skorzeny is not the representative of *VÖEST* for Spain and South America and has never been. But Skorzeny has in several instances served as occasional business go-between—which was accepted by *VÖEST* only so far as it was of interest to them. I admit that because of these deals abroad, conferences with Skorzeny in Austria were a necessity and that he once visited *VÖEST*."[7]

Finally the vice-chancellor also had to admit that in the transactions carried out in behalf of *VÖEST* by Skorzeny, the commando chief had realized at least 225,000 schillings.

When angry Austrians investigated to learn just who had written the opinion for the board of directors of *VÖEST*, they discovered it had been composed by the chief clerk of the firm, Dr. Franz Hueber. That answered a lot of the questions, because Hueber was the brother-in-law of Hermann Göring. During the *Anschluss* of 1938, Göring had insisted that Hueber be installed as justice minister. Later Hueber had moved to Berlin as state secretary in the Nazi justice system and eventually became president of the Reich Administrative Court. After the war he had been sentenced to eighteen years in prison by a Viennese people's court, but a Linz, Austria, court reduced the sentence. When the Western powers critically needed help during the postwar years, Hueber, like Gehlen, Schacht, Krupp, Skorzeny, and others, found himself a free man. Soon he was chief clerk of the state-owned *VÖEST* . . . and he didn't forget his Nazi friends.

To American intelligence agents Skorzeny was becoming more a man to be watched than a man to rely upon. When West Germany's political sovereignty was restored in 1955, after the statute legalizing the occupational rights of the Allies was rescinded, the new Federal Republic of Germany was established. The Gehlen Org, which had been so valuable to the United States as an espionage arm of the CIA, was transferred to the new West German government and Reinhard Gehlen concentrated on German affairs. Hjalmar Schacht continued the mysterious travels required by his work in assembling the Nazi funds scattered around the globe. But now he made certain the funds were used for the benefit of the new government and for Nazi survivors interested in reestablishing Germany's prestige. Skorzeny's SS organization, once so valuable an asset to the Western powers, now became a liability and an embarrassment as the Federal Republic of Germany was permitted to rearm. The new government was given the right to raise half a million troops to be commanded by the supreme NATO head. Skorzeny, realizing the change in the situation, also altered his goals. He spent more time and money on personal projects and on projects dealing with his SS companions and the new West German government. And some of his projects caused considerable concern among officials in the West, concern that his actions might bring about a revival of fascism in the new West German government based on the same principles as the Third Reich, concern that he might reveal some of the actions he had taken in behalf of the United States, France, and Great Britain in previous years. Various steps were taken to curb him. The U.S. Department of the Treasury froze all profits from the U.S. edition of his book, basing the decision on the law that all German assets were frozen. The French no longer permitted him to cross their frontier and, later, Great Britain also barred him from entering the country. This made him furious.

"Because of this stupid ban," he told Christopher Morris of the *London Express,* "I am finding it extremely difficult to conduct busines deals with my British friends. When I am passing through London I have to stay in the customs area. I am not going to get down on my knees and beg for permission to enter, however."[8]

When the U.S. Embassy in Madrid learned that the U.S. Army planned to interview Skorzeny for a film about spectacular events of World War II, the ambassador immediately notified Washington that he thought it would be a serious mistake for the army to "involve itself with this unsavory and unabashed Nazi."[9]

The U.S. Department of State concurred, saying such an involvement "would be inappropriate and unwise."[10]

The film was cancelled.

The greatest concern over Skorzeny's actions, however, was stated in an air intelligence information report by a U.S. agent who wrote, in part:

The ability of Skorzeny to remain in contact with large numbers of prominent members of the Nazi "Old Guard" of whom a great many undoubtedly reside in Spain is of interest. It is entirely possible that

Skorzeny can lead to the whereabouts of many "wanted" Germans who have faded away from Germany via clandestine means in an effort to lose their former identities.[11]

No more accurate report was ever written about Skorzeny, but it only scratched the surface.

15 THE SWASTIKA SYNDICATE

Long before Skorzeny escaped from the Darmstadt internment camp in July 1948, there was evidence he was organizing former SS members into an underground movement. This organization was first known as the "Skorzeny Movement" and was mentioned in an official report from the Headquarters, U.S. Constabulary, to the Deputy Director of Intelligence at Headquarters, European Command. The second paragraph of the report explained the suspected purpose of the "Skorzeny Movement":

> A group of former SS and paratroopers have attached themselves to an underground movement which is under Skorzeny's direction. According to reliable sources, the movement's headquarters is located in Tyrol, Austria. This movement has a two-fold purpose: (1) Active resistance to Bolshevism and (2) Evacuation of Western occupation troops. The Skorzeny movement is also maintaining direct contact with an underground movement in the Soviet zone known as "Grief."[1]

The Western powers were not too concerned with the "Skorzeny Movement" at this time because it was small enough for their occupation troops to handle easily. Later, when the "Skorzeny Movement" became known as the *Bruderschaft* (Brotherhood) and the membership continued to grow, the West, instead of being apprehensive, encouraged its growth. The international crisis caused by the

178

Soviet's covert and direct aggression had created a vital need for help and Skorzeny, by this time a member of the silent conspiracy with the U.S. intelligence, promised his cooperation. From his cells at Dachau and Darmstadt and from hiding after his escape, Skorzeny very efficiently guided the organization until by the early 1950s it was a group to be reckoned with by those opposed to fascism and Third Reich principles.

The original idea for such a postwar organization came not from Skorzeny but from Martin Bormann, Hitler's private secretary and close associate. Late in 1944 when it became evident that no miracle was going to save the Third Reich, Bormann, who handled the Nazi treasury, began thinking of the future. At the secret meeting of the industrialists on August 10, 1944, at the Hotel Rotes Haus in Strasbourg, which Bormann was aware of but Hitler was not, a far-reaching agreement was made, one which affected the free world in the years after the Third Reich. Bormann agreed that the German industrialists should immediately begin transferring money, machine tools, specialty steel, and secret blueprints abroad for use after the war. In addition, the industrialists were encouraged to set up firms in neutral countries. Bormann promised them Nazi funds for this purpose with the understanding that the Nazi survivors would be able to draw from the profits of these firms later. Skorzeny and Schacht were a part of the plan. Skorzeny handled the physical transferring of the assets to neutral countries while Schacht used his great financial skill to advise the industrialists how to camouflage their foreign assets on paper, although at the time he was imprisoned in a concentration camp by Hitler on suspicion of conspiracy. However, when the end of the Third Reich came, Bormann disappeared. Years of investigation after Bormann was tried and convicted *in absentia* during the IMT trials at Nuremberg failed to solve the mystery of his disappearance. Did he escape from Berlin and establish a secret headquarters in South America? Was he killed trying to get out of Berlin? Is he alive today? No verified answers to those questions were ever discovered but one fact is certain: Skorzeny took over the role Martin Bormann had reserved for himself after the end of the Third Reich.

Skorzeny and his uncle by marriage, Hjalmar Schacht, fell heir to the secrets of the Nazi treasure: where it was located; how it got there; who controlled it; and the purpose for which it was intended. The one important change that Skorzeny made in Bormann's original plan was his strong emphasis on the welfare of the former SS members.

The *Bruderschaft* eventually became known as *Odessa*, a code word meaning *Organization der Entlassene SS Angehorige* (Organization for the Release of Former SS Members). As another U.S. intelligence report stated, imprisonment didn't stop the commando chief.

"The leader of this movement is Otto Skorzeny, who is directing it out of the CIE in Dachau," the report explained. "The Polish guards are helping the men that receive orders from Skorzeny to escape."[2]

But what did they do after they escaped? For this part of the operation Skorzeny organized *Die Spinne* (The Spider), whose personnel were responsible for maintaining the escape route from Germany to Italy. There were "safe houses" or sanctuaries every fifty miles, and the route was so secret that the staff at one station only knew about the next "safe house" up or down the line. Only Skorzeny and a few of his close associates knew the details of the entire escape path. One investigation of *Die Spinne* by U.S. intelligence agents revealed that the SS members usually moved from certain German cities such as Stuttgart, Munich, Frankfurt, or Bremen south to Bavaria. Further investigation verified that no matter from what city the escapee started his trip, he usually ended up in the medieval town of Memmingen in the Allgäu section of Bavaria. Simon Wiesenthal, who gained fame as the world's most relentless Nazi hunter after World War II, discovered in the course of his searches for escaped war criminals of the Third Reich that from Memmingen there were two routes, one going to Bregenz, Austria, and the other to Switzerland. The Bregenz route skirted Lake Constance and then continued on to Innsbruck, across the Brenner Pass and into Italy.

"The Nazis called this the B-B axis," Wiesenthal said. "It was a code name for the Bremen-Bari route."[3]

Later, Skorzeny simplified the routes into two main ones, both departing Bremen: either to Rome by land, or to Genoa by water. In order to transport the SS members to Bremen, various methods were devised. One involved the U.S. military. The trucks delivering the immensely popular American army newspaper *Stars and Stripes*, were driven by Germans. Skorzeny made certain that most of the drivers were *Die Spinne* members or sympathizers. The U.S. military authorities were so lax when they hired the drivers that they never discovered most of the Germans were using false names. At the various checkpoints between cities in Germany, the drivers would smile at the military police, hand them a few copies of the newspaper, and be motioned through the checkpoint. The Americans were unaware that hidden behind the bundles of *Stars and Stripes* were usually escaping SS members.

Once the escapees reached Austria or Switzerland during the early days of *Die Spinne,* when the routes went that way, they had little trouble continuing their journey. They were furnished forged documents prepared by former Skorzeny commandos from Friedenthal who had specialized in such documents during the war. In later years when Wiesenthal questioned an Austrian police officer about his knowledge of the escaping SS members, he readily admitted he knew who they were.

"We couldn't stop them. Their documents were in order and we were glad to get them out of our territory."[4]

Obviously, Skorzeny had an excellent organization, one that became even more efficient as the years passed. At the inception of *Die Spinne* in 1946 at the Karlsfeld hospital, the organization consisted of SS members still imprisoned by the West but who planned to escape. Later, the U.S. 66th Counter Intelligence Corps, Region IV, listed the leading members of the organization as Skorzeny; Hasso von Manteuffel, a tough German commander who had distinguished himself on the eastern front during the war; Helmut Beck, a former Panzer division commander; SS Captain Franz Röstel; Hermann Lauterbacher, formerly a member of Himmler's staff; and others. Röstel obtained a Syrian passport, changed his name to Haddad Said, and directed the escapees from his headquarters in Munich and Lindau. Lauterbacher handled the affairs of *Die Spinne* in Italy, concentrating on overseeing the so-called "monastery route" between Austria and Rome. This route consisted of religious "safe houses" between Austria and Italy and culminated in Collegio Teutonico di Santa Maria dell' Anima in Rome, where Monsignor Alois Hudal, Bishop of Eila, welcomed the escapees. Hudal's reply to those who questioned the morality of a priest helping SS members escape from Germany where they faced trial for war crimes was: "I am neither police nor carabinieri. My Christian duty is to save whoever can be saved."[5]

Shortly after his escape from Darmstadt, Skorzeny visited Italy to check on the efficiency of *Die Spinne* and renew his wartime contacts there. Those who believe Martin Bormann eluded the Russian troops in Berlin during the final days of the Third Reich are convinced that

Skorzeny met with Bormann in Italy at this time. Since Bormann has never been found, dead or alive, this meeting has never been verified. It is known by his own statements after his capture in 1960 by the Israeli secret service that Adolf Eichmann, the SS officer in charge of the destruction of millions of Jews, used the "monastery route" to get out of Germany after the war. So did numerous other infamous Nazi war criminals, and Skorzeny's "inspection" trip satisfied him the route was successful and he owed a debt of gratitude to Hudal for his Christian attitude.

There was an ironic similarity between the *Die Spinne* escape routes and those used by *Bricha,* the Jewish refugee organization that transported Jews to Palestine illegally. It wasn't unusual for the two organizations to have escapees and refugees in the same "safe house" the same night! Isser Berman was in a small inn near Merano one night in the company of six other Jews en route to Italy. Their guide told them to stay quietly on the upper floor of the inn; there were "guests" on the lower floor who did not want to be bothered. Berman, however, had to urinate during the night. Since there were no facilities on the upper floor and he had reached a point where he thought his bladder was going to burst, he slipped down the steps of the inn and went out into the darkness. As he stood near the outside wall of the inn and relieved himself, he became aware that another man nearby was doing the same. They both finished at the same time and walked back into the inn. In the dim light they came face to face.

"I was petrified," Berman said. "The man I had been standing beside in the darkness was an SS staff officer from Auschwitz whom I knew well. Many times he had slapped me or pushed me while I was in the death camp and he had done much worse to others. The very day the camp was liberated, this SS officer had told me I was going to die before nightfall."

Berman and the SS officer looked at each other for several seconds without saying a word then each went his own way.

"I couldn't sleep the remainder of the night," Berman said. "I expected him to come after me at any minute. It wasn't until several weeks later, after I was safe in Italy, that I realized he, too, was escaping from Germany. He probably was as scared as I was."[6]

Skorzeny and his associates later set up a legal arm of *Odessa* just as they had set up *Die Spinne* as the escape arm. The legal arm was known as HIAG, an acronym for *Hilfsgemeinschaft auf Gegenseitigkeit* or

Mutual Aid Association. HIAG used political and financial pressure in the best interests of former SS members. Where did the money come from to finance HIAG, *Odessa, Die Spinne,* and other SS protection organizations? Who financed the neo-Nazi international newspapers such as the *Suchdienst* and *Der Freiwillige?* Where did the large sums of money come from that Skorzeny used to finance his political activities in behalf of the SS members in the Federal Republic of Germany? Schacht's clandestine financial chicanery concealed the sources very well, but the minutes of the meeting of industrialists in Strasbourg in 1944 gave a clear indication of the postwar plan. One section of the minutes states:

> The Party [Bormann] leadership expects that some members will be con-
> victed as war criminals. Thus preparations must now be made to place less
> prominent leaders as "technical experts" in various German key enterprises.
> The Party is ready to supply large amounts of money to those industrialists
> who contribute to the postwar organization abroad. In return, the Party
> demands all financial reserves which have already been transferred abroad
> or may later be transferred, so that after the defeat a strong new Reich can
> be built.

When Bormann disappeared after the war, Skorzeny made certain the industrialists adhered to the 1944 plan. His office in Madrid became the collection agency for *Odessa*. Schacht funneled all the funds he obtained to Skorzeny, who then decided where and how to use the money. In this he was helped by Léon Degrelle. Since a U.S. Treasury Department report, made the year after the war ended, listed 750 different enterprises scattered around Europe, the Mideast, and Central and South America that were financed by Nazi money, Skorzeny and his associates were recipients of huge sums when the postwar repayments began. An East German investigator estimated that at a low rate of return of 5 percent, Skorzeny received at least 83 million deutsche marks within three years.[7]

But this flow of money didn't satisfy Skorzeny. He used several other methods to obtain extra financing for his postwar Nazi cause. Any German in Spain involved in the import-export business had to pay a percentage of his profits to Skorzeny. Blackmail was also used. Dr. Albert Pietzsch of Munich was shocked one day to check his mail and discover he had a letter asking him to collect one million deutsche marks for Operation Skorzeny-Berlin. The letter stated:

For the Operation Skorzeny-Berlin about one million D-mark is still needed, to be ready by December 15. You take over the collection of the highest sum possible for the district of Munich. Pick among our people those who have not suffered too much financially and who above all things are reliable. Obligate everyone to silence with personal word of honor. On November 25 send the money in a little package registered to Gerhard Ponnerewitsch at Wendlingen, Neckar. You are requested not to confide in any one of your relatives.

Long live the Führer[8]

Pietzsch, former president of the *Reichswirtschaftskammer* (Secretary of Economics), at first ignored the letter and was going to throw it away. A friend, however, suggested he turn the letter over to the German police. They wanted nothing to do with the matter, so they promptly gave the letter to the American counterintelligence unit in Munich. When the Americans questioned Pietzsch, he said he had no idea why he had received the letter unless someone was trying to blackmail him.

"Perhaps they think that because I knew Hitler personally I am still an ardent Nazi," the doctor said. "I am not."[9]

A couple of days after he talked with the American intelligence agent Pietzsch received a telephone call from an unknown person asking him if he had received the letter. The caller wouldn't give his name and became aggravated when Pietzsch did not answer his question concerning the letter. Pietzsch later told the American intelligence agents that the caller had to be someone who knew him well because only a few people were aware that he had to make and receive his telephone calls at a neighbor's house. After a great deal of painstaking investigation, agents and police suspected one Hans Gunther Seeger. Brought to the Munich police headquarters for questioning, Seeger quickly admitted he had once belonged to Operation Skorzeny-Berlin but had severed his relationship with the SS organization. He also admitted that it was still in existence. Seeger was finally released for lack of evidence, but the intelligence agents were convinced that Skorzeny was probably blackmailing many Germans who were paying off because they didn't want their past records made public.

Nor did Skorzeny confine his activities to Germany and Spain at this time. One Region IV American counterintelligence report stated that a Dr. Karoly Ney, a Hungarian who had been an ardent Nazi during the Third Reich years, had founded an organization called KABSZ (Comradeship of Eastern Front Fighters) in Hungary under Skorzeny's direction. The KABSZ was very active in behalf of former SS members, as well as Nazis in general, and followed much the same procedure to raise funds as Skorzeny did in Spain. Skorzeny also viewed Ireland as an ideal spot for his operations. When Hitler planned to invade England during the war, he had ordered that a cadre of Irish fighters sympathetic to Germany and the Third Reich be trained by the SS in Germany and then sent back to Ireland to organize an underground movement. This pro-Nazi Irish underground movement was expected to establish airfields for use by the Luftwaffe and to sabotage British harbor installations in Ireland. When Operation Sea Lion, the code name for the planned 1940 invasion of England, was abandoned, so was the plan to form an Irish underground movement. Three years later, in 1943, Skorzeny had sent two Irish parachutists, who were members of his commando unit, to Ireland, but they were captured shortly after they landed. In 1957, however, Skorzeny decided to try again. This time he went to Ireland himself, posing as a man merely seeking a restful spot to live out his remaining days, and bought Martinstown House at Kilcullen in County Kildare. He purchased the estate from a British colonel who had fought in Italy against the German troops but held no grudge. When Dr. Noel Brown of the Irish Parliament learned that Skorzeny was in Ireland, he publicly questioned the propriety of permitting the infamous Nazi to live in the country, declaring that Skorzeny was still a very dangerous man. Skorzeny hastened to vow that all he wanted to do in Ireland was raise sheep and horses and to relax.

The Irish government found itself in a dilemma. Officially it encouraged foreigners to reside in the country—even offering a twenty-five-year tax-free status—in the hope they would bring more prosperity to the financially strapped population. Skorzeny took advantage of this policy and in a few months he had seventy large estates occupied by his associates, including Prince Ernst Heinrich von Sachsen, Alexander von Dörnberg, Albert Schmidt, and others. Dörnberg, former Himmler and Ribbentrop staff member, was Skorzeny's main courier. He made regular trips between his home in Glengariff, Ireland, and Gersfeld, Rhön. Schmidt was his contact man in Dublin, managing the Amsterdam Coffee Bar on South Anne Street as a front. Before long Skorzeny had his "German colony" in Ireland well organized and was ready for business, the same clandestine business he operated in Spain.

The Irish organization was actually meant to be a beachhead of the SS organization for operations in England. Since Skorzeny was banned from England because of his Nazi activities during the Third Reich, Ireland was an ideal spot from which he could conduct business there. But the Irish are a much too independent people to accept one of Hitler's close associates as one of their own and in the end Skorzeny felt their anger in a thousand ways. Political pressure mounted and life became miserable for him. Knowing he could no more change the Irish minds than he could force himself to give up his SS friends, Skorzeny sold his Irish holdings and returned to Madrid. His indirect attack on England from a German base in Ireland was a failure but Skorzeny earlier had launched an assault on one of England's greatest war heroes, Hitler's nemesis, Winston S. Churchill.

Churchill, perhaps more than President Franklin D. Roosevelt and as much as Soviet dictator Joseph Stalin, insisted on the Nazis accepting an unconditional surrender at the end of World War II. The English had taken the brunt of the Luftwaffe during the early years of the war and the V-1 and V-2 during the latter years. British soldiers had endured great hardships; British prisoners had been tortured to death. The SS had been responsible for much of the terror, so when the American officials began releasing Nazi war criminals from prison during the crucial years of the Korean conflict, Churchill was not in agreement. There wasn't much he could do to prevent the Americans, but he told his intimates he would not condone such leniency in England. So when Skorzeny, through his American contacts, insisted that SS Obersturmbannführer Fritz Knöchlein be released, Churchill angrily refused to even consider such an action. The lieutenant colonel had been tried and found guilty of ordering the massacre of approximately 100 British prisoners, in part wounded members of the King's Scots and Norfolk Regiment, on May 27, 1940, near the French village of Le Paradis. The trial, held at the Altona Curie House before a military tribunal, lasted fourteen days and Knöchlein was sentenced to death. Churchill, dismissing Skorzeny's request through the Americans to release Knöchlein, ordered the death sentence carried out. It was.

Skorzeny waited almost a year before he made his move to even the score with Churchill. As he said later, "I decided to wait until an opportune moment, and that moment came when the old man wanted to be reelected to office." [10]

Skorzeny's scheme was simple. According to him, he possessed letters Churchill had written to Benito Mussolini between 1927 and 1944 that were filled with praise for Mussolini's actions against Communism. That Churchill corresponded with Mussolini for nearly five years after the war began was not known to most Englishmen and certainly would not have been condoned, since during these same years thousands of British soldiers were dying at the hands of the fascists.

If he had them how did Skorzeny get the letters? If Skorzeny is to be believed the long trail of the correspondence began on April 25, 1945, when Mussolini departed Milan to make his final stand in the north. Claretta Petacci, his mistress, went with him but his wife stayed behind. Mussolini supposedly left his wife all his documents, including the Churchill letters, which could have been her passport to safety.

"If they try and stop you or harm you," the Duce reportedly told his wife, "ask to be handed over to the English."[11]

According to Skorzeny, however, Mussolini took the letters with him on his flight from Milan. "He never let them out of his sight; they were his political capital, the documents that he expected to weigh the judicial scale in his favor after the war."[12]

Skorzeny explained that when he rescued Mussolini from the Gran Sasso in 1943 Mussolini's briefcase in which the letters were stored was too bulky to squeeze into the overloaded Fiesler *Storch*. The briefcase was turned over to the commandos returning to Friedenthal by regular transport aircraft. As soon as Skorzeny was notified about the contents of the case, he understood the value of the letters sent and received by both Mussolini and Churchill. From that moment Skorzeny had at least one of his SS commandos at Mussolini's side wherever the Duce traveled, keeping his eyes on the letters.

When Mussolini fled Milan on April 25, 1945, he took both of his most valued possessions: his mistress and his Churchill letters. SS *Obersturmführer* Franz Spögler was with Mussolini's party carrying out Skorzeny's orders to keep a constant surveillance on the case containing the Churchill letters without alerting the Duce that he was doing so. Spögler, a young and handsome German, was very friendly with Claretta Petacci and she, in turn, trusted him. When she decided she wanted more clothes to take with her, she had sent Spögler back to Milan with a letter requesting her friends at the Villa Mirabella to give them to him.

"Unbeknownst to Mussolini or his mistress," Skorzeny said, "Spögler also took the Churchill letters. He knew the end was near and he didn't want the partisans to get the letters."[13]

Three days later Mussolini and Claretta Pettaci were executed by Italian partisans near Lake Como, and the Churchill letters disappeared.

After the war the letters—and rumors of the incriminating correspondence—became the object of worldwide interest. Those who hated Churchill wanted them for blackmail purposes; others believed the letters were invaluable as collectors' items; opposing politicians knew publication of the letters would eliminate Churchill as an opponent in any election; and the Russians wanted to discredit the Western powers by proving that one of their greatest leaders during World War II had documented his admiration for Mussolini in personal letters to the Duce as late as 1944.

In August 1951, as the elections approached in England, Churchill traveled to Venice. Many in his political party thought it was a bad time for Churchill to be out of the country since the election campaign was in full swing but Churchill insisted. Later Skorzeny vowed that he and Churchill met secretly during this trip.

"It was a pleasant meeting," he explained. "We discussed personal business."

Paul Förster, who accompanied Skorzeny, is the only known witness to the meeting that has spoken out. He was more explicit than Skorzeny. "Sir Winston received some wartime items he wanted very badly and in return we received hope that some of our comrades in prison might obtain early releases."

When the Conservatives defeated the Labor Party, which had been in power for six years, Churchill was named prime minister. During the following years orders came from Churchill's office as well as the office of the American high commissioner to open prison doors and release such Nazi prisoners as Gottlob Berger, the SS general who had been sentenced to twenty-five years in prison and served less than two; Hans Lammers, former chief of Hitler's Reich Chancellery, whose twenty-year sentence was rescinded; Paul Körner, state secretary with Göring and former head of the "Hermann Göring Works," a profitable wartime business, was released as was Heinz Jost of the SS security service; Franz Alfred Six, who was Adolf Eichmann's superior; Edmund Veesenmayer, SS comrade of Skorzeny; and others. Kurt Meyer, a general in the Waffen SS who had been sentenced to death for the massacre of Canadian prisoners of war, was released despite the protests of the Canadians. Meyer, as arrogant as ever, went directly to a meeting of the SS after he left prison where he vowed: "We do not intend to stand at the back door, not at the rear entrance which is for messengers and servants. We intend to enter the state through the front door. Yes, my comrades, the Federal Republic is our state."[14]

Despite Skorzeny's contention that most of these Germans were released because of his "deal" with Churchill regarding the Mussolini correspondence, there is no factual evidence to support it. They may have been a factor, of course, but so was the world situation. Many Nazis were released from prison during this period because they were needed to help re-establish German industry or the German military, both of which were needed to offset the Soviet tactics of the time.

Meyer's statement was an exaggeration but it was an indication of Skorzeny's goal. And slowly but surely, he managed to get more and more influence in the very government from which he was a fugitive. When Skorzeny called a meeting of the *Odessa* group on January 25, 1957 to be held at Kronenstrasse 47 in Stuttgart, even Dr. Eugen Gerstenmaier of the Bundestag attended. Gerstenmaier had served in Canaris's espionage unit during the Third Reich and after the war had entered politics. As a prominent member of the government of the Federal Republic of Germany, he looked after the interests of the SS members. He rebuffed every criticism in the Bundestag concerning the SS and led the battle to permit the SS members to join the German army of the Federal Republic of Germany with at least the same rank as they had held in the SS. The measure was passed in 1956, much to the delight of Skorzeny. At the meeting in Stuttgart a year later, Gerstenmaier; Paul Hausser, former right-hand man of the senior Waffen SS general, Sepp Dietrich; Helmut Sundermann; Paul Wegener, a former gauleiter; Werner Naumann, former state secretary in the Ministry of Propaganda; Skorzeny; and other former SS members discussed the agenda, which included:

1. Rehabilitation of the SS and NSDAP
2. Possibilities of a stronger inclusion of National Socialism in Bonn politics[15]

The attitude of those former SS members present at the meeting was expressed by SS *Brigadeführer* Karl Cerff when he said, "We have done nothing which needs to be kept secret or is disreputable, but we have placed value on everything being done discreetly and in confidence because there are things which the press does not need to report."

Cerff also made it clear to Gerstenmaier that whoever in Bonn granted the most concessions to the former SS members would have the votes of the members in the elections. That this statement, in many ways a veiled threat to all German politicians, was understood is verified by later actions of Adenauer's government. Through the efforts of Gerstenmaier, with the backing of many other SS sympathizers in the Bundestag, a measure was passed that all former SS men who had served at least ten years in Himmler's organization would be eligible for a state pension. In appreciation of this measure and others, many former Nazis received the wholehearted support of *Odessa* members at the polls. Willie Stegmann, corps judge of the Waffen SS, became attorney-general in Hamburg and was in a position to decide whether or not to prosecute former SS members for war crimes; Dr. Gerhard Schröder, who served with Schacht during the Third Reich, became Interior Minister in the Bonn government; Kurt-Georg Kiesinger, a Nazi since May 1933, was elected chancellor in 1968; and today many former Nazis have great influence in the West German government because of Skorzeny's *Odessa*.

From his office in Madrid, Skorzeny's influence in the Federal Republic of Germany was duly noted by every chancellor from Adenauer on and the West German government used his worldwide fame and his commando experience to reestablish German prestige and power in other parts of the world. It was on an earlier mission to South America that the secret relationship between Skorzeny and Evita Perón had begun.

16 EVITA AND SKORZENY

In June 1949, not quite a year after Skorzeny had escaped from the German internment camp at Darmstadt, George R. Eckman, acting commander of the 7970th Counter Intelligence Corps, European Command, wrote the American consulate general at Frankfurt that Skorzeny was probably in Argentina.

> Skorzeny's whereabouts have not been known since his escape in 1948. Over the past year, however, a number of reports have been received from various sources indicating that Skorzeny has managed to emigrate illegally to Argentina with the aid of an unknown agency. He is allegedly living there under an alias at present. These reports have originated from a number of sources including international businessmen, residents of the U.S. zone having relatives in Argentina, and former close friends of Skorzeny.[1]

Argentina was a natural place to go for a Nazi on the run, as Skorzeny was in 1949. Evita and Juan Perón ran the country with the same brutal tactics that Hitler had used in Germany during the Third Reich. Why not? Perón had learned his lessons well from both Hitler and Mussolini, and when the fascists were defeated in 1945 he opened the door to those trying to escape. When the U.S. ambassador to Argentina, Spruille Braden, criticized Perón's actions, Perón declared: "Some say that what I am doing follows the policy of Nazism. All I can say is if the Nazis did this, they had the right idea."[2]

But Perón had another reason for offering asylum to the Nazis escaping from defeated Germany after 1945, a reason that few persons were aware of. Skorzeny was one of those persons. He knew about the Perón-Bormann conspiracy that had started a year before the end of the Third Reich. Another principal in the scheme was Evita Maria Duarte, Perón's mistress and later his wife. When Bormann gave the German industrialists tacit approval in 1944 to transfer money, machine tools, specialty steel, and secret blueprints abroad for use after the war, he also set up a plan to assure his personal future in case Germany was defeated. Bormann had discovered in late 1943 that there was a large secret Nazi fund hoarded in the Reichsbank in Berlin, a fund derived from the gold, jewels, and currency taken from Jews killed in the extermination camps. Nearly a hundred shipments were made to the Reichsbank during the last two years of the war and deposited under the fictitious name of "Max Heilger." Dr. Walther Funk, president of the Reichsbank, was in charge of the fund and Skorzeny aided in many of the shipments to the Reichsbank. He was aware that millions of gold marks, pounds sterling, Swiss francs, and dollars, as well as a fortune in platinum, diamonds, and other precious stones were hidden away in the vaults of the Berlin bank.

When Bormann discovered the Reichsbank fund, he recognized an opportunity to accumulate a fortune for himself from the secret fund of the Third Reich. But he also recognized that if the Third Reich collapsed, the secret fund would be confiscated as enemy property. Without Hitler's knowledge, Bormann began playing a two-handed game. Professing undying loyalty to Hitler—and, in fact, he stayed with the Führer until the very end of the Third Reich, more than many of Hitler's other associates did—Bormann, at the same time, began dipping into the secret fund and shipping it out of Germany. He had Dr. Helmut von Hummel, his aide, who in 1945 also hid a quantity of gold for Bormann in the Bavarian Alps, go to the Reichsbank and withdraw money from the secret fund for "party expenses." Over the following twelve months the withdrawals were made periodically and each withdrawal became larger than the previous one. But instead of using the money to cover the expenses of the Nazi party, Bormann, with the help of Skorzeny, shipped the money in armored trucks to ports in southern Spain, where German U-boats were waiting. The money, and later diamonds and other precious stones, were transferred to the U-boats and taken to Argentina.

Why did Bormann feel safe in shipping his ill-gotten fortune to

Argentina? The answer: Juan Perón. The handsome, tall army officer with the jet-black hair and friendly smile, who had been sent to an Andean mountain garrison by his superiors in 1940 to keep him away from the seat of power in Buenos Aires, was an opportunist who always had his palm open when money was mentioned. He was also politically ambitious. While he was at his "Siberian" post in the mountains, Perón formed a political organization called the GOU (United Officers Group) and enlisted most of the officers in the area. Emphasizing his disgust with the conservative government and its corruption, Perón went from army post to army post selling his GOU, while the more sophisticated military elite smiled at his amateurish attempt to gain power, certain that he was doomed to fail. By 1943, however, shortly before Bormann discovered the secret fund in the Reichsbank, Perón had signed up nearly all the 4,000 officers of the Argentine army. While the government headed by President Ramon S. Castillo was still wondering what it should do about Perón's organization, the GOU organized a military coup and ousted Castillo. Perón handpicked General Pedro P. Ramirez as president of the country, but the army was well aware that the power behind the president was Juan Perón. And Perón was profascist, a firm supporter of Hitler.

By 1943 the United States suspected Argentina, and especially Perón, of aiding Nazi Germany despite the fact that it was a neutral country, and applied pressure on the new president to halt German spy activities in Argentina. While Ramirez was publicly denouncing the Nazi spies and ordering their arrest in blustery, dramatic speeches, Perón, behind the scenes, was helping the Nazis set up additional *Abwehr* posts in the country. When Johann Siegfried Becker, one of Canaris's *Abwehr* agents, arrived at Buenos Aires in 1943 after having stowed away aboard the ship *Rita Garcia*, Perón arranged for him to get ashore although Becker had no identity papers. Becker was helped by Perón aides in setting up a spy network in the country and establishing a headquarters in the city. More and more German spies arrived in Argentina with Perón's blessing, but pressure from the United States, in the form of warships in the harbor of Montevideo and the threat to freeze all funds, forced Argentina to sever official diplomatic relations with Germany early in 1944. Under Perón the largest and most elaborate Nazi espionage organization in Latin America was estab-lished, and the suave army colonel won the absolute trust of Bormann. When he sought a place to send the money and other valuables he took from the Reichsbank, Bormann selected Perón as his clandestine treasurer.

Bormann, however, knew little or nothing about Perón's mistress Evita. If he had, he would have given a great deal more thought before putting his personal fortune where she could get her hands on it. Nor did he know that the slender, well-dressed actress, who had learned how to please men in the waterfront dives of Buenos Aires, was at that moment taming the colonel to whom he was sending his fortune. Evita Duarte arrived in Buenos Aires from the country in 1933, when she was fourteen years old. She had no money, no friends, and very little acting or singing talent, but by mid-1943 she was making $1,000 a week, lived in a fashionable apartment on the calle Posadas, and wore clothes ordered from Paris. She still had no acting skill, but she was featured in films and the theater. The key that opened the door to success, Evita discovered, was pleasing men who could, in turn, help her. Actors who could get her film parts, producers who promised her stardom, radio station owners who featured her in soap-opera roles. No bed was too small, no bed too big if, after she did her part, the man under the sheets with her did his. And the one man she decided she wanted to bed down with was Juan Perón. Evita was working for Radio Belgrano in 1943, and every time she appeared on a talk show, the name mentioned most was that of Juan Perón, the strongarm of Argentina. When Radio Belgrano gave a party for the military, she finally met Perón. He was forty-eight, she was twenty-four, but she had learned enough in those years to satisfy a man twice her age, and that is exactly what she did. However, Evita had a decision to make. She had already formed a liaison with one army officer who was a member of the government, Colonel Anibal Imbert, the minister of communications, and the man who controlled all the radio stations in Argentina. Should she give up a sure thing to gamble on a good-looking colonel who wanted to be president of the country? It didn't take her long to make up her mind. She and Perón slipped away from the party together. The following morning she showed up at the radio station in a government limousine. She never left Perón's side again as long as she lived, figuratively speaking. Nor did he want her to leave.

Evita and Perón were married on October 18, 1945, and on June 4, 1946, Perón became the twenty-ninth president of Argentina. Soon both Perón and the public discovered that Evita had no intention of sitting back and acting as the demure first lady of the country while her husband wielded his power. She immediately demanded a piece of the action and got it. She became involved in charity work, feeding and caring for the poor; fought for and obtained the right for women to vote; built a beautiful orphanage; and supported the church. On the other hand, she became involved in seizing nearly $200 million of British holdings in Argentina, became known as the "Woman with the Whip" because of her practice of torturing others, and skimmed funds off the top of the Argentine treasury and deposited them in her own name in Swiss banks. Nor did she change her habit of taming men with sex. There was little wonder that she was fascinated with the Bormann treasure when she learned about it and with the man who came to Argentina to reclaim it, Otto Skorzeny.

Evita first learned about the money being transferred by Bormann from Germany to Argentina from Rudolf Ludwig Freude, a German-Argentine banker who aided Hitler during the war in any way he could. Freude was handling the shipments as they arrived in Buenos Aires, depositing much of the fortune in Banco Alemán. He was assisted by a fomer aide of Schacht, Heinrich Dörge. Evita and Perón were living together at this time, and she was so busy trying to get the colonel to marry her that she ignored the mention of the Bormann gold at first. After her marriage, however, when the subject was mentioned again, she became very interested and soon discovered that she had come upon a "mother lode" of unbelievable value. Using her sex-and-persuasion technique and now backed by the power of the president of Argentina, Evita convinced Freude and Dörge it would be much safer for everyone concerned if the money was deposited in her name until Bormann came for it. Consequently, the treasure was deposited under the name of Evita Duarte in various banks throughout Buenos Aires, including the Banco Germánico, Banco Alemán Transatlántico, Banco Tornquist, and the Banco Alemán. One estimate of the treasure at the end of 1945 was more than $800 million in bank deposits, plus 4,600 carats of diamonds and other precious stones, 90 kilograms of platinum and 2,500 kilograms of gold. Evita Perón had access to it all.

As the weeks passed after the Nazi defeat and Martin Bormann did not show up in Argentina, both Evita and Perón acted as though the money was their own personal fortune. They also took steps to make certain it didn't slip through their fingers. Perón appointed himself alien-property custodian, planning to confiscate the Bormann treasure for himself and his wife. In addition, Evita let both Dörge and Freude, who considered themselves trustees of the Bormann treasure, understand that they had no claim to the money or valuables, and it would be best if they forgot completely about the matter. After being harassed by the police and the military, both men took her advice . . . temporarily.

One man who knew the details of the shipment of the money and valuables to Argentina by Bormann as well as the clandestine investments of German industrialists in South America was in prison awaiting trial before an American military tribunal. Skorzeny, the man who knew the secrets of the Nazi financial camouflage along with Schacht, had learned that Bormann had not been seen since the end of the war. This report only made him chafe more because he was behind bars. And it didn't make him any happier when he learned in 1947 that Evita Perón was on a goodwill trip to Europe, visiting Switzerland, Italy, Spain, France, and Portugal. His *Odessa* associates had briefed him on the Perón regime in Argentina, emphasizing that Evita was the "brains" behind the president, a tough-minded woman who was both greedy and ambitious.

"One report I got at this time," Skorzeny said, "was that the only way she could be softened up was to get into bed with her when she was lonely. After being in prison for several months and not able to get near a woman, I replied that I was an ideal man to soften her up. But what really worried me was her purpose for traveling to Europe. I thought she might be disposing of some Nazi party money deposited in Argentina."[3]

That was the closest Skorzeny ever came to admitting there was such a thing as the Bormann treasure!

While he received no definite information on any financial arrangements Evita might have made on her European trip, Skorzeny did learn through the prison grapevine that she could be very difficult with those who opposed her. When one leading Argentine family who lived part of the year in Paris, the Federico Bembergs, did not give a party in her honor while she was in France, Evita was furious. As soon as she returned to Argentina, Perón's government declared that Bemberg owed $32 million in back taxes and seized Bemberg's holdings in Argentina. Later, when she hinted she wished to visit Great Britain and King George rebuffed her by stating he and his family would be in Scotland during the time of her proposed stay, Evita vowed revenge. Less than a year after her return home, Argentina nationalized the British railroads and other British holdings in the country. Skorzeny was convinced she was a difficult woman with whom to deal, but he was determined to try to get the Bormann funds as soon as he got out of prison.

After his escape in July 1948, Skorzeny's whereabouts were unknown for a considerable time. Not until he established a residence in Madrid and appeared in public again did anyone know where Skorzeny was hiding. Now it appears that he was in Argentina no later than January or February of 1949. Gilberto Rivas, an engineer who lived in Austria during 1937 and 1938 and had met Skorzeny at that time, says that he saw Skorzeny in Buenos Aires early in 1949.

"I first saw him on the last day of January," Rivas explained. "As I got off a plane at the Moron Airport, I saw Skorzeny entering the terminal. I caught up with him and we had a drink and talked over old times. Naturally, I didn't say anything about his escape."[4]

Rivas said that he was often in contact with Skorzeny during the next six years when Skorzeny was in Argentina. "He traveled quite often and sometimes I didn't see him for three or four months. But on the other hand, he spent a great deal of time with the Peróns."

Another Skorzeny acquaintance, Oscar Bracker, verified that Juan Perón and Skorzeny were very friendly from 1949 to 1955. Bracker, a German who had lived in Argentina since 1936 and was pro-Nazi, was on Perón's staff as a financial advisor. After Perón's ouster in 1955, anti-Perónists issued a warrant for Bracker's arrest, based on charges that he had diverted government money to Perón's private bank account in Geneva. Bracker escaped to Paraguay where he lived with other exiled Germans. Because of his intimate association with Juan Perón while Perón was in power, Bracker's description of Skorzeny's maneuvering to reclaim the Bormann treasure is probably the most accurate account available:

"Skorzeny was very, very smart. When he arrived in Argentina in 1949, Perón welcomed him personally because he admired the big commando. Perón considered the Mussolini rescue one of the greatest feats of the war. At the same time, Perón was concerned whether Skorzeny was aware of the Bormann treasure deposited in Argentina. Skorzeny was clever. He never mentioned the money at first. He just tried to establish a good relationship with Perón and explained to Perón how he could help him maintain order in Argentina. Perón was receptive because there was a great deal of unrest in the country."

Bracker explained that Skorzeny trained the Buenos Aires police in

Nazi torture tactics and Gestapo interrogation methods. Perón was so delighted with the results that he insisted that Skorzeny oversee the training of the police in all parts of Argentina.

"But the smartest move Skorzeny made when he arrived in Argentina was to ignore Evita Perón," Bracker said. "Skorzeny was very polite with her, very formal. Evita was the toast of Argentina, perhaps the most notorious woman in all the world, and she wasn't accustomed to being ignored. It made her very angry but Skorzeny pretended not to notice. In my opinion, he was playing a game with her, a damn deadly game. Somehow he had found out that she controlled the Bormann treasure, and if he was going to get his hands on the money, it would have to be through her."[5]

According to Bracker and Rivas, Skorzeny's opportunity to make his move to regain the Nazi funds occurred in July 1949. Through an informant sympathetic to the Nazi cause, Skorzeny was tipped off that two navy officers were planning to murder Evita. The Argentine navy personnel had never forgiven Perón for killing several navy men when he led the military coup in 1943 that forced the ouster of President Castillo. Nor did they like the power and influence Perón had given his wife. They had decided to remove her from the Argentine scene. When Skorzeny was given the details of the plot, he led a police raid on the apartment where the men were living. The police discovered guns, ammunition, a detailed sketch of the Home for Working Women, one of Evita's proudest creations, and a map of the city with various times marked on it. The two naval officers were not in the apartment, however. Skorzeny promptly dismissed the police and went directly to the Casa Rosada, the presidential palace. He was told that Evita was in her office at the Ministry of Labor, a few blocks away. Hurrying there, he arrived just as Evita was leaving the building.

"I was with her," Bracker said. "We were making an inspection of the Home for Working Women so that Evita could decide how much additional money she should donate to the home from the Evita Perón Foundation. I had complained that too much money had been spent on the home already. My god, each bedroom looked like a Hollywood boudoir. There were satin sheets, lovely drapes . . . and these women were supposed to be on charity. Evita wasn't very happy with me, so when she saw Skorzeny she turned her attention to him."

Skorzeny, in a very formal manner according to Bracker, explained that he felt her life was in danger and suggested that she cancel her trip.

"Evita just laughed at him. She said no one in Argentina would want to harm her. When Skorzeny insisted she was a target for assassins, she laughed harder. Finally she invited him to go along, saying he could protect her. He got into the back seat with Evita and me."

As they neared the Home for Working Women Skorzeny suddenly ordered the driver to stop.

"Skorzeny leaped from the limousine, ran into a nearby building and disappeared," Bracker explained. "As I got out of the car to see where he had gone and why, he came back out of the building with two men, directing them at gunpoint toward the limousine. He told me to get on the radio in the car and notify the police."

Skorzeny admitted later to Bracker that he knew exactly where the men were hiding from the map and sketch he had found in the navy men's apartment earlier. In the eyes of Evita, Skorzeny was a hero, the man who had saved her life. He never told her, and she never learned from any other source, that the two would-be-assassins had been captured before her arrival by former SS members Skorzeny had dispatched to the scene after finding the sketch and map in the apartment of the two men. Skorzeny took all the credit for himself. It was the first verified incident that as he got older Skorzeny became less and less involved personally in terroristic and violent incidents, preferring instead to do the planning and let others carry them out.

After the Home for the Working Women incident, Evita and Skorzeny became close friends.

"Very close," Bracker explained. "I know for certain that they often went on two- or three-day trips together, supposedly to inspect various government installations. Actually, they were holed up in one of Evita's secret residences, either near the ocean or high in the mountains. She was fascinated by his reputation, his huge size, and his manliness. He was always interested in beautiful women, and if they had power and influence, so much the better. In Evita's case his interest was much greater because she controlled the Bormann treasure."

The attraction between the pair was not all sexual. Skorzeny showed her how to keep dissidents in the labor unions in line, one of her special responsibilities. He taught the secret police Nazi torture tactics that had proven effective during the Third Reich. Electric prods to the genitals and soles of the feet, whips, chains, freezing water—the same devices and methods used by the SS, SD, and Gestapo in Berlin, Dachau, Auschwitz, and other places during Hitler's reign became common in Argentina. A U.S. Foreign Service dispatch from the U.S.

Embassy in Brazil to the Department of State in Washington reported on the police tactics.

O Cruzeiro, the illustrated weekly magazine owned by Diários Associados, the Chateaubriand newspaper chain, began publication on September 13 of a series of articles written from Montevideo by reporter David Nasser and based on information received by Nasser from Dr. Alberto Caride, exiled Argentine physician and other Argentine exiles in Uruguay.

The fourth article accuses the Perón government of using former Nazis, who have migrated to Argentina as refugees, as instructors in Gestapo methods. This article also gives a list of former figures in the German Nazi party who are alleged now to be in' Buenos Aires, among them Otto Skorzeny, an ex-officer in the Elite Guard, and Ante Pavelic, former Croatian quisling.[6]

By early 1950, according to Bracker and the Reverend Egido Esparza, a Catholic priest who opposed the Perón government, Evita and Juan Perón had given Skorzeny approximately one-fourth of the Bormann treasure, which he immediately funneled back to Madrid for use by *Odessa* and other Nazi groups. Yet, Skorzeny was determined to obtain all of the Nazi money, or at least all of it that was still available. Schacht, through his banking contacts, had learned that Evita Perón and her associates had at least forty numbered Swiss bank accounts. Skorzeny was convinced that many of these accounts, if not all, held Bormann funds. Before he could lure the tough-minded Evita into divulging more information about the Nazi money, however, she became ill of cancer and died on July 26, 1952. Her will left her jewels to the poor and all else to Perón. But Juan Perón had a problem. Many of Evita's assets were tied up in foundations and organizations over which her cronies had control. Perón had to act quickly if he was to get his hands on this money. He asked Skorzeny to help.

Skorzeny's first move was to obtain the estimated $100 million in assets of the Evita Perón Foundation. When Evita's former associates in the foundation formed a group, the Association of Friends of Evita Perón, to administer the fund immediately after her death, Skorzeny advised Perón to use his influence as president of Argentina to outflank them. He had Perón announce that he was taking control of the Evita Perón Foundation and all its assets. When Evita's cronies protested, Skorzeny's Nazi-trained Argentine secret police moved in and backed up Perón's claim. The Association of Friends of Evita Perón gave up the fight and disbanded.

Another problem faced by Skorzeny on Perón's behalf was Juan Duarte, Evita's brother who had become the richest bachelor in Argentina through his sister's protection and who now was claiming half of Evita's fortune. Under Argentine law, he had a claim, since a wife's estate was to be divided equally between her husband and her family. Since her Swiss bank accounts held several hundred million dollars and her jewels were estimated to be worth $30 million more, Juan Duarte became a serious threat to the Bormann funds, which Skorzeny was determined to reclaim. The fact that Evita's will had donated her jewelry to the poor was ignored by both parties. A visit to Duarte's lavish country estate, which was always inhabited by beautiful film starlets, by Skorzeny and several of his former SS members residing in Argentina convinced Duarte it would be best for his future health to cooperate with his brother-in-law in the disposal of his sister's fortune. Skorzeny had to be discreet because he had learned through his Nazi grapevine that Juan Duarte had been Evita's courier between Argentina and Switzerland. For a three-year period Duarte had been responsible for delivering an estimated $20 million and several suitcases full of jewelry to a bank vault in Zurich in addition to other monies deposited in her Swiss bank accounts. Before anything happened to Duarte personally, Skorzeny needed the key to the vault or documentation from Duarte which would permit him access to the vault.

Shortly after Skorzeny's visit to Juan Duarte, Evita's brother traveled to France and Switzerland. In Paris he was his usual playboy self, squiring beautiful women to clubs and restaurants, staying at the Ritz, and, in general, acting as though he had more money than he knew what to do with. In Switzerland, however, he was more subdued, more serious. He signed the necessary documents that gave Perón access to Evita's money and jewels hidden in a bank vault in Zurich, as well as to the Swiss bank accounts in her name. It was the same as signing his own death warrant. As soon as Duarte returned to Argentina, Perón, at the urging of Skorzeny, forced Duarte to resign from his government posts, accusing him of corruption and involvement with the members of a black market ring. In addition, Skorzeny learned from Maliza Zini, an actress whom he knew, that while Duarte was in Paris he had sold a large part of Evita's jewel collection. To the former Nazi commando chief this was the same as stealing money from the Nazi treasury.

Duarte, wise to the ways of both the Nazis and the Argentine dictator, tried to run, but everywhere he went the police were waiting or former SS members were watching for him. On the morning of April 9, 1953, Duarte was found stretched across his bed in the apartment he often used in Buenos Aires when entertaining starlets. He was dead, a .45-caliber bullet in his head. Officially, the cause of death was suicide; unofficially, another victim had been added to the long list attributed to Skorzeny, except this time he was collaborating with Juan Perón instead of Adolf Hitler.

Nor was the death of Juan Duarte the only one connected with the Bormann treasure and Skorzeny's determination to reclaim it after Bormann disappeared. Heinrich Dörge, the former aide of Schacht who had helped Evita conceal the Bormann funds as they arrived from Germany, made the error of thinking he could get a share of the treasure for himself. He was found dead on a street in Buenos Aires, and no official reason for his death was ever announced. Freude, the banker with Nazi sympathies during the Third Reich years but anti-Skorzeny sympathies after the Third Reich collapsed, had two problems. He knew too much about the Bormann funds and their intended use, and he expressed a firm desire to control the ultimate disposition of the fortune. His involvement with the Nazi money and jewels ended abruptly when he drank a cup of poisoned coffee. According to the Argentine authorities, it was never learned how the poison got into Freude's cup!

It soon became evident to Skorzeny and others that the death of Evita Perón had sounded the death knell for the Perón regime. Juan Perón quickly lost the loyalty of the *descamisados* (the shirtless ones) who, through Evita's efforts, had elected Perón president. He spent more time fondling young girls than he did handling government documents. Skorzeny, predicting a quick downfall for Perón, made certain that the Bormann funds, now in Perón's control, were transferred to European banks to which he, too, had access.

But there was another matter Skorzeny had to take care of before Perón lost his control of the Argentine government, and that was the Nazi funds invested in German-controlled industry in the country, an investment that was to be repaid generously after the war. One Nazi deal was an indirect "investment" by German industrialist Dr. Fritz Thyssen. Thyssen was an early supporter of Hitler. He had given the Führer millions of dollars and had personally joined the Nazi party as early as 1931, but he later became completely disgusted with Hitler's actions. He made the mistake of writing Hitler a letter in 1940 explaining his feelings and shortly found himself in a concentration camp. Bormann, recognizing a financial opportunity, negotiated a deal with Thyssen whereby for a sum reported to be over $1 million—how much more has never been determined—Thyssen and his wife would not be put to death. Hitler, of course, was completely unaware of the deal and Bormann had to keep the details secret. He extracted a promise from Thyssen that the ransom would be payable after the war. When the German industrialist was released from the concentration camp in 1945, he went to Argentina with his family, completely ignoring his deal with Bormann when Hitler's right-hand man disappeared during the last days of the Third Reich, not realizing that Skorzeny knew about the agreement. When Thyssen was approached by Skorzeny, he shrugged his shoulders and explained that he had no money, that the Argentine government had impounded his fortune under the Alien Property law. Thyssen was convinced that in later years he would regain the fortune and the Nazis would never get their hands on a penny of it. He didn't reckon with the influence of Skorzeny, however, who soon had Perón release the Thyssen fortune. Thyssen paid, and paid well, for his protection while in the concentration camp, although the exact sum was never revealed. Whatever it was, it was added to the coffers of *Odessa* and Skorzeny's other Nazi-dominated organizations.

The Krupp deal was somewhat different. Hitler had made concessions to Dr. Gustav Krupp for various reasons: he needed the war weapons produced by Krupp; he needed the influence Krupp could exert over other German industrialists; and he needed Krupp's cooperation in handling the workers, many of whom were forced to labor in the plants by the Nazi government. Bormann, monitoring the Krupp dynasty and the fortune piling up, decided that Krupp should not only pay a considerable fee to the Nazi party for his favored position but also to Bormann's personal bank account for the help he provided as Hitler's private secretary. He patiently waited for the right moment to present his demands and found it when Krupp asked him to help get a new law passed under which he could will his dynasty to his son, Alfried. Under a German law passed in 1920 the "line of succession" inheritance was illegal. Bormann agreed with the understanding that he would be well compensated later. The law was passed—actually it was a directive from Hitler—on November 12, 1943. And as the Perón regime wound down in Argentina, Skorzeny collected the funds promised Bormann for his aid in convincing Hitler to issue the directive. It wasn't difficult. Skorzeny was already serving as liaison officer between his friend Alfried Krupp and Perón regarding the huge Krupp assets in Argentina. He spent a great deal of time at the Krupp ranch, the Rancho Grande, in the Province of Salta, when he was in Argentina, so it was a simple (but secret) matter to have the funds transferred from the Krupp accounts to an account available to Skorzeny.

There was one embarrassing incident involving Krupp and Skorzeny, an incident that revealed to the public the still-close connection between German industry and former Nazi officers. In 1954, the Argentine newspaper *Epoca* published a photograph of Perón greeting representatives of the Krupp firm. One of the men in the photograph was Otto Skorzeny! His height, his face, his scar, made identification positive despite his use of an alias. The Krupp office in Buenos Aires issued a statement explaining that "Skorzeny was in Argentina for the Krupp firm to carry out a special task unknown to the Krupp office in Buenos Aires."[7] A few hours later the Essen headquarters of the firm stated: "Skorzeny has no relationship with the firm."[8]

Skorzeny's activities in Argentina were seriously impeded by the publication of the photograph, but he was already preparing to return to his residence in Spain anyway. The Perón regime was nearing its end. Although Perón still controlled part of the military and the Skorzeny-trained secret police, his opponents were getting stronger and stronger. In September 1955, with his government in a complete shambles, Perón escaped to the safety of a Paraguayan gunboat with the aid of Skorzeny, former SS members, and the Nazi-trained secret police. There was no way Skorzeny was going to permit his enemies to murder Perón as long as Perón still had control of the remainder of the Bormann funds. At this time Skorzeny played his trump card. He arranged for Perón to live in exile in Spain through his intercession with his influential friends in the Franco government. The price? The remainder of the Bormann funds!

17 PYRAMIDS AND NAZIS

If there were any doubts that Skorzeny's allegiance to the United States was of an opportunist nature and temporary, they were dispelled by his actions in Egypt and the Mideast. Even his deep hatred of the Soviets was forgotten when it interfered with his personal ambitions. Egypt presented Skorzeny the opportunity to promote fascism; to establish a Nazi clique whose influence would be felt by the West German government, to restore German prestige in the Mideast, and to become a wealthy man. He didn't allow the opportunity to pass. It was no wonder Gilberto Rivas didn't see him for three or four months at a time in Argentina during the Perón regime. Skorzeny was also spending a great deal of time in Egypt.

King Farouk, who ruled Egypt during the Third Reich years, was pro-Nazi, even though his country was occupied by the British. When the Germans and Italians were threatening to capture Cairo in 1942, Farouk had been forced by the British to dismiss a pro-Nazi prime minister, but this did not stop his clandestine cooperation with Hitler. After the war, the king made his anti-Western feelings public, and in October 1951, denounced the country's 1936 treaty with Great Britain which permitted the British to station military forces in the Suez Canal zone. The resulting rioting and anti-American and anti-British feelings among the Egyptians convinced the United States and England that Farouk had to be replaced. The CIA, under the influence of Allen Dulles, selected Egyptian army General Mohammed Naguib to head the government. He was a soldier with an impeccable military record and a man who would take suggestions from the Western countries. Unfortunately, the CIA didn't realize that the real power in the Egyptian army was a lieutenant colonel named Gamal Abdel Nasser. Nasser hated the British. The scar on his forehead was a vivid reminder of his 1935 demonstration march against British rule when he was clubbed on the head by Egyptian police and British troops. He had formed an organization of junior officers in the Egyptian army who had a like hatred of the British, an organization known as the Free Officers Corps. By 1952 Nasser's group numbered 750 members and, in addition, he had the support of the Egyptian Communists and the Moslem Brotherhood, a fanatical religious group. Yet, Dulles and the CIA ignored Nasser as a hothead with little or no influence, and mistakenly placed all their bets on Naguib.

On Wednesday, July 22, 1952, with the help of the CIA, Naguib sent the Egyptian army into the streets of Cairo and Alexandria, proclaimed himself commander-in-chief of the military forces, and challenged King Farouk to oppose him. Three days later, when Farouk refused to give up his power to dissolve Parliament and appoint prime ministers, Naguib ordered his troops to encircle the summer palace where the king was staying. While the soldiers kept Farouk's personal bodyguard under control, he marched inside and gave the king six hours to get out of Egypt. Farouk was on his royal yacht sailing away from the country long before the deadline.

The takeover of the country by Naguib, with Nasser playing the role of a shadowy dictator in the background, opened the door wide for the three silent conspirators of Hitler's regime: Gehlen, Schacht, and Skorzeny. As Gehlen stated in his memoirs: "We found Arab countries particularly willing to embrace Germans with an ostensibly 'Nazi' past." [1] And Naguib was quick to ask for help. Since his revolt had the backing of the CIA and he was aware that Gehlen was collaborating with the U.S. intelligence agency, his request for someone to train his security forces went to Pullach, Gehlen's headquarters south of Munich. Gehlen and Schacht were in complete agreement that the man for the job was Otto Skorzeny. Dulles, aware of Skorzeny's anti-Soviet role during the immediate postwar years when the Western nations desperately needed help, concurred. Skorzeny went to Egypt as Naguib's military advisor. It was a decision the United States would regret in later years.

There was, of course, another reason former Nazis were quick to accept the Egyptian invitation. It once again pitted them against the Jews and the newly established Israeli nation. As the *Jüdische Rundschau* stated in 1951: "As for Skorzeny's anti-Semitic and fascist propensities, this is undoubtedly true. Skorzeny readily admits his strong anti-Semitism."[2] Gehlen, too, had reservations about the relationship between the new West German government and Israel.

"I have always regarded it as something of a tragedy that West Germany was inevitably dragged into an alliance with the state of Israel against the Arab countries," he stated in his memoirs. "I always regarded their [Arabs] traditional friendship for Germany as of immense value for our national reconstruction. And at the request of Allen Dulles and the CIA, we at Pullach did our best to inject life and expertise into the Egyptian secret service, supplying them with the former SS officers I have mentioned."[3]

If there was any doubt that Naguib was pro-German, his public statements cleared up the misunderstanding. "I want you to believe me when I say that I have not changed the great admiration I have for the Germans. Their efficiency, their extraordinary gifts as scientists and technicians, and their loyalty are quite unique. I have been noticing all these qualities in recent times, watching the work of the German officers and experts in my army."[4]

Dr. Noureddine Tarraf, one of Naguib's most important supporters and later Minister of Health, was even more explicit when speaking of the Germans, particularly the Nazis.

"Hitler is the man of my life. The German dictator had been an ideal leader who dedicated his life to the realization of his noble ambition. He never lived for himself but for Germany and the German people. I have always wished to live like him."[5]

Skorzeny felt at ease among Egyptian officials with this attitude. His first task was to organize a staff of former SS and Wehrmacht officers to train the Egyptian army and security forces. He selected carefully, making certain that each officer he brought to Egypt was a diehard Nazi, an expert military tactician, and was anti-Semitic. Among those recruited by Skorzeny were SS General Oskar Dirlewanger, who had commanded a brigade composed of poachers, criminals, and men under the sentence of court-martial during the Warsaw ghetto uprising and whose actions against the Jews had earned him the nickname "Butcher of Warsaw"; SS Colonel Adolf Eichmann, the officer Himmler charged with the destruction of millions of Jews and who later would be kidnapped from Argentina by the Israeli secret service and smuggled back to Israel to stand trial; SS General Wilhelm Farmbacher; Panzer General Oskar Munzel; Leopold Gleim, former chief of Hitler's personal guard and Gestapo security chief of German-occupied Poland; and Joachim Daemling, former chief of the Gestapo in Düsseldorf. To handle medical problems, Skorzeny recruited Dr. Hans Eisele, who had been chief medical officer at Buchenwald concentration camp, and Heinrich Willermann, former medical director at Dachau.

U.S. officials, many of them unaware that Allen Dulles had encouraged Gehlen to provide Naguib with German military advisers, became worried when so many infamous Nazi officers appeared in Egypt. Even Dulles became concerned when it was reported to him that Skorzeny was meeting often with Gamal Abdel Nasser, the Egyptian army lieutenant colonel who seemed to be giving more orders than Naguib. A secret letter, Embassy Dispatch 2276, from Jefferson Caffery of the U.S. Embassy in Cairo to the Department of State in Washington, indicates that inquiries concerning Skorzeny's activities in Egypt were being conducted.

On June 14 the local press announced that Otto Skorzeny had an hour's interview with Gamal Abdel Nasser on June 12. Aside from recalling that he was in charge of the special commando unit which kidnapped Mussolini and pointing out his experience in the training of commandos, the press gave no further details.

The Counselor of the German Embassy states that he and his colleagues had no previous information concerning the visit. They are trying now through contacts among the German Military Mission to find out what Skorzeny is up to. The German Counselor remarked that it was difficult to keep track of this individual because he resides in Spain but the German Embassy knew that when he was here the last time, four or five months ago, he talked to the Egyptians about the supplying of small arms and the training of commandos.

On the general subject of the activities of German officers in Egypt, the German Counselor said that a foreign office official came to Egypt recently to investigate them following Sir Winston Churchill's speech in which he mentioned their activities. Working in close cooperation with the British Embassy, this official was unable to turn up any evidence concerning illegal activities by the German military experts. Moreover, he and British

Minister Creswell agreed that it was better to let the present group of experts remain here since the overwhelming majority of them were doing a straightforward and legitimate job rather than advise them to leave. They made this decision because they believed that persons like Skorzeny would have no difficulty in replacing them with 100 or 200 former SS officers with whom the Embassy would have no contact and over whom it would have no control.

According to the German Counselor, Skorzeny visited Dr. Wilhelm Voss before seeing Nasser. The German military experts here immediately sent a written protest to Voss objecting to his having received Skorzeny. Voss replied that he agreed that it was undesirable but that he only accepted Skorzeny's request to see him in order to tell him to keep out of the commando business and to leave the country.[6]

This secret dispatch and others that followed from Egypt indicate that U.S. officials and even CIA agents were woefully unaware of what the Nazis were *really* doing in Egypt. The Adenauer government was well aware of Skorzeny's presence in Egypt and condoned his actions in behalf of the new Federal Republic of Germany. The pretended "ignorance" of the German Counselor was merely a face-saving move and an effort to deceive the U.S. Embassy. As for the statement by Voss that he told Skorzeny to stay out of the commando business and leave the country, nothing could be further from reality. Skorzeny was already training an Arab foreign legion in commando tactics. This secret unit was comprised of 400 former Nazis and Gestapo veterans and used a training base at Bilbeis in the Delta. He also helped organize and train the first Palestine terrorists and planned their initial forays into Israel by way of the Gaza Strip about 1953–1954. Voss was aware, too, that Skorzeny had no intention of leaving Egypt except for his periodic trips to Argentina and other countries where *Odessa* had business and political interests and to his home base in Madrid.

Who was Wilhelm Voss and why did the official West German ambassador to Egypt, Dr. Gunther Pawelke, later resign in anger protesting that the Adenauer government had more confidence and cooperated more with Voss and Skorzeny than it did with its own official representative? Voss was a former director of the Skoda arms complex in Czechoslovakia and was very knowledgeable about the operation of steel mills. Naguib invited him to Egypt to oversee a new special weapons factory being opened in the suburbs of Cairo, the

Helwan complex, and a Demag steel mill constructed in the same area. Voss, working with Gehlen, Skorzeny, and Schacht, soon wove a web of intrigue that increased Germany's trade with Egypt, which was very profitable not only for the new Federal Republic of Germany but for himself, Skorzeny, and Schacht as well. Voss and Skorzeny channeled their export-import business through the H.S. Lucht firm in Düsseldorf, which was directed by another former SS official, Werner Naumann. Naumann at one time was secretary of state in the Gestapo, working directly under Heinrich Himmler. Naturally, the firm's business and financial transactions passed through Schacht's bank in Düsseldorf so he, too, could reap his share of the monetary rewards. The profits were excellent. Skorzeny sold Egypt several hundred 1942-model German machine guns he had secretly obtained in Germany after the end of the war. He acted as go-between in a $3½ million sale of military equipment by Franco to Egypt and participated in many other deals involving both arms and vitally needed industrial and consumer products. The sale of arms to Egypt particularly concerned Great Britain and the U.S., since the anti-Semitic feelings of both Naguib and Skorzeny were well known. Washington and London, committed to defending the new nation of Israel but at the same time wanting to protect their military and political interests in the Mideast, tried to learn more about the H.S. Lucht firm which Skorzeny was using as a "front." It was a difficult task. One report stated: "Skorzeny carries on great activities and is tied up with half the world. Officially, he figures as the representative of German machine tool factories and is also export-import manager of a Düsseldorf firm, H.S. Lucht. These jobs serve as a pretext to cover his numerous movements."[7]

Another worry to the Western powers at this time was the evidence that Skorzeny, despite his hatred for the Soviets, was now in touch with contacts behind the Iron Curtain. The CIA had known for some time that Skorzeny had a special employment unit established in Leipzig, East Germany, with the full knowledge of Moscow, to recruit military technicians for Egypt. Then, during the investigation of the H.S. Lucht firm, it was also discovered that the Frank Gallati whom Skorzeny's wife had been seen visiting in Düsseldorf was in charge of the foreign department of the Otto Wolff Company, a firm very interested in trading with East German companies and other firms behind the Iron Curtain. It was also learned that Otto Wolff von Amerengen, one of the firm's owners, was chairman of the Russian committee of the *Ost-Ausschuss* (Eastern committee) of the Federal German Industry Association. Gehlen assured the CIA that Skorzeny was devoted to keeping the Soviets out of the Mideast, but by this time even Gehlen's organization was suspected of having several Soviet agents who had infiltrated his espionage net during the past several years. With vital military bases and control of the oil fields of the Mideast at stake, the investigation of Skorzeny's activities in Egypt was stepped up.

On February 27, 1953, a young man claiming to be a former Waffen SS officer who had been living in Argentina since the end of the war visited the U.S. consulate general's office in Marseille. He told the consul, J. Roland Jacobs, that he was unhappy with the actions of his former SS comrades and wanted to give the consul some information. Jacobs listened bemusedly at first as the young SS officer, who would not give his true name but used the pseudonym "Kluf," told about the secret organization of former SS officers and their activities. The consul was well aware of *Odessa* and the other Nazi groups. But, as his report indicates, he became intently interested when Kluf added some new facts about the Nazis.

> Kluf revealed the existence of a secret international organization composed of former SS officers and partially financed by the Soviets. They are supposed to work with the Russians against the Western orbit. He said, in addition, that the organization is presently planning an armed insurrection against American oil companies to begin during the next two or three months in Teheran.

> He said he had been living in Buenos Aires and about two months ago, along with other former SS officers in Argentina, he said he received orders from the organization to return to Germany via Spain. He estimated that 180 persons left Argentina in response to these orders. He said he went to Madrid where he reported to former SS officer Viy who lives in Madrid/Elviso, calle Oria. He said he knows Skorzeny, had served with him during the war. He said Skorzeny had recently returned from a trip to Cairo.

> Kluf said he did not like the Russians and told Skorzeny he was not in favor of working with them. Skorzeny allegedly promised him he could return to Germany to work independently (not for Russia, nor for America, but for Germany) but that Viy gave him different instructions. These were that he, accompanied by a courier from the Russian zone, would return to Germany

and report to the organization's headquarters in Hamburg. Kluf said he was not in accordance with this so he left the courier after crossing the French border and came to the consulate in Marseille.[8]

He also told Jacobs that the SS organization had been receiving financial support from Russia since 1951 and that it also received funds from German industry, including the Princess Isenberg in Munich and the Countess Faber Castell of the large German pencil-manufacturing firm. Another surprising fact that he revealed was that Otto Remer, the major who had played a leading role in thwarting the July 20 assassination plot against Hitler and who had founded the neo-Nazi *Sozialistische Reichspartei* (SRP) after the war, was cooperating with the Russians now that his party had been banned in Germany. Jacobs knew that Remer was in Egypt with Skorzeny's SS group.

U.S. authorities, aided by British agents, immediately checked on Kluf's information that two pleasure yachts had left Marseille a few days earlier, carrying SS officers who were specialists in commando tactics and had served with Skorzeny during the Third Reich. Also on board was a large supply of weapons, mostly pistols of Belgian manufacture individually packed in aluminum boxes, bought with Soviet funds. No official report was ever made about their findings, but it is known that a ship called the *Astrid,* sailing under a Swedish flag, was stopped and searched. And there were no riots protesting against the American oil companies in Teheran at that time.

Yet, American and British authorities knew that they had been lucky to receive the tip from the German officer who was disillusioned with the Soviets and were able to act upon it in time. With Nasser gaining strength and his Free Officers Corps encompassing most of the Egyptian army officers, the CIA decided to try to win him over to their side, too. Miles Copeland, an agent, contacted Nasser and later reported he had turned over $3 million to him.[9] Later, Kermit Roosevelt became friendly with Nasser and in the next few years was instrumental in convincing Washington to provide $20 million worth of army equipment, mostly personal gear for the soldiers. Behind the "gifts" to Nasser was the CIA's belated appraisal of the colonel which led the intelligence officials to the conclusion that he would soon oust Naguib and take over control of Egypt. His chance to overthrow Naguib came in 1954 and Nasser took it. While making a speech in Alexandria, Nasser was wounded in the shoulder by a would-be assassin. He blamed the attempt on "government plotters" though he knew the gunman was a member of the Moslem Brotherhood, one of his own supporting organizations. With the army backing him, Nasser deposed Naguib, sending him into domestic exile in a luxury apartment, and moved into the royal palace.

With Nasser in firm control of the country, Skorzeny had more influence than ever in Egypt. He had the unlimited support of both Nasser and the Egyptian army. For Nasser's State Security Cadre (SSC) commander he selected Gleim, chief of Hitler's personal guard during the Third Reich. Daemling, the Gestapo chief from Düsseldorf, became Advisor on Special Activities for Nasser. His responsibilities included the Egyptian secret police and the concentration camps at Abu-Sabal and El-Kanater, which were patterned after the Third Reich concentration camp at Dachau. The former chief of the Wehrmacht security division in the Ukraine during World War II, Bernhardt Bender, was chosen to head the Egyptian Security Police, the organization in charge of the prisons. One by one, Skorzeny, Schacht, and Gehlen placed their Nazi associates in positions of responsibility in Nasser's new regime. Yet, though this procedure concerned the Western powers, U.S. and British officials still relied on Skorzeny's deep-rooted hatred of the Soviets to keep the Russians out of the Mideast. Washington and London authorities were convinced they could adequately protect Israel from Nasser and the Nazis while Skorzeny and the Nazis protected Egypt from the Soviets. They underestimated Nasser's three obsessions: build the great Aswan Dam; force the British out of the Suez zone, and eradicate the state of Israel.

The withdrawal of funds for the Aswan Dam in July 1956 by the United States and Great Britain infuriated Nasser, as did the condemnation of the raids by his Nazi-trained Egyptian and Palestinian commandos into the Gaza Strip. While the Western powers waited patiently for Nasser to calm down and take the advice being issued in Washington and London, Nasser turned to the Soviets. In this abrupt about-face he was aided, surprisingly, by Skorzeny. U.S. Embassy Dispatch 2276 revealed that Skorzeny's associate, Wilhelm Voss, was a go-between with the Soviets in behalf of Egypt.

Dr. Voss has been playing a double game since October 1952. Among the group of German military experts closely cooperating with each other are Voss, Skorzeny, Major Mertins, and Colonel Ferchl. The latter was a former member of the German General Staff and curiously enough was liberated by the USSR in 1950. No other members of the German General Staff have been liberated since 1946. Ferchl was employed shortly after his liberation as a military expert in Egypt.

Ferchl and Mertins are in touch with two Russian women. One (married) lives in Port Said and visited Rumania and Bulgaria. The other lives in Cairo. Voss has four Czechs working with him. He pretends these are Sudeten Germans and has asked the German embassy to give them passports (refused).

The German ambassador recently commented: "If we don't get busy we have another Operation Cicero." [10]

Cicero was the German code name for Elias Basna, an Albanian who sold British secrets to members of the German embassy in Ankara, Turkey, during World War II. Now it appeared to the German ambassador in Cairo that Voss, Skorzeny, and their associates were selling out to the Soviets.

Bolstered by the promise of Soviet aid and relying on the Nazi-trained military forces at his disposal, Nasser completely shocked the Western powers by seizing and nationalizing the Suez Canal on July 26, 1956. Three months later Great Britain, Israel, and France attacked Egypt in an effort to regain the canal and their lost prestige. The U.S. State Department was taken by surprise and urged the three Western nations to withdraw from the canal zone but they refused. Caught between its desire to protect the oil fields of the Mideast and its ties with Israel, Great Britain, and France, the United States submitted the question to the United Nations Security Council. What happened next is conjecture, but it is known that a letter was received at the White House from Russian Premier Nikolai A. Bulganin. Unofficial reports state that Bulganin threatened both France and Great Britain with intercontinental rocket attacks unless they withdrew their troops. They did . . . and Nasser and Skorzeny were in a stronger position than previously.

The Soviets continued to send Nasser arms and agreed to underwrite the multimillion-dollar Aswan Dam. Between 1955 and 1966 Russia sent a total of $1.2 billion worth of arms and military equipment to Egypt. Skorzeny made certain he got his share of the profits despite the fact the material was coming from the east not the west. One of his largest and most complicated deals was the swap of $85 million of Russian-made munitions from Czechoslovakia for Egyptian cotton which was sent to Moscow. From this one deal alone, Skorzeny made a small fortune, and there were many other such transactions with the Soviets.

Skorzeny, however, still kept in close contact with influential Germans in the Adenauer government in Bonn, primarily Walter Hallstein and Dr. Herbert Blankenhorn. His dealings with the Soviets were strictly business. His ultimate aim of creating a German-Egyptian dominated bloc that could restore German prestige in the Mideast and help the Federal Republic of Germany gain world status once again was not forgotten. The one stumbling block to the plan, however, was Israel and Skorzeny aided Egypt in every way possible to overcome it. When Israeli agents Dr. Moussa Marzouk and Samuel Azzar were caught in Egypt, Skorzeny urged that they be hanged and they were. Another Israeli agent was found dead in his cell in Cairo's Central Prison, a "suicide" resembling many of the "suicides" that occurred during the Third Reich, aided by Gestapo agents. Skorzeny also supported the Palestinian terrorists and helped train them in commando techniques which they in turn used successfully in behind-the-line missions in Israel. In a plot reminiscent of the assassination plans of the Nazis during the Third Reich, one Palestinian Arab went to Paris with the assignment to kill French President Charles de Gaulle. The plan was canceled when an informer notified the French government, yet it was an indication that in 1961, sixteen years after World War II, Skorzeny still had the same boldness as when he was Hitler's commando chief.

One of Skorzeny's toughest assignments during the postwar years was his protection of German scientists, technicians, and engineers recruited to operate Nasser's special military program. Voss brought the first group to Egypt. As the need for rocket scientists became acute after 1956, when Nasser decided he wanted operational rockets in his military arsenal, a more complex and secret recruitment program was formulated. Want ads about a North African aviation industry appeared in many German newspapers. Answers to the ads, mailed to a post office box in Zurich, were forwarded to Egyptian-born Swiss industrialist Hassan Sayed Kamil for processing, and those qualified were offered positions in Egypt. Among those who accepted the offer were three rocket scientists considered the best in the world: Paul Goercke, Wolfgang Pilz, and Hans Kleinwachter. Altogether an estimated 450

German scientists, engineers, and technicians moved to Egypt. Their pay was excellent, with salaries ranging from $1,000 to $2,500 per month, high for the 1960 era, and many of them lived in air-conditioned penthouses, had expensive sports cars, and belonged to the Heliopolis Sporting Club. But they also had a problem. Mossad, Israel's secret intelligence service, considered the German scientists a serious threat to the nation of Israel. If and when Nasser succeeded in placing operational rockets in his military arsenal, perhaps rockets with nuclear or other unconventional warheads, Egypt would have a distinct advantage in any conflict between the two nations. Mossad agents were sent to harass or, if necessary, to kill the German scientists in Egypt.

Kleinwachter, a short, stocky man who wore glasses and looked more like a college professor than a rocket expert, had his own office complex at Helwan, the city where the missile factory was located. As he was driving home from Helwan to his villa in Heliopolis one evening, he spotted a car parked on the side of the narrow road. One man blocked his way, and when Kleinwachter stopped, the stranger walked to his car, stuck a gun in the window and fired. The bullet ripped a hole in the woolen scarf around the German scientist's neck but missed his throat. Kleinwachter grabbed the barrel of the gun and turned it aside. With his other hand, he grabbed the pistol he always carried in his pocket and fired back. The ambushers fled.

Skorzeny was immediately notified about the attack on the German scientist, and each of the rocket experts was provided with Nazi-trained Egyptian security guards who accompanied them at all times. This helped protect the Germans but the Israeli agents didn't give up. Heinz Krug, a German who owned the Intra-Händel firm, located in the German offices of United Arab Airlines, and who provided materials and patents to the Egyptians, went to lunch one day with a stranger and was never seen again. The young secretary to Wolfgang Pilz was blinded in one eye and had her hearing impaired when she opened a letter that exploded. The letter, of course, was meant for Pilz. Skorzeny retaliated directly and indirectly against the Jewish agents, using the same tactics he had used for Hitler. He convinced Nasser to make life more miserable for the 45,000 Jews remaining in Egypt. When one of the German scientists was attacked or threatened, hostages were taken from the Jewish ghettoes, imprisoned in the Dachau-like concentration camps and tortured by former Gestapo agents. Many synagogues, Jewish schools, and hospitals were closed;

Jewish doctors and other professionals were harassed and sometimes forbidden to continue their work; and even some Jewish property was seized. These actions were reminiscent of the Nazi days in Germany which led to the Holocaust.

Meanwhile, Israeli Security Chief, Isser Harel started an intensive propaganda campaign against the German scientists. He called in editors of the principal Tel Aviv newspapers and gave them classified information so they could write about the activities of the German scientists and their "criminal activities." Articles appeared hinting that Nasser was preparing for atomic, biological, and chemical warfare, and Foreign Minister Golda Meir stated the German scientists in Egypt were working on arms banned by international law because of their hatred of Israel and desire for the destruction of the Jews. The unauthorized propaganda campaign by Harel against the German scientists in Egypt made Premier David Ben-Gurion furious. It jeopardized his good relations with the new German government and his policy that the new government should not be blamed for the actions of the old—or Nazi—government. He forced Harel to resign.

It was a victory for Skorzeny but a short-lived one. At first he was secure in the knowledge that such influential men as the American Averell Harriman, at the time assistant secretary of state, felt the German scientists should remain in Egypt. As Harriman said: "The departure of German scientists from Egypt could lead to their replacement by teams of Soviet scientists able to accomplish the same tasks and would not alter in any way the situation in the Mideast, other than increase Egypt's dependence on the USSR."[11]

But the desire of the Western powers to keep the Soviet influence minimized in Egypt was dealt a severe blow in 1965 when Nasser invited East German President Walter Ulbricht to visit Egypt. The invitation was made under pressure from Moscow. When the Adenauer government protested, Nasser was in no position to withdraw it. He was already too deeply in debt to the Soviets for the Aswan Dam funds and other aid. Consequently, Bonn broke off diplomatic relations with Egypt, cut off all economic aid, and established normal diplomatic relations with Israel. This action put an abrupt end to Skorzeny's activities in Egypt and dealt a death blow to the rocket work at Helwan. But the after effect of the Nazi activity in Egypt, and especially the activities of Skorzeny, is still in evidence in the Mideast today.

18 THE ENFORCER

While Skorzeny roamed the world during the three decades after the end of World War II and exerted considerable influence on various countries through his SS organization, the Nazi hunters were constantly on his trail and the trail of his associates. The best known of the Nazi hunters and the most persistent has been Simon Wiesenthal, but he was not the only one to track down war criminals during the postwar years. The beautiful Beate Klarsfeld, Howard Blum, Tuvia Friedman, Julius Mader, Tony DeVito, and many others less well known have dogged the footsteps of Skorzeny and other Nazi survivors day and night. It has been a secret war, largely unnoticed by the public, that has been in progress in all parts of the world for more than thirty years and will continue for years to come, since the Federal Republic of Germany abolished the statute of limitations that would have made it impossible to prosecute Nazi war criminals after December 31, 1979. To the observer it would seem that the intelligence agencies of the world, plus the dedicated individuals who have spent their lives searching for the Nazi war criminals, would be able to overwhelm their opposition, the former SS members, but this is not the case. Though outnumbered, Skorzeny and the *Odessa* were and are today a slippery, shadowy enemy very difficult to trap and decisively defeat. Battles are lost but so far the war has been won by Nazi war criminals. The "general" who outsmarted and outmaneuvered the Nazi hunters for three decades was Otto Skorzeny.

Wiesenthal, who works from a three-room office at No. 7 Rudolfsplatz in the old part of Vienna, has sought out Nazi war criminals since 1946 and has an outstanding record. During that period he has provided evidence leading to the arrest of more than 1,000 war criminals and is still working on 500 or more cases.

"But recently I was handed a list of names of former SS officers who committed crimes during the Third Reich," he said. "Do you know how many names were on the list? Ninety thousand!"[1]

Yet, Wiesenthal and the others doggedly keep investigating, harassing, and, as in the case of Adolf Eichmann, even use the techniques of James Bond or Skorzeny himself to kidnap a Nazi war criminal. Wiesenthal was a successful Jewish businessman and architect before the Third Reich. The Nazis arrested him and he was shunted through Buchenwald and various other extermination camps for several years, avoiding execution twice by last-minute reprieves. When he finally was released from the Mauthausen death camp in Austria in 1945, he weighed only ninety pounds and had lost most of his relatives in the gas chambers. After his liberation he went to work for the U.S. Army's War Crimes Division and eventually set up his Jewish Documentation Center in Vienna, devoting his time and money to tracking down the Nazi criminals and gathering evidence. It was at this time that he discovered he had formidable opposition in the person of Skorzeny. Skorzeny used legal, illegal, and violent means to thwart the Nazi hunters, to protect his SS associates.

The case of Franz Paul Stangl, the former commander of the Treblinka extermination camp, seemed open-and-shut to Wiesenthal when Stangl was finally located. After all, there was irrefutable evidence that he had been in charge of the execution of at least 400,000 Jews at the camp and had run Treblinka with an iron hand. He was an on-the-spot killer, not one who sat behind a desk and ordered the executions from a distance. But he was a wise murderer, one who sought no limelight or publicity, and was so successful at keeping a low profile that when he was held prisoner in the American camp near Salzburg after the war, little attention was paid him. Consequently, when the opportunity arose at the carelessly guarded Camp Marcus W. Orr, Stangl walked away and with the help of *Odessa* and Skorzeny, went to the Mideast. There he worked with Skorzeny and Gehlen, spending a great deal of time in Syria. Then he moved on to Brazil, where Skorzeny arranged for him to obtain a position in the São Paulo

Volkswagen factory. For twenty years Stangl went about his business as though nothing of a criminal nature had happened at Treblinka, as though the world were ready to let bygones be bygones. Wiesenthal, with the patience and determination that has marked his long and distinguished career, was determined to bring Stangl to trial. He traced Stangl to the quiet residential section of São Paulo named Brooklyn through the cooperation of a cousin of Stangl's who did not like him. There he located Stangl living in a comfortable home with his wife, four children, a Brazilian son-in-law, and a grandson.

It was then Wiesenthal discovered the influence of Skorzeny and his organization of former SS members. Brazilian police would not arrest Stangl, Austrian authorities did not want to extradite him, and the Volkswagen officials refused to believe Stangl was guilty of the crimes charged. Skorzeny was behind all three obstacles, using pro-Nazi contacts in both governments and the plant to shape the attitude expressed about Wiesenthal's exposure of Stangl. Primarily, Skorzeny insisted too many years had passed for such charges to be brought against Stangl. The statute of limitations had elapsed, and there were no witnesses reliable enough, after the passage of so many years, to actually tie Stangl to the executions at Treblinka. Even his SS dossier, which stated Stangl had delivered to Berlin from the camp within the space of a year, 2,800,000 U.S. dollars, 11 million Soviet rubles, 250,000 kilograms of gold wedding rings, 350,000 pounds sterling, and 20 freight cars of women's hair, among other items, didn't impress those authorities determined not to arrest Stangl.

"I started hunting Stangl in 1946, found him in 1964, and it took me three more years before the authorities would act," Wiesenthal said. "Very discouraging."[2]

How much money Skorzeny provided from the treasury of *Odessa* to bribe Brazilian officials, support Austrian politicians, and hire top level lawyers was never revealed, but from 1964 until 1967 the Stangl affair was stalemated. Then Wiesenthal finally got the break he wanted. There was a change in the political situation in the São Paulo state. Roberto Abreu Sodré, an anti-Nazi, was elected governor. When Wiesenthal managed to get Stangl's dossier into Sodré's hands, so the new governor could examine it personally, the battle was won. Stangl was arrested on February 28 by Brazil's secret police and flown to Brasilia a few days later. Skorzeny was aware that there was no extradition treaty between Brazil and Austria. The only way Wiesenthal could get Stangl out of the country was to apply to the Brazilian Supreme Court under the international principle of reciprocity. Skorzeny quickly made certain that all Third Reich SS records referring to Stangl were kept from the Austrian authorities, knowing the Brazilian Supreme Court would not extradite Stangl on the material provided by Wiesenthal alone. When Stangl's case received wide publicity, the Federal Republic of Germany decided that to protect its own image, it, too, should request extradition and did so through the Land Court in Düsseldorf on March 17, 1967. However, members of *Odessa*, through their contacts in Germany, made certain the evidence they supplied the Brazilians was so inconsequential that it was certain the Brazilian authorities would *not* agree to the extradition. Wiesenthal found out about this Skorzeny plot at the last minute and made a hurried trip to the Berlin Document Center, where he was provided with a complete official dossier of Stangl's activities in both the Nazi party and the SS. The dossier reached Brazil in time for the German extradition hearing, but the matter was far from settled.

Poland decided that since Stangl's crimes were committed on Polish soil, he was their man, and sent official evidence of Stangl's actions at Treblinka and a three-man delegation to pick him up and return him to Poland for trial. Skorzeny definitely didn't want the SS prisoner in the hands of the Communists and was willing to make certain Stangl committed "suicide" in his cell before he permitted the Polish delegation to take him from the prison. This step was avoided when suddenly the Brazilian Supreme Court agreed to extradite Stangl to Germany, but attached certain restrictions to the extradition at the urging of Skorzeny and his associates, restrictions which they thought would cause Germany to withdraw their request. The first condition for extradition required that the German court sentence Stangl to a definite number of years in prison, not a vague, indefinite sentence. Secondly, after Stangl completed his term in a German prison and was released, he had to be turned over to the Austrians so they could try him for crimes committed in Austria during the Third Reich. The German officials customarily sentenced Nazi criminals they were forced to prosecute by public opinion to life sentences then released them within a short time, but the Brazilian Supreme Court restrictions made such a move impossible in Stangl's case. Germany promptly dropped all action in the extradition case and Skorzeny seemingly had a victory.

Not quite. The Israelis planted a rumor which was never verified but is believed to have been based on fact) that they intended to kidnap Stangl from Brazil and take him to Israel to stand trial. The rumor was spread on June 15, and the following day Bonn cabled Brazil that they would accept the restrictions placed on the extradition order. Seven days later Stangl was flown to Germany. Skorzeny and *Odessa* fought to keep the German trial of Stangl from starting for three more years, but in 1960 Stangl was found guilty. He died of natural causes in prison, however, before the second restriction could be tested.

"The case of Franz Stangl was a tragedy," Skorzeny said in 1973. "He was a sick man and should never have been sent to prison. Just before he died we had arranged for him to be released within a few weeks so he could receive medical treatment at a clinic in Argentina. We were too late." [3]

No mention was made of the Brazilian Supreme Court restriction, which prohibited an early release for Stangl, nor the condition that if he was released he had to be turned over to the Austrians. The betting was that Stangl actually would have been released after a short prison term, just as so many of his SS comrades had been, and that he would have gone to South America and stayed there. Altogether, from crime to trial, twenty-seven years had elapsed! And the Stangl case was a success. Multiply this one difficult investigation and follow-up action through the trial to actual sentencing by the 90,000 names in Wiesenthal's files, and the complexity of the war between the former Nazis and the Nazi hunters can be appreciated.

Unconscionably long trial delays was another Skorzeny tactic that worked wonders for the Nazis scheduled to stand trial in Germany. By convincing German judges, either by bribes, brotherhood sympathy, or national loyalty, to accept defense excuses for postponements that often delayed cases for a decade or more, Skorzeny managed to keep many former SS members from behind bars. Horst Wagner, an SS member who held a position in Hitler's German Foreign Office and was accused of sending Jews from countries outside the Third Reich to the concentration camps, was arrested in 1958 but German prosecutors took nine years to prepare his case. Just as his trial date of May 1968 approached, the high-priced lawyers of HAIG, the legal arm of *Odessa,* managed to obtain one postponement after another based on ill health. In July 1972, fifteen years after he was arrested, he underwent an eye operation and the trial was called off again. Dr. Horst Schumann, who conducted medical experiments at Auschwitz, was finally extradited from Ghana after a long delay masterminded by Skorzeny. Six years later he had still not been in court because of alleged high blood pressure. Dr. Werner Best was charged with involvement in the death of over 8,000 Poles during the Third Reich but his case was dropped because of "old age." Best was sixty-eight years old when the decision was made.

Another technique used by Skorzeny was to keep the whereabouts of the Nazi criminal hidden. The best known case of a phantom Nazi is the intriguing and mysterious now-I-see-him-now-I-don't situation of Josef Mengele, the elusive Auschwitz concentration camp doctor whose flick of a cane sent new arrivals to instant death. Those he saved usually suffered a worse fate as human guinea pigs for medical experiments. Known as the "Angel of Death," Mengele was responsible for the death of millions in the gas chambers. For more than thirty years Wiesenthal and other Nazi hunters have made him Number One on their most-wanted list of Nazi criminals.

"Mengele was the perfect SS man," Wiesenthal said. "He would smile at pretty girls while he sent them to their death. In front of the Auschwitz crematorium, he was once heard to say 'Here the Jews enter through the door and leave through the chimney.'"[4]

Skorzeny took good care of Mengele after the collapse of the Third Reich not only because he was a former SS man but because Mengele's family was wealthy and influential in Germany. They owned a large farm equipment factory in the Bavarian town of Günzberg and Skorzeny was looking toward the future when such a family could return the favor by helping him. He smuggled Mengele out of Germany with Adolf Eichmann to Rome by an *Odessa* escape route, then moved him to Buenos Aires. As long as Evita Perón was alive Skorzeny had no trouble protecting Mengele, Eichmann, and a large number of former SS members in Argentina. When Evita died and the Perón regime began to fall apart, he moved Mengele to Brazil and then, in 1959, to Paraguay, where President General Alfredo Stroessner, a Nazi supporter, granted Mengele citizenship card No. 809. With the aid of Skorzeny, he became a security advisor to Stroessner in addition to establishing a timber operation near the Paraguay-Brazil border, where he had the option of crossing into Brazil at a moment's notice.

During his South American postwar odyssey, Skorzeny set up a hideout for Nazi war criminals such as Eichmann, Mengele, and others at a farm twenty miles from Asunción, Paraguay. Arvin Krug, a German who was always supplied with money, food, and transportation for the farm, managed the secret hideout. It was extremely well guarded by watchdogs, fences, and armed guards so that the curious and the Nazi hunters couldn't get near the place. When questioned about the farm and about Mengele, Skorzeny just smiled.

"I have stayed at the Krupp ranch in Argentina, a villa in Brazil, a beachhouse in Spain, and perhaps a farm in Paraguay, I don't remember," he said. "As for Mengele, I just know what I read in the newspapers."

"They say you are protecting him," Skorzeny was asked. "Are you?"

The big Austrian shrugged his shoulders. "I am also supposed to be protecting Bormann and sometimes the Israelis say I am hiding Hitler himself. You can't believe everything you hear, you know"[5]

The closest the Nazi hunters came to capturing Mengele was in 1960, when Mengele's companion Eichmann was found living in Buenos Aires. The kidnapping of Eichmann by the Israeli secret police was a great victory for the Nazi hunters and a serious defeat for Skorzeny. For years, ever since Eichmann's escape from Germany in 1945, Skorzeny had "taken care of him." First in Italy, then in Egypt, and finally in Argentina where under the pseudonym of Richard Klements he lived with his family in the San Fernando district of the city. Eichmann was a colorless person even while he was an SS Elite Guard colonel in charge of the section for Jewish affairs under Himmler. In 1960, however, the Mossad checked and rechecked and discovered that Richard Klements was actually Adolf Eichmann. Once they were certain—the final verification came when Klements celebrated his birthday with a party on March 21, the date of Eichmann's birthday—Issel Harel was notified. The agents were ready to liquidate Eichmann and reported to Harel that it would be no problem to do so, but the Mossad chief had other ideas. He ordered them to kidnap Eichmann and bring him back to Israel to stand trial! This, of course, was a much more difficult operation to pull off in Argentina, a country known for its sympathy for the Nazis. And the Mossad was well aware of the capabilities of Skorzeny and *Odessa* to thwart such a kidnapping plan.

Why did Harel want Eichmann to stand trial instead of just die with a bullet from a Mossad agent's gun in his brain? He wanted the public trial so the world would hear and remember the enormity of the crime against humanity instigated by Eichmann and his associates under the orders of Adolf Hitler. Death by a bullet on a street in Buenos Aires would soon be forgotten, while a public trial where the details of the charges against Eichmann could be presented for the world to see, hear, and read would be a record for history. As Michael A. Musmanno, who presided at the trial of Eichmann's battalion leaders in 1948 at Nuremberg, explained: "The loss of any one person can only begin to be measured in the numbing realization by surviving kin and friends that he is gone forever. The extermination, therefore, of one million human beings is beyond one's capacity to feel. One cannot even begin to calculate the full cumulative terror of murder one million times repeated."[6]

Some realization of the horror of the action taken by Eichmann, the inhumanity of man against other human beings, can be felt by understanding his method of operation. In early 1941, for instance, Eichmann was already responsible for the murder of thousands of Jews, but he had a complaint. Too much time was lost and it was much too expensive, according to him, to transport the Jews the great distances between their homes and the death camps. But he had an idea: take the executioners to the Jews! Hitler and Himmler agreed. Eichmann was given permission to organize four *Einsatzgruppen* (Special Action Groups) made up of rifle sharpshooters which would follow German troops into conquered territories in the east and solve the Jewish problem. Moving into a city or town the *Einsatz* commander would summon the prominent Jewish leaders and inform them of plans to resettle them in an area out of the war zone. The Jewish leaders would then order all Jews to assemble at a given point with all their possessions in preparation for moving to the "safe" area. When they arrived at the assembly point, their possessions were confiscated and they were ordered into trucks, which took them to prearranged execution grounds, a wood, usually, where there was an antitank ditch already dug. The Jews were lined up in front of the ditch and shot by the rifle squads. Always resourceful, Eichmann also had a variation on the procedure. He had vans equipped as mobile gas chambers, and some Jews were gassed instead of shot.

This was the man Skorzeny protected for fifteen years and was confident would never be arrested for his actions during the Third Reich. The Israelis had other ideas, and on the night of May 11, 1960, when Eichmann stepped from a bus near his home on Garibaldi Street in Buenos Aires, they were waiting. He was seized by the Mossad squad only a few feet from the front door of his home, bound and gagged, and taken to a hideout in another part of the city. There he was interrogated. He offered no resistance, readily admitted his identity and, among other facts, gave the Mossad agents Mengele's address in Buenos Aires. Agents rushed to the Mengele home but they were too late. Skorzeny, alerted to the fact that Eichmann was missing, sent a warning to Mengele and other Nazis in the city to leave for safer areas immediately. So once again Mengele slipped out of the net the Nazi hunters had been trying to snag him with for years.

Eichmann, however, was hooked for good. On the morning of May 20 he was taken to the airport, smuggled past customs, passport, and security officials and put on an El Al airliner. Twenty-four hours later he was in Israel. The following day Ben-Gurion made a short but shocking announcement in the Knesset:

> I have to announce that a short time ago one of the greatest of Nazi criminals was found by the Israeli secret police. Adolf Eichmann who was responsible together with the Nazi leaders for what they called the "Final Solution of the Jewish Problem"—that is the extermination of six million Jews of Europe.[7]

Shortly after the kidnapping of Eichmann, Skorzeny placed an announcement in the Bonn newspaper *Volunteer* stating:

1. It was reported that I had met Eichmann in Austria in 1949 and helped him on his flight. Both assertions are untrue.
2. It was reported from Israel that I had burned five synagogues in Vienna. This, too, is untrue.
3. According to a report from Tel Aviv, a certain Friedmann was supposed to have said that he would "bag" me like Eichmann. My whereabouts have been known officially for some time. If Friedmann should look me up, I shall receive him appropriately.
4. In other respects I have had nothing to do with the persecuting of the Jews.[8]

However, a few days later Skorzeny held a meeting of *Odessa* leaders from around the world in Beirut, Lebanon, to discuss the impact of the Eichmann kidnapping on other Nazis still at large. They also debated various actions they could take in regard to the upcoming trial of Eichmann. Arrangements were made to provide funds for Eichmann's legal defense, a committee was set up to take care of his family, and a list of officials in Israel and Germany sympathetic to Eichmann was made.

"Skorzeny didn't want Eichmann to reveal the secrets of *Odessa* which he knew," Musmanno said later. "I heard through my contacts in Israel that one option Skorzeny was considering was Eichmann's murder if he began talking too much. That is one of the reasons Eichmann was behind bulletproof glass all the time."[9]

Some of the most dramatic testimony given at the two-month-long trial was that of Musmanno, a non-Jew who had traveled from Pittsburgh, Pennsylvania, to testify. His statement on the witness stand tied Eichmann in with the Jewish massacres more than that of any other witness. When Musmanno related that at Nuremberg Göring, Kaltenbrunner, Ribbentrop, and Hans Frank had all told him personally that Eichmann was at the head of the murder machine which ended the lives of six million men, women, and children, Eichmann was doomed. Skorzeny knew it. He decided to take another propaganda approach to the situation. He resolved to try to convince the world that such trials, including the Nuremberg trials of 1947, were the revenge of the victors on the loser and had no legitimacy. Eichmann, he insisted, was merely a small-minded bureaucrat who was only a cog in the machine. This description by Skorzeny was in conflict with his actual feelings toward the man, but by this time he had written Eichmann off. His efforts were partially successful. Musmanno and Hannah Arendt, the historian and author, became embroiled in a public argument after she had written her account of the Eichmann trial. Many other jurists, historians, and political figures debated the method the Mossad used to get Eichmann to Israel for a trial, a clear violation of Argentine law, and the justification or lack of justification of such a trial so long after the war. The controversy has never ended and today, nearly two decades after Eichmann's capture and trial, some say he was misjudged, misrepresented, misunderstood and, finally, on May 31, 1962, mistreated. On that date he was hanged on the gallows of Ramleh Prison outside Tel Aviv. Skorzeny was proud of his last words. Hailing Germany, Austria, and Argentina, Eichmann declared: "I had to obey the rules of war and my flag. I am ready."[10]

"Adolf Eichmann died as he lived," Skorzeny said, "a brave man."[11]

When they missed Mengele in Buenos Aires the night they kidnapped Eichmann, the Mossad lost their best opportunity to capture the doctor. In 1966, when Paraguay became a member of the United Nations Security Council, Israel dropped all efforts to have Mengele arrested and extradited, trading the "Angel of Death" for the support of Stroessner's government in the council. Wiesenthal, however, never gave up his search for Mengele, and in the summer of 1979, nearly thirty-five years after the end of the Third Reich, he offered a $50,000 reward for information leading to his capture.

Was Skorzeny merely talking when he suggested at the meeting in Beirut in 1960 that it would be best to kill Eichmann rather than permit him to reveal the secrets of *Odessa*? No, he was not. In fact, there are some investigators who believe Skorzeny and the *Odessa* might even have instigated the tip to the Israelis about Eichmann's whereabouts that led to his kidnapping and trial because Eichmann was becoming a liability to them. The bizarre death of another Nazi war criminal living in South America gives credence to this theory. Hubert Cukurs, the SS member known as "The Monster of Riga" because he took a leading part in the massacre of 32,000 Latvian Jews in 1941, was a good friend of Mengele's and saw him quite often. Cukurs lived in Buenos Aires, too, but when Eichmann was kidnapped he quickly abandoned his fashionable home, just as Mengele did, and moved into a bungalow on the shore of Paulista Riviera near Rio de Janeiro. He operated a boat and seaplane concession at the fashionable resort. While it was a profitable business, he didn't make the fortune he wanted. Cukurs often flew other Nazis to various interior areas of Brazil and had a mental list of the war criminals and where they were located. One day he decided he could make his desired fortune by putting that mental list to use, and he selected Josef Mengele to be the fall guy. He knew that Mengele was hiding in Paraguay, across the Parana River from the small Argentine town of El Dorado, so he contacted Jewish agents with a deal. For $150,000 and a guarantee of his own security, he offered to lead them to Mengele. He even suggested a plan to capture the wanted "Angel of Death." Since Mengele's hiding place in Paraguay was near the town of Carlos Antonio Lopez, a haven for Nazis, it would be impossible for the Jewish agents to reach Mengele by a ground route. Cukurs volunteered to fly them to a landing spot on the Parana River near Mengele's home and they could attack from the river side. The agents replied they would take the offer under consideration.

Skorzeny's intricate and efficient network of Nazis in the area discovered Cukurs's scheme before the Jewish agents made their decision. A few days after Cukurs had contacted the Jewish agents, two strangers arrived in Uruguay from Düsseldorf, carrying phony passports identifying them as Heinz Oswald Taussig and Anton Kunzle. The ticket agent at the Lufthansa office said later they spoke German with an Austrian accent. On February 23, 1965, a note arrived at the Associated Press office in Bonn announcing that Hubert Cukurs's body could be found at the Casa Cubertini in Montevideo, Uruguay. A check by Montevideo police, who were notified by cablegram, turned up Cukurs's body in a trunk. He had been tortured and his skull had been crushed. At first the police thought he had been murdered by Jewish agents who had tried to kidnap him, just as they had kidnapped Eichmann five years earlier, but other evidence soon revealed the true story. Cukurs was slain by *Odessa* members who learned he was trying to hand Mengele over to the Israelis for a price. Since Skorzeny controlled *Odessa* he was a prime suspect as the planner of the operation. Interpol, however, refused to investigate the murder because it was believed to be a political killing and Interpol doesn't intervene in political matters. Cukurs's death and the circumstances surrounding it provided ample proof that the Nazi war criminals led by Skorzeny were capable of murdering one of their own if he betrayed their trust.

If any doubt about the brutality of Skorzeny and the *Odessa* members remained, the case of Professor Werner Heyde and Friedrich Tillmann removed it. Heyde, in 1941, was chief of the neurological clinic in Würzburg at the university's medical school. When Hitler decided to enlarge on his euthanasia program to include Jews who had no physical or mental defects, Heyde was one of the men appointed to select the Jews for death. A test group of Jews numbering 285 were removed from Dachau to a mental institution, the Bernberg Institute, and given lethal injections. Hitler considered the test so successful and satisfying that he gave orders for the program to continue. Heyde was one of four psychiatrists chosen to go to the various death camps in Germany, select Jewish inmates, and send them to the "nursing homes." One of his assistants was Tillmann, who provided the necessary ambulances to carry the "patients" from the camps at Dachau, Buchenwald, Auschwitz, or Flössenburg to the "nursing homes" at Bernburg, Sonnenstein, Andernach, Brandenburg, or elsewhere where they were "put to sleep." This was the prelude to the "Final Solution," a test to see whether such a diabolical plan would work or not. It did. Heyde, Tillmann, and their associates killed tens of thousands of Jews under this bogus "mercy killing" program, until Eichmann finally took over and put the extermination process on a production line basis.

As the war neared its end, Heyde and Tillmann escaped from Germany and the advancing U.S. Seventh Army. After a stay in Denmark, Heyde was captured and taken to Frankfurt, where he was imprisoned awaiting trial at Nuremberg. In November 1946, while being transported from Frankfurt to the courtroom at Nuremberg, Heyde escaped from the jeep in which he was riding and disappeared. Actually he slipped into the German city of Plön, assumed the name of Fritz Sawade, and once again built up a lucrative medical practice. In 1959, however, he was arrested during a new drive to round up Nazi war criminals led by Dr. Fritz Bauer, a fifty-two-year-old jurist who had become prosecutor general of the State of Hesse.

Tillmann, meanwhile, had lived in Argentina under the protection of Skorzeny and the *Odessa* until Perón's fall from power. He decided at that time he would probably be safer in Germany and returned to his old haunts. Both he and Heyde were protected in Germany until the determined Dr. Bauer, whom Skorzeny could not influence, decided to bring Heyde to trial. Once Heyde was in prison he began to talk. He gave Bauer information about the *Odessa*, about Skorzeny's activities, addresses of other Nazi war criminals, and the future plans of the survivors of the Third Reich. It was the same as signing his own death warrant. On February 13, 1964, a few days before his trial was to start, Heyde was found hanging by his belt in his cell. He was dead. Only a few hours before Heyde's "suicide," Tillmann fell from an office window eight floors above the streets of Cologne. Accident? Dr. Bauer's only comment was that the deaths were provoked by some people behind the scenes. Most of those persons involved believe Skorzeny could have provided the answers to the reason the two men died and how.

The "feeding and caring" of former SS members by Skorzeny and his associates since the end of the Third Reich has been a marvel of patience, intrigue, and meticulous planning, as well as a display of brutality and terrorism learned under the Führer. Hitler left a legacy of violence to the world; Skorzeny made certain it was preserved.

19 THE FINAL MISSION

In 1973 Skorzeny wrote to an acquaintance: "It is a pity that I have no time at the moment to write a new book, but I have in mind to write one day a book about all the political and military persons I have met. You would be astonished to know all the names of kings, presidents of states, dictators, and fieldmarshals I have known."[1]

Skorzeny never wrote the book and, in fact, never intended to write it. To do so would have meant a betrayal of the principles he had held to all his life: loyalty to those with whom he associated; secrecy about his actions; and silence, except among friends. But there was a more compelling reason for his not writing the book. In 1970 he became seriously ill. His problems began with a sore back which he ignored at first, since his back had bothered him for years, ever since he had been wounded by Russian artillery shells during the early part of the war. After the wounds healed he had felt much better, but two years later, while involved with the rescue of Mussolini, his reconnaissance plane crashed and he reinjured his back. From the time of the plane crash in 1943 until 1970 he suffered recurring back pains. In 1970, however, the pain became so intense that he couldn't walk at times, so he made an appointment to see a doctor in Madrid. The Spanish doctor examined him and shook his head.

"There is nothing seriously wrong with you except you are getting older and have a touch of arthritis," the doctor said. (Skorzeny was 62.) He gave Skorzeny a few pills and sent him home.

The pills had no effect on the pain and for the first time since the end of the Third Reich, Skorzeny felt helpless. The man who had kidnapped a regent, rescued a dictator, and kept the Allied supreme commander locked in his quarters during the Christmas season now couldn't walk to the bathroom to relieve himself. Several other Spanish doctors examined him and shrugged. They agreed with the initial diagnosis: age and arthritis. As Skorzeny's condition worsened his wife became desperate. When she heard that a young German doctor had opened a practice in Madrid, she made an appointment for her husband. The German physician listened to Skorzeny's explanation about how he felt and what the Spanish doctors had told him, then gave Skorzeny a thorough examination. During the examination he took several X rays of Skorzeny's back. When the X rays were developed, the problem the German doctor saw was completely different from the one the Spanish doctors had diagnosed.

"You have a tumor on your spine," he told Skorzeny.

It was grim news. The possibility that the tumor was malignant only made the situation worse. The German doctor told Skorzeny that his only chance of survival was an immediate operation.

"However, you must remember that such an operation is very risky," the physician said. "If your spine is injured during the operation you will be paralyzed."

It was a difficult decision for Skorzeny but Hitler's former commando chief didn't back down when he was faced with his greatest challenge.

"Make the arrangements," he said.[2]

Even making the arrangements for him wasn't easy. The specialist Skorzeny wanted for the operation did his operating at the University Clinic of Hamburg, and even in 1970 Skorzeny had to be careful when he traveled in Germany. Anti-Nazi groups and organizations as well as the small but determined group of Nazi hunters from France, Austria, Israel, and other countries were constantly awaiting an opportunity to repay Skorzeny for his Third Reich and postwar activities. While he often made trips to Germany on business, Skorzeny always was on guard, always planned his routes carefully, and never followed a set routine. This time, however, he would be lying helplessly in a hospital bed and unconscious a large part of the time. The answer to his problem was *Odessa*. His former SS members escorted him to Hamburg and stood guard at the clinic while he was in the operating room and during his recovery period.

While operating the surgeon discovered not one tumor on his spine but two! One on top of the other. This added complication resulted in Skorzeny being paralyzed from the waist down, a seeming catastrophe for a man who had spent his life involved in physical action. In addition, both tumors were malignant.

"I thought he would be so discouraged that he'd just give up," Alois Wirmer said. Wirmer, a former SS member and commando who had spent part of the war with Skorzeny, was one of the security agents who had accompanied him from Madrid to Hamburg. "He certainly surprised me. Within hours after he had regained consciousness, he was hollering for a therapist. He vowed he would walk again."[3]

Skorzeny did. A physical therapy expert who had been a former commando at Friedenthal came to Hamburg and worked with him. It was very slow, tedious, and at times painful work, but within a month Skorzeny had advanced from a shuffle to his first hesitant step. Six months later he was walking again, not with the same speed or confidence as before the operation, but walking. And, of course, involved again with *Odessa*.

He returned to Madrid after finishing his therapy, knowing that the tumors had been cancerous. His actions didn't give the public any indication that his greatest battle had just started. In addition to thwarting the Nazi hunters at every opportunity by providing funds and legal help to former SS members through *Odessa*, Skorzeny's name was linked with a series of mercenary and undercover operations ranging from illegal arms traffic to Africa and the Middle East to an assassination plot against Fidel Castro. But it was all downhill for Otto Skorzeny after the operation in Hamburg. Some days and weeks he felt well, others were painful reminders that the cancer was spreading through his body.

"As close as I was to him," Wirmer said, "he never indicated in any manner that he had cancer. I thought the tumors were benign, that he was recovering. When he had a bad spell he told me he had a cold or the flu or indigestion. I never thought otherwise."

When Hans Bauer, Hitler's personal pilot for years, fell ill in Germany in 1974, Skorzeny made a trip back to visit him. He also attended several meetings of his old SS comrades in Spain, South America, and Germany during this period. Whenever a report was published stating that Martin Bormann had been seen in one country or another, Skorzeny would take time to deny vehemently that the stranger was Bormann. When one writer insinuated that Bormann and Eva Braun, Hitler's mistress, had had an affair, he was furious, insisting that Bormann would not have dared to make any advances toward the

Führer's mistress or he would have been shot. His interest in Bormann never waned, but after keeping Skorzeny under surveillance for years, the Nazi hunters never obtained any hint from him whether Bormann was dead or alive. Many believe Bormann survived the Berlin bunker, escaped to South America, and is still there today, although every clue that has been investigated through the years has failed to produce any verification that he is still alive. Skorzeny played games throughout the postwar years with Bormann's name, first saying he was alive, then saying he died in Berlin in 1945. Was he acting as an agent for Bormann when he obtained the Bormann treasure from Perón? Or did he know that Bormann was dead and was acting in his stead? When asked this question pointblank in 1973 his answer was immediate and decisive.

"Bormann died trying to escape from Berlin," Skorzeny stated. "There is no doubt about that. All the other stories about him over the years are not true."[4]

Of course, this was at the time Germany announced that the remains of Bormann had been dug up near the bridge at Invalidenstrasse in Berlin. Was he hoping that the official German announcement and his own statement would put the Bormann-is-alive rumors to rest once and for all? This would allow Bormann to live out his life in relative peace in South America if he was still alive.

The cancer had sapped Skorzeny's strength so relentlessly that when Juan Perón returned to power in Argentina in 1973, Skorzeny couldn't play a direct role in the new regime. However, he did one last favor for Evita Perón. He made certain that her body was returned to Argentina for proper burial. When she died in 1952, Evita's body was turned over to the Confederation of Labor (CGT), the union organization of bus drivers, truck drivers, wine workers, metal workers, road workers, and other members of the laboring class who idolized her. After Perón's fall from power in 1955, however, her body disappeared from public view and was not seen again by the general public until sixteen years later. Skorzeny had insisted that the Argentine intelligence service, which he had helped organize, take her body from the CGT and protect it from the anti-Perónists who threatened to destroy the corpse. In 1956 he arranged for Evita's body to be shipped to Bonn, where it was hidden in the Argentine Embassy unbeknownst to the ambassador. Later the body was shipped to Rome where the *Odessa*, under Skorzeny's direction, had the corpse buried in a cemetery in Milan under an assumed name. Fifteen years later, after Skorzeny received reports that terrorists in Argentina were on their way to Italy to search for Evita's body, he ordered former SS members to have the coffin dug up, placed in a hearse, and escorted to Madrid. Juan Perón and his new wife, Isabel, took charge of Evita's body, and the casket remained in Spain until after Perón returned to power.

Perón's health was bad, also, and he died on July 1, 1974, as Skorzeny himself was weakening. But with the assistance of Isabel Perón, Skorzeny arranged for Evita's body to be flown from Madrid to Buenos Aires, where she lay in state beside her husband. Later she was laid to rest in Recoleta Cemetery.

Léon Degrelle, Skorzeny's longtime collaborator who lived in Madrid in a luxurious apartment, was close to Skorzeny during these last months. When it became evident that Skorzeny was weakening and couldn't defend Hitler, the Third Reich, and the former SS members as he had during the nearly three decades since the end of the war, Degrelle became more voluble. Still under a death sentence in Belgium but protected in Spain by Skorzeny, Degrelle decided to express his views on a Dutch television show which he knew would be beamed to Belgium. His remarks to the interviewer were supported by Skorzeny, and indicate how Hitler's former commando chief felt despite the fact he knew he was dying.

"I am a racist. I believe in racial purity and I do not want my race to be polluted. The Jews? It is their own fault. They never did want to be true citizens of one country. It is a legend that six million of them were killed."[5]

Degrelle's words, approved by Skorzeny, proved that he was still a dedicated fascist. He praised Hitler and the Third Reich, and stated he was proud of his own actions as Belgium's leading Nazi collaborator during World War II.

"I am only sorry that I didn't succeed, but if I had the chance I would do it all again but much more forcefully."

Shortly after the television interview, Degrelle and Skorzeny were at a memorial service in Madrid to pray for the souls of Hitler and Mussolini, when a former French resistance fighter accosted Skorzeny. Calling him an obscene name, the Frenchman struck Skorzeny across the face. In earlier years, it would have meant the Frenchman's death, but in his deteriorated physical condition Skorzeny could not strike back. Instead, in a voice loud enough for everyone nearby to hear him, Skorzeny said, "I am proud to have served my country and my Führer."[6]

To an acquaintance in the United States who wanted to visit with him in Madrid in early July 1975, Skorzeny wrote in April of that year:

For two weeks I have been in the hospital because during most of the winter I had a fever which would not leave me. Now my doctor forced me into a hospital and they found the reason for the fever and I feel much better. At the same time they gave me a complete check-up which at my age is necessary.

It would be really nice if we could see each other during the summer and I am surely until the twentieth of July in Madrid.[7]

For one final time Otto Skorzeny used the deception that had marked his entire life. He was *not* feeling better. He did *not* stay in Madrid until July 20. He died on July 7, 1975, and, after a cremation service, his ashes were flown to his native Vienna.

Death, however, did not still the controversy about Otto Skorzeny, who believed in speaking his mind, not what he thought others would like to hear. He didn't state, as so many other Nazi survivors did, that he had tried to stop Hitler, that he had tried to lose the war simply to brighten his own image. He always said that he did his best to win, fought to the last second as well as he could—and didn't care who knew it.

To his admirers Otto Skorzeny was a courageous adventurer, a German James Bond who was willing to accept any assignment that involved action and an element of danger; to his foes he was nothing more than a violent, brutal Nazi who had a long string of luck until cancer cut him down. Some called him the "cloak-and-dagger" man of the Third Reich, the master of ambush, the crazy raider who was not afraid of death. Others vow he was a rather simple-minded, dangerous Nazi officer who was willing to kidnap and murder for Hitler. Each opinion is partly true and each is partly false. But one fact is certain: Skorzeny's actions during and after the Third Reich had a serious impact on history, perhaps second only to that of Adolf Hitler, although he was not nearly as well known. Hitler set policy during the Third Reich but he had to depend upon others to carry these policies out. Otherwise the effect of his decrees and policies would not have been important. Skorzeny was Hitler's choice for shouldering the responsibility of commando terrorism. Hitler set policy for twelve years; Skorzeny committed, planned, and taught others terroristic actions for those twelve years plus thirty additional years. It was Skorzeny who was responsible for the continuity of Nazi terrorism during the postwar years and for the extension of Hitler's Third Reich policies around the globe.

It has become evident during recent years that major wars in this nuclear age will be fewer than in the past but individual and group terrorism will increase steadily. Skorzeny and his commandos during the Third Reich and Skorzeny and his *Odessa* members during the postwar years were leaders in modern day terroristic tactics. Skorzeny's followers and students adhere to his teachings today. The students in Teheran, when they stormed the American embassy in 1979 and held U.S. employees hostage, used a technique that Skorzeny used in Hungary during World War II, when he stormed the Burgberg in Budapest and held the Hungarian regent Admiral Milós Horthy hostage. The legendary Entebbe raid by the Israelis in 1976 brought back memories of Skorzeny's rescue of Mussolini thirty-three years earlier. Secrecy, derring-do, and surprise brought the more than two hundred hostages out of Uganda just as it brought Mussolini off the peak of the Gran Sasso. The kidnapping and murder of former Italian prime minister Aldo Moro in 1978 was reminiscent of the fate of Hubert Cukurs in South America when Cukurs broke the unwritten law of secrecy of the *Odessa* and revealed the hiding place of Josef Mengele.

These and similar incidents of violence and terror have roots in the Skorzeny technique. A quick rundown of the major terrorist and guerrilla organizations which use commando tactics today reveal that Skorzeny was directly or indirectly involved with most. The IRA? Skorzeny spent considerable time in Ireland during the postwar years, advising the leaders of this organization, and many of their actions follow Skorzeny-pioneered tactics. The PLO? Skorzeny advised both the Al Fatah and PLO while he was in Cairo involved with the Nasser regime and was well acquainted with Yassir Arafat. The Baader-Meinhof group, despite having a different ideological approach to the world situation, benefitted by adopting several Skorzeny techniques, such as kidnapping and political disruption. The Black Liberation Army, the Symbionese Liberation Army, and the Weather Underground took encouragement from the Third Reich techniques of Hitler's commando chief and copied them, consciously or unconsciously when the situation was similar.

The violence and brutality of Skorzeny's actions during the Hitler era have been well documented and are known throughout the world. In the long run, however, it is his clandestine activities with *Odessa* after the Third Reich collapsed that has had the greatest effect and will continue to do so in the future. His determination not to allow the members of the SS to forget their oaths of allegiance to Hitler and the

Führer's principles and his ability to organize them into a smooth functioning, efficient group was his master stroke. *Odessa* is undoubtedly one of the most dangerous threats to man's freedom today. The organization's low-profile approach is successful and the surreptitious manner in which the members of *Odessa* gain their objectives usually is unnoticed by the public. Seldom do the former SS members leave their calling card or brag about their achievements as many other terrorist organizations do. In fact, when the six-year-old Renault belonging to Nazi hunter Beate Klarsfeld was blown apart on July 5, 1979, in Paris, the public was amazed when *Odessa* claimed credit for the bombing. Usually there is only silence. Nor, of course, is there any public jubilation in evidence when Skorzeny's *Odessa* manages to get another member elected to office or appointed to a high position in the German government.

It is in the political realm that Skorzeny's contribution to neo-Nazism may pay off the best. His *Odessa* members, by contributing funds, pressuring other Germans, campaigning, and voting, have managed to place many ex-Nazis in influential positions in West Germany. Naturally, not all ex-Nazis adhere to the policies or principles of Hitler or the method of enforcing them used by Skorzeny, but some do. Somehow, some way, many of the Führer's Third Reich tenets once again are being approved by the government! In the 1978 presidential election in West Germany, for instance, the leading candidates were Walter Scheel, who had been president since 1974, and Karl Carstens of the Christian Democratic Union party. Both were former members of the Nazi party. Another candidate, Hans Filbinger, withdrew from the race when his Nazi background was revealed. Both Scheel and Carstens were cleared by a German denazification court after the war. But critics of the two reminded voters that Skorzeny did them one better—he was cleared by a U.S. military tribunal! So the suspicions, justified or not, of ex-Nazi leaders in the government continue, a tribute to the controversy Skorzeny caused in both life and death.

Terrorism, the Skorzeny syndrome, is flourishing in the modern world, a reminder that Hitler and Nazism are still taking their toll more than three decades after the Third Reich collapsed. The "most dangerous man in Europe in 1944," "Scarface" Skorzeny from Vienna, made certain of that. It is said he died with a smile on his face. If so, was it because he knew the terrorism he left behind would continue after him?

APPENDIX I
GLOSSARY

Abwehr   Counterespionage service of the German High Command, headed by Admiral Canaris. After Canaris was executed as a spy in 1941, the Abwehr was disgraced.

Allgemeine SS   The overall SS organization composed of full-time, part-time, active, and inactive members. It was distinct from the Waffen SS.

Amt   An office, branch, or directorate of a ministry.

Auswärtiges Amt   The Foreign Ministry.

Beamter   Official or functionary.

Burgermeister   Mayor of a town or city.

CSSD   Chief of the secret police.

Dienststelle   Headquarters, office, or station.

Ehrenführer   Honorary SS officer, usuallyaf17of senior rank.

Feldjägerkorps   A shock formation of the SS.

Führer   Leader, chief, commander. Hitler was referred to as "Der Führer" (the leader).

Gauleiter   Highest ranking Nazi party official in one of the main territorial divisions of Germany. There were forty-two such territorial divisions in Germany.

Geheime Feldpolizei   Secret Field Police.

Geheime Staatspolizei   Secret State Police (Gestapo).

Gemeindepolizei   Municipal police.

Gericht   Court of law.

Gestapo   Geheime Staatspolizei (Secret State Police).

Gruppe   Group or wing in the Luftwaffe of about forty planes. Sometimes an *ad hoc* military formation.

Hauptamt SS   Central Office of the SS.

Hauptamt SS-Gericht   SS Legal Department.

HIAG   Mutual Help Association for former SS personnel.

Jagdverbände   SS sabotage and subversive units. Commandos.

Kriminalpolizei   The Criminal Police sometimes known as Kripo.

Liebstandarte SS Adolf Hitler   Adolf Hitler Bodyguard Regiment.

Nationalsozialistische Deutsche Arbeiterpartei   National Socialist German Workers' Party. Official title of the Nazi party. Also known as NSDAP.

Oberkommando der Wehrmacht   High Command of the Armed Forces (OKW).

Referat   Sub-section or "desk" within a group.

RSHA   Reich Central Security Department which combined the Gestapo, Kripo, and the SS Security Service known as the SD.

Schutzstaffel   The SS.

Sonderkommando   A special detachment of the SS assigned police and political tasks in occupied territory.

Sturmabteilung   Storm Detachment known as the SA.

Totenkopfverbände   Death's Head Formations. The concentration camp guard detachments.

Waffen SS   The militarized SS detachments.

Wehrmacht   The German armed forces.

APPENDIX II
COMPARATIVE RANKS

SS	British Army	U.S. Army
Reichsführer SS	Field Marshal	General of the Army
SS Oberstgruppenführer	General	General
SS Obergruppenführer	Lieutenant-General	Lieutenant General
SS Gruppenführer	Major-General	Major General
SS Brigadeführer	Brigadier	Brigadier General
SS Oberführer	Senior Colonel	None
SS Standatenführer	Colonel	Colonel
SS Obersturmbannführer	Lieutenant-Colonel	Lieutenant Colonel
SS Sturmbannführer	Major	Major
SS Hauptsturmführer	Captain	Captain
SS Obersturmführer	Lieutenant	First Lieutenant
SS Untersturmführer	Second Lieutenant	Second Lieutenant
SS Sturmscharführer	Regimental-Sergeant Major	Sergeant Major
SS Hauptscharführer	Sergeant Major	Master Sergeant
SS Oberscharführer	Quartermaster-Sergeant	Technical Sergeant
SS Scharführer	Staff Sergeant	Staff Sergeant
SS Unterscharführer	Sergeant	Sergeant
SS Rottenführer	Corporal	Corporal
SS Sturmmann	Lance-Corporal	Private First Class
SS Oberschütze	Private	Private

BIBLIOGRAPHY

PARTIAL LIST OF PERSONAL CONTACTS

Nicolaus von Below	Detmold, West Germany
Hans Barkhausen	Koblenz, West Germany
Harvey Berg	Buffalo, New York
Isser Berman	London, England
Ilse (Fucke-Michels) Braun	Munich, West Germany
Oscar Brecker	London, England
Thomas G. Charouhas	Asuncion, Paraguay
Peter DeShazo	La Paz, Bolivia
F. Joseph Donohue*	Washington, D.C.
Michele Ficarelli*	Bari, Italy
Paul Förster	Kassel, West Germany
Graham K. French	Brasilia, Brazil
Adolf Galland	Bonn, West Germany
Franz-Josef Giehl	Wittlich, West Germany
Rudi Gunter	Munich, West Germany
W. Averell Harriman	Washington, D.C.
Otto Heitmann	New York City
Giacinto Iusco	Bari, Italy
Hans Jaeger	Berchtesgaden, West Germany
Traudl Junge	Munich, West Germany
Julius Mader	East Berlin
Hasso von Manteuffel	Diessen am Ammersee, West Germany
Gustav Molders	Munich, West Germany
Michael A. Musmanno*	Pittsburgh

Hanna Reitsch*	Frankfurt, West Germany
Leni Riefenstahl	Munich, West Germany
Karl Ritter	Buenos Aires, Argentina
Gilberto Rivas	Zurich, Switzerland
Hans Ulrich Rudel	Kufstein, West Germany
William A. Rugh	Cairo, Egypt
Charla Saylor	Quito, Ecuador
Edward Shaefer	Washington, D.C.
Otto Skorzeny*	Madrid, Spain
Albert Speer	Heidelberg, West Germany
Donald Spencer	Washington, D.C.
Kurt Student*	Bad Salzuflen, West Germany
Mitchell L. Werbell III	Powder Springs, Georgia
George Whitmer	London, England
Simon Wiesenthal	Vienna, Austria
Alois Wirmer	Inglostadt, West Germany
Vaughn Young	Los Angeles
Norman Ziff	Buenos Aires, Argentina

*Deceased

Many other persons who provided information asked not to be identified publicly for fear of reprisal or other reasons.

SELECTED DOCUMENTS, REPORTS AND RECORDS

Berlin Document Center
  Letter from Schellenberg to Hitler about Skorzeny's Budapest Operation and urging Skorzeny be awarded the Gold Cross.
  Skorzeny's Nazi party records.
  Friedenthal records.
  Skorzeny's personal background questionnaires.
  Skorzeny's SS records.
Documents and Material Relating to Otto Skorzeny at Institut für
  Zeitgeschicht, Munich; Imperial War Museum, London; Bundesarchiv, Koblenz; Library of Congress, Washington, D.C.; Bayerisches Hauptstaatarchiv, Munich.
Central Intelligence Agency
  International Terrorism in 1977.
  International Terrorism in 1976.
  Combating Terrorism Today.
  Various miscellaneous documents pertaining to terrorism.
Correspondence between Glenn Infield and Otto Skorzeny, 1973–1975.

Letters, documents, and additional materials relating to Otto Skorzeny's career. This was in addition to personal visits to Madrid.
Department of Justice
Letter to Director, CIA, from J. Edgar Hoover.
Various telegrams and reports pertaining to terrorism.
Musmanno Collection
Interview with Julius Schaub, March 22, 1948.
The private papers of Michael A. Musmanno contain information he obtained during the immediate postwar years when he investigated Hitler's death. At that time he interviewed more than 200 persons, ranging from cooks to high-ranking military officers and Nazi party members. Later he was a jurist at Nuremberg when twenty-three *Einsatz* leaders of Adolf Eichmann's mobile death squads were tried. When Adolf Eichmann was kidnapped and taken to Israel for trial, Musmanno was a prosecution witness during the 1961 court proceedings when Eichmann was found guilty.
National Archives
Testimony of Otto Skorzeny at Nuremberg—September 11, 1945.
Testimony of Otto Skorzeny at Nuremberg—November 6, 1945.
Report from the Assistant Chief of Staff, G-2—June 13, 1951.
Interrogation of Otto Skorzeny—August 12, 1945.
An Interview with Otto Skorzeny—August 12, 1945.
Counter Intelligence Report on Werewolf—May 31, 1945.
Embassy Report on Skorzeny.
U.S. Army Security and Intelligence Command
Interrogation of Gottlob Berger.
German Sabotage Services.
Special Activities of the Skorzeny Group.
Anti-Nazi Plot that Ended with Attempt on Hitler's Life.
Interrogation of Martin Oberlander.
Summary of Information—September 9, 1945.
Spacil: Memorandum for Officer-in-Charge.
Otto Skorzeny, SS Obersturmbannführer, Chief of Amt VI/S.
Captured: Lieutenant Colonel Otto Skorzeny.
Subject: Movie Interview of Otto Skorzeny.
Request for Memorandum on German Intelligence Service and Reply.
Otto Skorzeny Interned.
Possible Underground Organization of Skorzeny.
Letter from Skorzeny to Colonel Potter.
Report on Hermann Fegelein.
Report of Interrogation of Otto Skorzeny.
Undercover Agent Report.

Letter from Otto Skorzeny to Camp Commander, Darmstadt.
Review of Skorzeny's Activities by G-2.
Report on Skorzeny from 66th CIC.
Letter from Bernard A. Tormey to Director of Intelligence, Headquarters, European Command.
Report of I.M. Belba, CIC Special Agent.
Report of Rudolf J. Geiser, CIC Special Agent.
Security Report: Otto Skorzeny.
Air Intelligence Report on Otto Skorzeny by Major Robert Bisck.
Investigation Report on Joachim Melchert.
Confidential Report from U.S. Constabulary on Otto Skorzeny.
Confidential Intelligence Report by Agent Fritz Fischer, Dachau.
CIC Report: Operation Skorzeny-Berlin.
Skorzeny's Whereabouts: Report by Lieutenant Colonel George R. Eckman.
Miscellaneous airgrams, telegrams and reports.
Department of State
Terrorism (GIST).
Problem of International Terrorism.
Letter to Senator Sheridan Downey.
Nicholson Secret Memorandum Re Skorzeny.
Secret Foreign Service Dispatch from Madrid Re Skorzeny.
Airgram: Madrid to Department of State Re Skorzeny.
Foreign Service Dispatch from Brazil Re Skorzeny.
Anti-Semitic Views of Skorzeny: Daniel V. Anderson.
Embassy Dispatch 2276 from Cairo Re Skorzeny.
Memorandum of Conversation: Julian P. Fromer, Bilbao, Spain.
Consulate General Dispatch 104: J. Roland Jacobs, Marseille, France.
Memorandum of Conversation: G. Lewis Jones, Cairo, Egypt.
Traudl Junge. Unpublished Memoirs.
OSS Hitler Source Book. Langer Report.

PUBLISHED SOURCES

Ascoli, Max., ed. *The Fall of Mussolini*. New York: Farrar, Straus & Co., 1948.
Barnes, John. *Evita, First Lady*. New York: Grove Press, 1978.
Bayne-Jardine, Colin Charles. *Mussolini and Italy*. New York: McGraw-Hill, 1968.
Boas, William. *Germany 1945–1954*. Cologne: Boas International Publishing Company, 1956.

Clark, Alan. *Barbarossa: The Russian-German Conflict 1941–1945*. New York: William Morrow, 1965.

Cole, Hugh M. *The Ardennes: Battle of the Bulge*. Washington, D.C.: Department of the Army, 1965.

Collier, Richard. *Duce*. New York: Popular Library, 1971.

Deakin, F.W. *The Brutal Friendship*. New York: Harper & Row, 1962.

Derogy, Jacques and Carmel, Hesi. *The Untold History of Israel*. New York: Grove Press, 1979.

Eisenberg, Dennis; Dan, Uri; and Landau, Eli. *The Mossad*. London: Paddington Press, 1978.

Eisenhower, Dwight D. *Crusade in Europe*. New York: Doubleday & Company, 1949.

Farago, Ladislas. *Aftermath*. New York: Simon and Schuster, 1974.

Foley, Charles. *Commando Extraordinary*. New York: Ballantine Books, 1955.

Gallo, Max. *Mussolini's Italy*. New York: Macmillan, 1973.

Gehlen, Reinhard. *The Service*. New York: Popular Library, 1972.

Hitler, Adolf. *Secret Conversations*. New York: Octagon Books, 1972.

Infield, Glenn B. *Eva and Adolf*. New York: Grosset & Dunlap, 1974.

Irving, David. *Hitler's War*. New York: Viking Press, 1977.

Mader, Julius. *Jagd nach dem Narbengesicht*. East Berlin: Deutscher Militar-verlag, 1962.

Manchester, William. *The Arms of Krupp*. Boston: Little, Brown & Company, 1964.

Marshall, Bruce. *The White Rabbit*. New York: Houghton Mifflin, 1953.

McKown, Robin. *7 Famous Trials*. New York: Vanguard Press, 1963.

Miller, Francis Trevelyan. *The Complete History of World War II*. Chicago: Progress Research Corporation, 1949.

Montgomery, Paul L. *Eva, Evita*. New York: Pocket Books, 1979.

Musmanno, Michael A. *The Eichmann Commandos*. Philadelphia: Macrae Smith Company, 1961.

Payne, Robert. *The Life and Death of Adolf Hitler*. New York: Praeger, 1975.

Reitsch, Hanna. *The Sky My Kingdom*. London: The Bodley Head, 1955.

Schirach, Henriette von. *The Price of Glory*. London: Frederick Muller, Ltd., 1960.

Sedar, Irving, and Greenberg, Harold. *Behind the Egyptian Sphinx*. Philadelphia: Chilton Company, 1960.

Shavelson, Melville. *Ike*. New York: Warner Books, 1979.

Shirer, William L. *The Rise and Fall of the Third Reich*. New York: Simon and Schuster, 1960.

Shtemenko, S.M. *The Last Six Months*. New York: Zebra Books, 1978.

Skorzeny, Otto. *Skorzeny's Secret Missions*. New York: E.P. Dutton, 1950.
Stevenson, William. *The Bormann Brotherhood*. New York: Harcourt Brace Jovanovich, 1973.
Toland, John. *Adolf Hitler*. New York: Doubleday & Company, 1976.
Wiesenthal, Simon. *The Murderers Among Us*. New York: McGraw-Hill, 1967.
Whiting, Charles. *Skorzeny*. New York: Ballantine Books, 1972.

NOTES

References are given in abbreviated form. Interview dates are listed for first reference. BA refers to *Bundesarchiv;* BDC to *Berlin Document Center;* NA to *National Archives;* DS to *Department of State;* MC to *Musmanno Collection;* USAISC to *U.S. Army Intelligence and Security Command;* DJ to *Department of Justice;* CIA *to Central Intelligence Agency.*

INTRODUCTION

1. International Terrorism in 1977, p.1. (CIA)
2. Author interview with Albert Speer, February 1973. Heidelberg, West Germany.
3. Ibid.
4. Author interview with Otto Skorzeny, February 1973. Madrid, Spain.

1. THE MOST DANGEROUS MAN

1. Author interview with Hanna Reitsch, June 1976. Frankfurt, West Germany.
2. Author interview with Gustav Molders, a former Me-109 pilot who test flew the piloted V-1, June 1978. Munich, West Germany.
3. Reitsch, p.193.
4. Foley, p. 12.
5. Testimony of Otto Skorzeny at Nuremberg, September 11, 1945, taken by Colonel Howard A. Brundage. (NA Record Group 238)
6. Whiting, p. 17.

7. Author interview with Skorzeny.
8. Foley, p. 14.
9. Ibid, p. 15.
10. Interrogation of Gottlob Berger, May 8, 1945. Berchtesgaden. (USAISC—S.R. GG 1289(c) CS/2235)
11. Testimony of Otto Skorzeny at Nuremberg, November 6, 1945, taken by Lieutenant Colonel Smith W. Brookhart, Jr. (NA Record Group 238)
12. Author interview with Hans Jaeger, June 1978. Berchtesgaden, West Germany.
13. Payne, p. 420.
14. Ibid, p. 421.
15. Clark, p. 44.
16. Author interview with Skorzeny.

2. HITLER'S COMMANDOS

1. Author interview with Skorzeny. Hitler made this complaint to Skorzeny in July 1943 when they met to discuss the Mussolini rescue.
2. Skorzeny, p. 12.
3. Testimony of Otto Skorzeny at Nuremberg—Brookhart, Jr.
4. Testimony of Otto Skorzeny at Nuremberg—Brundage.
5. Report from the Assistant Chief of Staff, G-2, June 13, 1951. (NA Record Group 238)
6. Testimony of Otto Skorzeny at Nuremberg—Brookhart, Jr.
7. Skorzeny, p. 29.
8. Ibid, pp. 29–30.
9. Ibid, p. 35.

3. THE RESCUE OF BENITO MUSSOLINI

1. Mussolini Event. Foreign Military Studies. D-318. (NA Record Group 338) p. 24.
2. Ibid, pp. 24–25.
3. Ibid, pp. 24–29.
4. Ascoli, p. 102.
5. Mussolini Event, p. 103.
6. Author interview with Skorzeny.
7. Ibid.
8. Ibid.
9. Ibid.
10. Ibid.
11. Skorzeny, p. 96.
12. Ibid, p. 99.

13. Author interview with Skorzeny.
14. Ibid.
15. Mussolini Event, p. 138.
16. Infield, pp. 212–213.

4. TERRORISM VS. MILITARY OPERATIONS

1. Foley, p. 55.
2. Author interview with Skorzeny.
3. German Sabotage Services, Annex IV, p. 33, dated July 23, 1945. (USAISC)
4. Ibid.
5. Miller, p. 135.
6. Testimony of Otto Skorzeny at Nuremberg—Brookhart, Jr.
7. Special Activities of the Skorzeny Group. Counter Intelligence War Room Report P.F. 600, 544/W.R.C. 2, dated January 6, 1945, p. 120. (USAISC)
8. Shirer, p. 957.

5. "YOU'RE IN COMMAND, SKORZENY!"

1. German Sabotage Services. (USAISC)
2. Anti-Nazi Plot That Ended with Attempt on Hitler's Life. Report by Special Agent James Ratliff, Jr., CIC, 970/3 Detachment, dated August 26, 1945. (USAISC)
3. Author interview with Skorzeny.
4. Irving, p. 662.
5. Author interview with Skorzeny.
6. Ibid.
7. Toland, p. 908.
8. Irving, p. 665.
9. Skorzeny, p. 154.
10. Author interview with Skorzeny.
11. Ibid.
12. Ibid.
13. Toland, p. 917.
14. Author interview with Skorzeny.

6. THE HORTHY KIDNAPPING

1. Hitler's Secret Conversations, p. 542.
2. Skorzeny, pp. 193–194.
3. Ibid, p. 195.

4. Author interview with Skorzeny.
5. Ibid.
6. Ibid. Skorzeny insisted that much of the credit for the successful overthrow of Admiral Horthy without an armed conflict was due to Veesenmayer, not only because he told Skorzeny about the Miki Horthy-Yugoslavian meetings but because of Veesenmayer's actions when he confronted Admiral Horthy.
7. Ibid.
8. Shtemenko, p. 252.
9. Author interview with Skorzeny.
10. Skorzeny, p. 213.

7. SKORZENY'S "AMERICAN" TERRORISTS

1. Shavelson, pp. 262–262.
2. Cole, p. 2.
3. Skorzeny, p. 219.
4. Ibid, p. 222.
5. Interrogation of Otto Skorzeny by Walter H. Rapp from 11:00 A.M. until 12:00 A.M. on March 8, 1948. (NA Record Group 238)
6. Skorzeny, p. 222.
7. Ibid, p. 225.
8. TWX message, Headquarters Command 2, ETOUSA, dated December 23, 1944. (NA Record Group 238)
9. An Interview with Otto Skorzeny, August 12, 1945. (NA Record Group 238)

8. THE HIMMLER CHALLENGE

1. Author interview with Skorzeny.
2. Ibid.
3. Ibid.
4. Ibid.
5. Interrogation of Otto Skorzeny—Rapp. (NA Record Group 238)
6. Manchester, pp. 576–577.
7. Skorzeny, p. 254.
8. Foley, p. 120.
9. Whiting, p. 118.
10. Author interview with Skorzeny.

9. WEREWOLVES AND THE ALPINE REDOUBT

1. Interview with Julius Schaub, March 22, 1948. (Musmanno Collection) Schaub, Hitler's personal adjutant for many years, was interviewed by Musmanno at Garmisch.
2. Whiting, p. 132.
3. Author interview with Skorzeny.
4. Ibid.
5. Eisenhower, p. 380.
6. Author interview with Skorzeny.
7. Ibid.
8. Author interview with Rudi Gunter, Munich, June 1978. Gunter, an SS Hauptscharführer, survived the war and today operates a men's clothing store in Munich.
9. Author interview with Skorzeny.
10. Traudl Junge's unpublished memoirs. Traudl Junge was the youngest of Hitler's female staff and his favorite. She escaped from the Berlin bunker and today lives in Munich.
11. Author interview with Skorzeny.
12. Counter Intelligence Report on Werewolf, May 31, 1945, p. 3. (NA Record Group 238)
13. Memorandum on Nazi Resistance Plans. OSS German Section. No. 2–290. No date. (USAISC)
14. Ibid.
15. Interrogation of Martin Oberlander. Report IV—206B, Dossier 4763, dated November 13, 1947. (USAISC)
16. Summary of Information, September 9, 1945. Case No. A-1-59. John L. Parkinson, Special Agent, CIC. (USAISC)
17. This poster was reproduced by Engineering Reproduction Detachment 12, A Group, U.S. Army, 1945. (U.S. Army)
18. Whiting, p. 135.
19. Schirach, p. 18.

10. THE CAPTURE

1. Author interview with Skorzeny.
2. Spacil: Memorandum for Officer in Charge, 307th Counter Intelligence Corps Detachment, Headquarters, Seventh Army, dated July 5, 1948. (USAISC)
3. Author interview with Skorzeny.
4. Ibid.

5. Otto Skorzeny, SS Obersturmbannführer, Chief of Amt VI/S. Report No. S-975, 307th Counter Intelligence Corps Detachment, May 23, 1945. (USAISC)
6. Captured: Lt. Col. Otto Skorzeny. Document 470, cablegram from Commanding General, G-2, Seventh Army. (USAISC)
7. Subject: Movie Interview of Otto Skorzeny. Document 471, cablegram from Commanding General, G-2, Seventh Army to U.S. Conference Detachment, Berlin. (USAISC)
8. Otto Skorzeny Interned. Document 521. Thomas H. Buckley Report to Commanding Officer, CIC Region IV, 970 CIC Detachment. (USAISC)

11. THE TRIAL

1. Author interview with Skorzeny.
2. Ibid.
3. Interrogation of Gottlob Berger. (USAISC)
4. Author interview with Skorzeny.
5. Ibid.
6. Ibid.
7. Foley, pp. 151–153 and author interview with Skorzeny.

12. ESCAPE

1. Author interview with George Whitmer in London, June 1978. Whitmer is now retired and resides at Bovington, near London.
2. Letter from Skorzeny to Colonel Potter. Document 039, Office of the Chief Historian, U.S. Army, dated September 16, 1947. (USAISC)
3. Report on Hermann Fegelein. Documents 388–400, Report of Conversation with Mr. and Mrs. Hans Fegelein by Walter Hirschfeld, CIC Undercover Agent. (USAISC)
4. Report of Interrogation of Otto Skorzeny. Document 033, Headquarters, European Command Intelligence Center, U.S. Army, February 28, 1948. (USAISC)
5. Document 224, Dossier File 4763, Counter Intelligence Corps, Region IV. (USAISC)
6. Author interview with Skorzeny.
7. Ibid.
8. Mader, p. 176.
9. Letter from Skorzeny to Camp Commander, Darmstadt. Document 512, Letter to Spruchkammer, Darmstadt Camp, July 26, 1948. (USAISC)
10. Mader, pp. 178–179.

NOTES255

13. THE PHANTOM COMMANDO

1. Letter to Senator Sheridan Downey. Document 762.5235/2-750. (DS
2. Report of Jack K. McFall, Assistant Secretary of State, February 24, 1950. Document 8906. (DS)
3. Report about Skorzeny from 66th CIC. Document 439, Letter to Assistant Chief of Staff, G-2, U.S. Army, Europe, from George T. Nakamura, Adjutant, 66th CIC. (USAISC)
4. Document 536, Letter, Internal Division of 66th CIC to Eucom. (USAISC)
5. Letter from Bernard A. Tormey to Director of Intelligence, Headquarters, European Command. Document 334. (USAISC)
6. Mader, p. 190.
7. Report of I.M. Belba, CIC Special Agent, 7970th CIC. Document 00124. (USAISC)
8. Mader, p. 192.
9. Report of Rudolf J. Geiser, CIC Special Agent. Document YE 000417. (USAISC)
10. Security Report: Otto Skorzeny. Document 335. (USAISC)
11. Ibid.

14. THE FRANCO CONNECTION

1. Charles Foley interview with Skorzeny. *London Daily Express*, April 7, 1952.
2. Air Intelligence Report on Otto Skorzeny by Major Robert Bisck. Document 346. (USAISC)
3. Memorandum of Conversation: Julian P. Fromer, Bilbao, Spain. Document 154. (DS)
4. Letter to Director, CIA, from J. Edgar Hoover. Document 352. (DJ)
5. Secret Foreign Service Dispatch from Madrid Re Skorzeny. Document 762.5252/7-251. (DS)
6. Airgram: Madrid to Department of State Re Skorzeny. Document 14, Pol 27-12 GER. (DS)
7. Mader, p. 256.
8. Christopher Morris interview with Skorzeny, *Pittsburgh Press*, October 19, 1967.
9. Telegram from U.S. Embassy in Madrid to Department of State with copies to Bonn, Vienna, and Paris. Document 16, Pol 27-12 GER. (DS)
10. Telegram from Department of State to U.S. Embassy in Madrid. Document 18, Pol 27-12 GER. (DS)
11. Air Intelligence Report—Bisck. (USAISC)

15. THE SWASTIKA SYNDICATE

1. Confidential Report from U.S. Constabulary on Otto Skorzeny. Document 425. (USAISC)
2. Confidential Intelligence Report by Agent Fritz Fischer, Dachau, Counter Intelligence Corps. Region IV. Document 214. (USAISC)
3. Wiesenthal, p. 77.
4. Ibid, p. 81.
5. Mader, p. 193.
6. Author interview with Isser Berman, London, June 20, 1978.
7. Mader, p. 239.
8. CIC Report: Operation Skorzeny-Berlin. Exhibit A, Letter from Headquarters, Sub-Region Württemberg, Counter Intelligence Corps, Region I to Commanding Officer, 7970th Counter Intelligence Corps Group, European Command. Document 424. (USAISC)
9. Ibid, Exhibit C. Document 391. (USAISC)
10. Author interview with Skorzeny.
11. Toland, p. 992.
12. Author interview with Skorzeny.
13. Ibid.
14. Mader, p. 233.
15. Mader, p. 273.

16. EVITA AND SKORZENY

1. Skorzeny's Whereabouts: Report by Lieutenant Colonel George R. Eckman, Acting Commander, 7970th Counter Intelligence Corps, European Command to the American consulate general, Frankfurt, West Germany. Document 373. (USAISC)
2. Barnes, p. 37.
3. Author interview with Skorzeny.
4. Author interview with Gilberto Rivas, Zurich, Switzerland, July 1975.
5. Author interview with Oscar Brecker, London, June 1978.
6. Foreign Service Dispatch from Brazil Re Skorzeny. William T. Briggs, Second Secretary of U.S. Embassy, Brazil, to Department of State. Document 10-2052. (DS)
7. Mader, p. 251.
8. Krupp, p. 740.

17. PYRAMIDS AND NAZIS

1. Gehlen, p. 203.
2. Anti-Semitic Views of Skorzeny: Daniel V. Anderson, First Secretary of

Embassy, Madrid. Paragraph 3. Document 762.5252?7-251. (DS)

3. Gehlen, p. 260.
4. Sedar and Greenberg, p. 58.
5. Ibid, p. 59.
6. Embassy Dispatch 2276 from Cairo Re Skorzeny. Jefferson Caffery of the U.S. Embassy in Cairo to Department of State. Document 774.52/6-1553. (DS)
7. Memorandum of Conversation—Fromer. (DS)
8. Consulate General Dispatch 104: J. Roland Jacobs, Marseille, France. Document 762.5200/3-253. (DS)
9. Derogy and Carmel, p. 135.
10. Memorandum of Conversation: G. Lewis Jones, Cairo, Egypt. Subject: "Dr. Voss and his Friends." Document 774.52?4-2853. (DS)
11. Derogy and Carmel, p. 197.

18. THE ENFORCER

1. Author interview with Simon Wiesenthal, Pittsburgh, February 1977.
2. Ibid.
3. Author interview with Skorzeny.
4. *Parade* Magazine, November 19, 1978, p. 8.
5. Author interview with Skorzeny.
6. Musmanno, p. 104.
7. Eisenberg, Dan, and Landau, p. 35.
8. *Volunteer*, SS Newspaper published in Bonn, West Germany, May 29, 1960.
9. Author interview with Musmanno, June 1961.
10. *Pittsburgh Post-Gazette*, June 1, 1962, p. 1.
11. Author interview with Skorzeny.

19. THE FINAL MISSION

1. Letter to author from Skorzeny, May 30, 1973.
2. Author interview with Skorzeny.
3. Author interview with Alois Wirmer, Ingolstadt, West Germany, June 1978. Wirmer now operates a guesthouse in Ingolstadt.
4. Author interview with Skorzeny.
5. *Time*, April 2, 1973, p. 37.
6. *Daily Telegraph*, July 8, 1975.
7. Final letter to the author from Skorzeny, April 10, 1975, approximately three months before his death.

INDEX